THE
ZEEBRUGGE
RAID

ABOUT THE AUTHOR

Philip Warner (1914-2000) enlisted in the Royal Corps of Signals after graduating from St Catharine's, Cambridge in 1939. He fought in Malaya and spent 1,100 days as 'a guest of the Emperor' in Changi, on the Railway of Death and in the mines of Japan, an experience he never discussed. A legendary figure to generations of cadets during his thirty years as a Senior Lecturer at the Royal Military Academy, Sandhurst, he will also be long remembered for his contribution of more than 2,000 obituaries of prominent army figures to *The Daily Telegraph*.

In addition he wrote fifty-four books on all aspects of military history, ranging from castles and battlefields in Britain, to biographies of prominent military figures (such as *Kitchener: The Man Behind The Legend*, *Field Marshal Earl Haig* and *Horrocks: The General Who Led from the Front*) to major histories of the SAS, the Special Boat Services and the Royal Corps of Signals.

The D-Day Landings was republished by Pen & Sword Books to mark the 60th Anniversary of this historic event and was adopted by *The Daily Telegraph* as its official commemorative book.

By the same author

Alamein: Reflections of the Heroes
 (republished by Pen & Sword, 2007)
Auchinleck: The Lonely Soldier
 (republished by Pen & Sword, 2006)
Battle of France
Battle of Loos
Best of British Pluck
British Battlefields 1: The North
British Battlefields 2: The South
British Battlefields 3: The Midlands
British Battlefields 4: Scotland
Daily Telegraph Book of British Battlefields
British Cavalry
Castles in Britain *(illustrated edition)*
Civil Service
Crimean War
The D-Day Landings
 (republished by Pen & Sword, 2004)
Disputed Territories
Distant Battle
Famous Scottish Battles
Famous Welsh Battles
Field Marshal Earl Haig
Fields of War: Letters Home from the Crimea
The Great British Soldier

Growing Up in the First World War
A Guide to the Castles in the British Isles
Horrocks: The General Who Led from the
 Front *(republished by Pen & Sword, 2005)*
Invasion Road
The Japanese Army of World War II
Kitchener: The Man Behind the Legend
The Medieval Castle in Peace & War
Panzer
Passchendaele *(republished by Pen & Sword, 2007)*
Phantom *(republished by Pen & Sword, 2005)*
Political Parties
Roman Roads
Secret Forces of World War 2
 (republished by Pen & Sword, 2004)
Sieges of the Middle Ages
 (republished by Pen & Sword, 2004)
Soldier: His Life in Peace and War
Special Air Service (Official History)
Special Boat Service
Stories of Famous Regiments
World War One: A Chronological Narrative
 (to be republished by Pen & Sword, 2008)
World War II: The Untold Story

THE
ZEEBRUGGE
RAID

Philip Warner

Pen & Sword
MILITARY

940·458

First published in Great Britain in 1978 by William Kimber and Co. Limited
Reprinted in this format in 2008 by
PEN & SWORD MILITARY
an imprint of
Pen & Sword Books Ltd
47 Church Street
Barnsley
South Yorkshire
S70 2AS

Copyright © Philip Warner, 1978, 2008

ISBN 978 1 84415 677 1

The right of Philip Warner to be identified as author of this work
has been asserted by him in accordance with the
Copyright, Designs and Patents Act 1988.

A CIP catalogue record for this book is
available from the British Library

Printed and bound in Great Britain
By CPI UK

Pen & Sword Books Ltd incorporates the Imprints of
Pen & Sword Aviation, Pen & Sword Maritime, Pen & Sword Military,
Wharncliffe Local History, Pen & Sword Select,
Pen & Sword Military Classics and Leo Cooper.

For a complete list of Pen & Sword titles please contact
PEN & SWORD BOOKS LIMITED
47 Church Street, Barnsley, South Yorkshire, S70 2AS, England
E-mail: enquiries@pen-and-sword.co.uk
Website: www.pen-and-sword.co.uk

Contents

Admiral Keyes' plan of the
British attack on Zeebrugge
appears on pages 20-21

List of Illustrations

Captain Ion Hamilton Benn
Lieutenant R. D. Sandford
Commander A. E. Godsal
Lieutenant Sir John Alleyne, Bt
Motor launches making smoke
Some of the men who returned from the raid
   (*courtesy Mrs E. Vinnicombe*)

Special thanks are due to Mr R. B. Goodall whose skill in reviving old, and often damaged, photographs has made it possible for this book to be fully illustrated.

Foreword

If you are in the Belgian port of Zeebrugge on any 23rd April you will see a short but impressive ceremony at the point where the Mole begins. At the memorial which is in front of the Hotel de la Victoire there will be two lines of elderly men, and two lines also of sailors from the Belgian Navy. Wreaths will be laid, and the Last Post sounded. Then the party moves away.

That is not all. The old men, for their ages range from 78 to 88, will then go to the Flemish church* by the military cemetery where a service will be conducted half in English and half in Flemish. The church will be full and in the congregation will be Flemish children dressed in national costume. Outside the church is a small cemetery and when the service is over each child lays a flower on a serviceman's grave.

Lastly the veterans move to the Town Hall† where they are given a reception by the Burgomaster and other officials.

The Belgians have not forgotten the Zeebrugge raid of 23rd April 1918, and like to show their gratitude on the occasion of the visit by survivors. They regard the raid as the first step to the liberation of Belgium after its occupation by the Germans in 1914.

There are not many veterans now left to make this annual pilgrimage and pay a tribute to their dead comrades. There never were many, for the number engaged at Zeebrugge was relatively small and the casualties high. But those who still come, and fall in behind their white silk flag with a dragon on it (a dragon with a twisted tail!) hold themselves steady and erect in spite of the effects of wounds and age. It is a sight you will not forget, nor should you.

* Sint-Donaaskerk.
† Gemeentelijk Gebouw.

Acknowledgements

In March 1976 the *Daily Telegraph* kindly printed a letter in which I asked survivors of the Zeebrugge Raid, or their relations, to get in touch with me. 182 replies came in, many from people who had taken part. They came from many places, including Canada, New Guinea and the West Indies. I would like to express my gratitude to the *Daily Telegraph* for thus making possible the presentation of the raid from many viewpoints.

I also wish to thank all those who wrote to me or telephoned, many of whom sent in personal accounts, photographs, and helpful suggestions. My thanks are also due to Major Alistair Donald and the staff of the Royal Marines Museum at Eastney.

Lord Keyes, son of Admiral of the Fleet, Lord Keyes, very kindly provided me with a copy of his father's plan of the Zeebrugge attack, and several other illustrations. He also supplied me with reference material from which I could check various details of the raid.

Every attempt has been made to trace owners of copyright material. Anyone who feels that unacknowledged copyright material may have been used inadvertently in this book is requested to get in touch with the author so that the matter may be resolved.

My thanks are also due to Lord Kennet who allowed me to quote from his father's account of the battle first published in *Sea and Land* (1920) to Messrs Chatto and Windus for permission to use an extract from J. Keble Bell's *The Glory of Zeebrugge* (1918) and to The Bodley Head for permission to use letters from Engineer Commander Bury and Commander Osborne first published in Stanley Coxon's *Dover during the Dark Days* and to Commander Rosoman's son, Mr R. C. S. Rosoman, for permission to use his father's letter in the same book.

Introduction

Zeebrugge is a small, busy, Belgian port which lies eight miles from Bruges and seventy-two miles from Dover. On 23rd April 1918 it was the scene of one of the most daring and skilful raids in naval history. In two and a half hours* heavy casualties were sustained by both sides and then the Royal Navy, battered almost beyond recognition, retired with its job well done.

The reason for this remarkable feat of superb seamanship and exceptional human courage was the strategic importance of Zeebrugge. Since 1914 the Germans had been developing a fortified triangle of which one side was the coastline between Zeebrugge and Ostend, another the ship canal to Bruges itself and the third the canal system linking Bruges with Ostend. Apart from the main canals there were minor waterways and important dockyard installations. Here submarines, destroyers and other small craft could shelter when not preying on Allied shipping.

Although the biggest menace from the Germans was their U-boat (submarine) campaign which inflicted crippling losses on Allied shipping, there were secondary problems in the shape of destroyers, mine-sweepers and torpedo-boats. If the German Grand Fleet ever ventured to sea once more it would need a host of minor craft for such duties as mine-sweeping and reconnaissance. Mine-sweepers were also of vital importance for keeping the U-boat routes clear of mines. Usually the Germans maintained thirty submarines and the same number of destroyers or torpedo boats in the Zeebrugge area.

But it was not merely the attacking potential of the Zeebrugge-Ostend-Bruges triangle which made it such an asset to the Germans; equally valuable were the repair and dockyard facilities. Damaged ships could put in for shelter, be repaired, and back to sea with minimum delay. Bruges was of vital importance as a repair centre. It is essential to comprehend just how important this area was to the Germans; its value as a submarine and small craft base, its value as a shipyard, its value as a spring-

* The majority of the action took place within an hour.

board for a large-scale naval venture, and its value, by virtue of its advanced position, as a fuel-saver. Thus, instead of having to move to and from Germany, three hundred miles away, with consequent expenditure of fuel, submarines and other small craft could operate from Zeebrugge.

It is necessary to emphasise this point because among the many superficial judgements of military and naval strategy made since the First World War ended, the Zeebrugge raid has been criticised as being a death-or-glory mission for a limited gain. In fact the gain was enormous, and attempts to minimise its achievement are as uninformed as they are unjustified. Regrettably it is all too easy for a military historian, who has never even heard a bullet whizz by, still less been engaged in any sort of campaign, to deliver sweeping and uninformed criticisms of strategy and tactics, and be applauded by others who know as little.

The Zeebrugge raid, let us be clear on this point, was a success in several different ways. One was that it achieved the immediate objective it set out to achieve; the second was that it was a tremendous boost for morale not only in the Royal Navy but in the Allied forces as a whole. In April 1918 the military tide was running heavily against the Allies. On the Western front the Germans were driving forward once more into areas from which they had been bloodily ejected during the three years since 1914. Shipping losses were high and shortages were helping to add to war weariness at home. Something was needed to show that the British war effort was not as jaded and weary as it appeared. That event was the Zeebrugge Raid. However, it should be clearly understood that the raid was not designed as a morale-raiser. It was planned as a risky though feasible naval operation. The fact that it cheered the armed forces and civilian population (and depressed the Germans to an equivalent extent) was purely a bonus.

Somewhat surprisingly, in an otherwise commendable history of the naval war entitled *From the Dreadnought to Scapa Flow*,* Professor Arthur Marder accepts the German official view of the raid. 'Was Zeebrugge more than a naval Balaclava?' he asks rhetorically and vaguely. Balaclava was in fact a port, there was no 'Battle of Balaclava' but three separate incidents – the Charge of the Light Brigade, the Charge of the Heavy Brigade and the episode of the Thin Red Line; two of these were successes. Marder quotes the German Official History as saying, 'Closer examination of the situation very soon showed that the conduct of the war from Zeebrugge had suffered only minor and temporary restrictions. . . .'

* Oxford University Press, 1970.

Nevertheless the facts are that although a number of shallow draught boats were able to leave the Zeebrugge Canal soon after the operation only intensive dredging operations managed to open the channel three weeks later and then only partly. Three weeks is a long time in a critical phase of a war. No one among the Allies believed the canals would be blocked permanently : the aim of the raid was to disrupt. Its effect would have been infinitely greater if the British Air Force had followed up the closing of the canal by bombing the imprisoned German craft, some of which, but not all, managed to slip out later. Unfortunately Admiral Keyes was at that time no longer able to apply the four bomber squadrons from Dunkirk to the task of destroying German shipping trapped in Zeebrugge. Twenty-three days before the Zeebrugge raid the Royal Naval Air Service had relinquished control of all air force matters except the design and construction of airships and aircraft carriers. This meant that nearly three thousand aircraft and 67,000 men trained to fly and maintain them, as well as 103 airships, had passed from the Royal Navy to the Royal Air Force.

The long-term results were, no doubt, all that had been hoped for, but the immediate effect on the Royal Navy of this loss of virtually every air-minded officer and man was not happy. This became all too clear at Zeebrugge when the air follow-up could not be arranged and thus did not take place until a month later when the Air Ministry allowed one squadron to be allotted to the task. But by that time most of the German craft had managed to disperse. However it should be noted that although this slender air component was too late to consolidate the Zeebrugge raid it did valuable work in harassing German surface craft and bases in the next two months before the U-boats abandoned the Channel route altogether.

Extraordinary though it may seem, the German assessment of the Zeebrugge raid, though subsequently proved to be almost as unreliable as a wartime communiqué after a disaster, was widely accepted even by our own official historians. Yet all the time the evidence both of aerial photography, and later of eye-witnesses (see below), was available for those who wished to know the truth – that it was a success.

And now, having assessed the effects of the raid, we turn to describe it, first giving the overall picture and then giving the eye-witness accounts, from many viewpoints, of those taking part.

Nevertheless the facts are that although a number of shallow draught boats were able to leave the Zeebrugge Canal soon after the operation only intensive dredging operations managed to open the channel three weeks later and then only partly. Three weeks is a long time in a critical phase of a war. No one among the Allies believed the canals would be blocked permanently : the aim of the raid was to disrupt. Its effect would have been infinitely greater if the British Air Force had followed up the closing of the canal by bombing the imprisoned German craft, some of which, but not all, managed to slip out later. Unfortunately Admiral Keyes was at that time no longer able to apply the four bomber squadrons from Dunkirk to the task of destroying German shipping trapped in Zeebrugge. Twenty-three days before the Zeebrugge raid the Royal Naval Air Service had relinquished control of all air force matters except the design and construction of airships and aircraft carriers. This meant that nearly three thousand aircraft and 67,000 men trained to fly and maintain them, as well as 103 airships, had passed from the Royal Navy to the Royal Air Force.

The long-term results were, no doubt, all that had been hoped for, but the immediate effect on the Royal Navy of this loss of virtually every air-minded officer and man was not happy. This became all too clear at Zeebrugge when the air follow-up could not be arranged and thus did not take place until a month later when the Air Ministry allowed one squadron to be allotted to the task. But by that time most of the German craft had managed to disperse. However it should be noted that although this slender air component was too late to consolidate the Zeebrugge raid it did valuable work in harassing German surface craft and bases in the next two months before the U-boats abandoned the Channel route altogether.

Extraordinary though it may seem, the German assessment of the Zeebrugge raid, though subsequently proved to be almost as unreliable as a wartime communiqué after a disaster, was widely accepted even by our own official historians. Yet all the time the evidence both of aerial photography, and later of eye-witnesses (see below), was available for those who wished to know the truth – that it was a success.

And now, having assessed the effects of the raid, we turn to describe it, first giving the overall picture and then giving the eye-witness accounts, from many viewpoints, of those taking part.

PART ONE

PART ONE

I

Why the Raid was planned

If few people nowadays have heard of the Zeebrugge Raid, even fewer have heard of the Dover Patrol. Yet the Dover Patrol was one of the most important features in the First World War and is closely connected with the Zeebrugge Raid. The Dover Patrol was a miscellany of escort craft whose task was to protect the transports which conveyed Allied troops and stores to and from France. The magnitude of this task will be appreciated when it is realised that by 1918, at Dover alone, one million wounded men had been evacuated and every day 12,000 to 15,000 men were transported. All this was through a Channel littered with wrecks, full of mines and vulnerable to enemy submarines, destroyers or air attacks. By the end of the war some 10,000,000 men had passed through Dover, and even more through Folkestone.

To protect this vital traffic the Dover Patrol had an assortment of shipping, which for most of the time comprised an obsolete battleship, a few cruisers, a varying number of destroyers, a cross-channel steamer which had been converted into a floating sea-plane base and a motley collection of trawlers, drifters, armed yachts and motor launches.

This little fleet was based at Dover and Dunkirk. It performed magnificently and went beyond the normal limits of human endurance, so much so that after the first few encounters German coastal shipping was reluctant to try any venture likely to bring it into contact with the Patrol. (On one occasion, the night of 13th February 1918, a German destroyer did take a chance and undetected, through signalling mishaps, sank several drifters and a trawler before streaking for home again; the success of this daring venture was largely due to the fact that British ships in the Channel could not believe that any surface craft heard or seen in the dark could be anything but their own.)

Not least of the achievements of the Dover Patrol was maintaining an illuminated route from England to France – protected by minefields and surface craft. Although an illuminated route was itself partly vulnerable, its drawbacks were nullified by the fact that the presence of this lighted

19

Submarine "C.1"did not arrive at Viaduct

"Moorsom" and "Melpomene"
Western Patrol

"Trident" and "Mansfield"
Patrol off Blankenberghe

Picket Boat
Rescued crew of "C.3"

4 Motor Launches
Guarding against attack from N.W.

6 Motor Launches and 1 Coastal Motor Boat
Western Smoke Screen

4 Coastal Motor Boats
Stokes gun attack on Mole
Then Patrol off "Vindictive"

Course of Submarine "C.3"

2 Coastal Motor Boats
Smoke Screen off Blankenberghe

Submarine "C.3"
Destroyed Viaduct

Trenches & Machine Gun

Gun Emplacements &
Harbour Masters Office

.37 m.m. Guns

Machine Gun &
Gun Emplacements

Dugouts
Wartemberg
(Zeppelin) Battery
● ● ●
4·15qm.
Naval Guns
● ●
3·10·5 c.m.
Guns

BLANKENBERGHE & ZEEBRUGGE
LIGHT RAILWAY

The shore artillery opposition to this attack
consisted of about 24 Batteries extending
from the Dutch Frontier to Blankenberghe
including heavy guns of 21 c.m., 28 c.m., and
30·5 c.m.

Cables

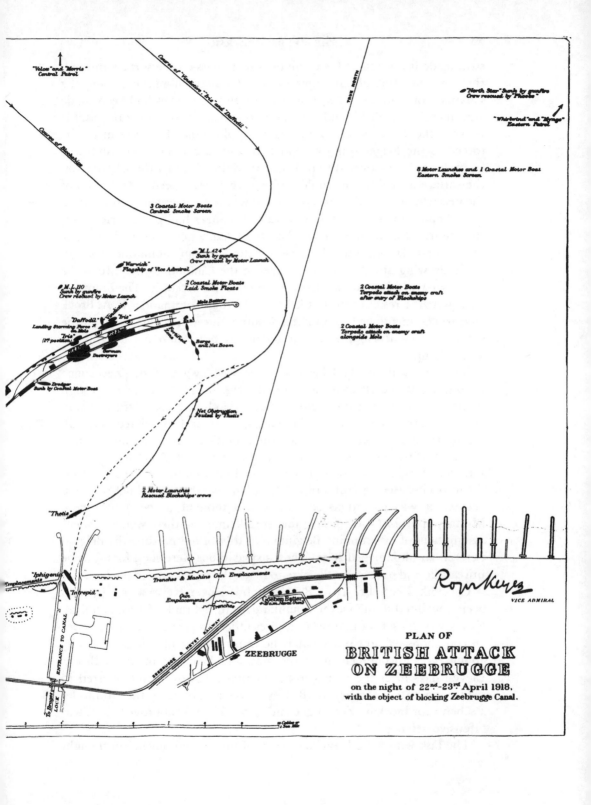

PLAN OF

BRITISH ATTACK
ON ZEEBRUGGE

on the night of 22ⁿᵈ-23ʳᵈ April 1918,
with the object of blocking Zeebrugge Canal.

strip made it impossible for German craft to pass on the surface through the Channel. Initially attempts to stop German submarines using the Channel route to the Allied transatlantic shipping lanes had been made with patrols, minefields and anti-submarine nets. It would not be possible to keep the U-boats out of the Atlantic altogether but they might be forced to the longer route around Scotland to get there. However the Germans soon discovered that if they travelled through the Channel on the surface at night, they could cruise at their best speed over the top of the nets which inevitably drooped in the water. In emergencies they could dive (hoping to avoid mines) and wait till danger had passed. However, surface travel came to an end when the Channel crossing was properly illuminated. During the whole period the German submarines tried to avoid drawing attention to themselves in the Channel as they would be much safer preying on merchant shipping in the Atlantic. The illuminations were the result of the fertile brain of Wing-Commander F. A. Brock who will be mentioned again later. A submarine which can travel on the surface avoids nets and below-surface mines, but it dare not do so if the area is lit up.

The Dover Patrol had been only too well aware of the Zeebrugge problem, and as early as the autumn of 1914 there had been a suggestion to block Zeebrugge and Ostend harbours. Nothing came of the first suggestion but the scheme was again raised in 1916 and considered in detail. Again it was rejected. In 1917 a more ambitious proposal was put forward; this involved the capture and occupation of Zeebrugge and its subsequent use for an expeditionary force to march to Antwerp and thus get in behind the German army. This plan was abandoned not so much because it was hazardous as that it was thought to be unnecessary. Military optimism was considerable at this time and there were confident assumptions of overrunning Belgium and thus of our needing the Belgian ports in an undamaged state. These expectations were soon found to be unrealistic and once again the plan to block the ports came to the fore.

On 28th December 1917 Rear-Admiral Roger Keyes, aged 45, had been appointed to the Dover Command, with the rank of Vice-Admiral. Keyes was the sort of man who inspires others to give of their best under all conditions. Almost immediately he improved the illuminated strip by giving every encouragement to the ingenious Wing Commander Brock. Eleven days after the embarrassing German destroyer raid referred to earlier, on 24th February 1918, Keyes was proposing to the Admiralty a scheme for blocking Zeebrugge and Ostend; it was approved. This was offensive defence.

The task which the Navy had set itself might well have been thought to be verging on the impossible. It was envisaged that Zeebrugge could be blocked simultaneously with Ostend at a date early in April. In the event the first plan was postponed, happily perhaps, because eventually it took place on St George's Day, 23rd April. It would be difficult enough to sail into an enemy-occupied and well-fortified port but it was infinitely more so at Zeebrugge which had the advantage of being screened by a long mole. That mole was, and is, the longest in the world. Its total length is just over 1½ miles. It begins on the west of the canal entrance and curves north-east in an arc. The Mole itself was joined to the shore by a causeway three hundred yards long. The fact that this was a viaduct made a most important part of the operations feasible. The Mole itself has subsequently been widened and dockyard buildings occupy part of the extension today. However it is perfectly possible to see the original form of the Mole and, as there is a plaque in the wall at the point, to see where HMS *Vindictive* came alongside. The visitor will note the considerable drop from the parapet to the lower platform; this proved to be no slight problem on the night itself in spite of suitable preparations for it.

Although the Germans did not expect the Mole to be attacked they had taken every precaution to make such a procedure highly dangerous for anyone venturesome enough to attempt it. This fact was known to the British through previous aerial reconnaissance. Preparations had included the installation of a dozen heavy guns (some 5.9 inch), anti-aircraft guns, machine-guns, blockhouses, barbed wire, a seaplane base, four hangars, a submarine shelter and accommodation for the garrison of a thousand. The raiding party would therefore not only be outgunned but also outnumbered if successful in setting foot on the Mole. There were additional hazards such as the constantly changing sandbanks which lay off the Belgian coast. Pre-war the hazards had been marked by buoys but the Germans had thoughtfully removed these as being likely to be of more assistance to a potential enemy than to themselves. This was not quite all a raider would have to contend with for in order to block the Bruges canal, which lay some distance back from the harbour, quite large – and thus easily hittable – ships would have to cover half a mile under intensive fire. Looked at with the advantage of hindsight the Zeebrugge Raid was not merely suicidal; it was attempting the impossible. But perhaps the Royal Navy's motto is: 'The difficult we do at once; the impossible takes us just a little longer.'

The aim of the raid was first to block the Bruges Canal by sinking several blockships at the point where it entered the harbour and at the same time damage the port installations at Zeebrugge as much as possible.

Simultaneously the canal to Ostend was also to be blocked by sealing up the harbour. In the event the Ostend raid, both on 23rd April and when attempted later on 9th/10th May, failed through unpredictable hazards. Nevertheless it should not be overlooked that as much courage and ingenuity went into the Ostend raids as did into Zeebrugge.

The core of the Zeebrugge problem was the Mole itself. Being of stone it could not be effectively damaged by bombardment, even from monitors. Monitors carried heavy guns on platforms which proceeded under escort to points at which they could bombard the enemy shore. Captain Coxon of the Dover Patrol described them thus : 'Of all the hideous monstrosities it is possible to conceive in the shape of naval architecture, commend me to them.' Nevertheless these ungainly monsters were used both at Zeebrugge and Ostend to 'soften up' (in modern parlance) the enemy before the raid and again during the raids when they fired into the area from which German reinforcements would be forthcoming. So that the preliminary bombardment gave no hint of forthcoming events, it had been started some time before as a routine operation.

As it was clearly impossible to neutralize the Mole itself by bombardment alone, its defences had to be tackled in some other way. It would be impossible to sail blockships through Zeebrugge harbour and into the canal entrance unless the attention of those manning the guns on the Mole was suitably occupied. Passing the end of the Mole the blockships would be engaged by five guns (4.1 and 3.5) and that would be only the beginning of their problems – if they survived the experience.

There was therefore mounted a 'diversion' in the shapes of an old cruiser HMS *Vindictive*, and two ferry steamers, *Iris* and *Daffodil*, specially brought from the Mersey. The ferry boats had the advantage of a very shallow draught, which would enable them to ride over and clear any mines (it was hoped). The inhabitants of Merseyside were not pleased when they saw their ferry-boats departing in early April but accepted their removal philosophically when told they were urgently needed to ferry more troops – mainly American – over to France. When they saw them after the raid and learnt the truth, pride and astonishment knew no bounds. One of the tasks of the ferryboats at the Mole was to press alongside the *Vindictive* and keep her in position.

HMS *Vindictive* was a curious looking ship even before she was converted for the raid. She had been commissioned in 1898 and at no time in her life had she looked an elegant craft. She had three large funnels, for she was a coal-burning ship. It was astonishing that after the battering she had received on the night of the raid she was still able to proceed back to Dover under her own power.

W. J. Maxey was a Stoker 1st Class on *Vindictive*. As he was working away in the stokehold in an inferno of noise, an exceptionally loud crash caused him to look upwards. To his surprise he could see the stars, for part of the deck had been blown clean off. As he said in 1977, 'Not many stockers have the benefit of a view of the night sky when they are doing their work.' After the First World War he joined the Territorial Army and became a machine gunner with the Middlesex Regiment. At 0630 on the morning of D-Day on 6th June 1944 he landed with his battalion on the Normandy beaches. Like many others he had taken part in the ballot for a VC after Zeebrugge but only a limited number were awarded and he was one of the unlucky ones. There were others on the Zeebrugge raid who also took part in the Second World War. One of them was Able Seaman R. S. Wright. He has a scar from a spear wound on his wrist, sustained in New Guinea in 1914. A naval party, of which he was one, had been despatched to eject the Germans from a wireless station they occupied there. The Germans had some local levies armed with spears. Wright served again in the Second World War in Combined Operations on the North African coast. Today, aged 88, he looks all the better for his experiences and could be mistaken for twenty years younger.)

To return to *Vindictive* and the operation. As soon as it was in position – and it was hoped that the smoke screen laid by the escorting craft would enable it to travel most of the way undetected (in the event this proved not to be) – an assault party would land on the Mole, deal with any opposition, and then destroy the German guns which would otherwise be preventing the three blockships *Thetis, Intrepid* and *Iphigenia*, from reaching the Bruges Canal where they planned to scuttle themselves. All three were obsolete cruisers, and for their task would be heavily loaded with cement, making them sink quickly; it would also make them very difficult to remove. Two other craft were to play an important part in the operation. They were two old C-class submarines and their assignment was to be loaded with explosives and proceed to the arches under the viaduct. There the explosives would be detonated taking a substantial portion of viaduct with them. Of this more later.

In addition to the main elements – the assault craft for the Mole and the blockships – there were a host of other craft involved. They included the two monitors, *Erebus* and *Terror*, whose duties were described above. There was a variety of destroyers: *Termagant, Truculent, Manly, Scott, Ullswater, Teazer, Stork, Phoebe, North Star, Trident, Mansfield, Whirlwind, Myngs, Velox, Morris, Moorsom, Melpomene,* and, of course, Admiral Keyes' flagship, the destroyer *Warwick*. There were thirty-three motor launches (MLs) which had a variety of tasks, but most of them were required to lay a smoke-screen for the approach. There was a patrol boat and a picket boat (to evacuate the crews of the submarines), there was a paddle mine-sweeper, and there were sixteen Coastal Motor Boats. In view of the vagaries of the Channel weather, which can match the worst in the world, the voyages of some of the small craft were likely to be nothing if not adventurous. In all there were seventy-eight craft of varying sizes engaged at Zeebrugge. (For Ostend there were fifty-nine.) Both raids were covered in case of interference by the enemy, going or coming, by a naval squadron from Harwich. For escort duties there was attached the 61st Wing of the Royal Air Force and for attacking duties there was 65th Wing. These were for the operation only, not for subsequent employment.

The old cruisers which were to be used as blockships and the aged C class submarines were regarded as expendable, but it was hoped that the ferry boats and the *Vindictive* might return under their own power, which they did. In view of their experiences *Iris, Daffodil* and *Vindictive* might well have thought themselves lucky. The destroyers were, of course, well able to look after themselves as well as others. Casualties among the MLs, which took impossible risks, were surprisingly low. The MLs and CMBs require a little explanation. MLs were mainly required for smoke-laying duties but they cheerfully took on other duties too. CMBs were faster than MLs but only, it seemed, because they were lighter. Their extra speed gave them a chance, when not laying smoke, of nipping in under the guns of enemy craft and despatching torpedoes to suitable destinations. No form of existence could be more hazardous and less comfortable than on these small craft, whizzing back and forth in the Channel, but no posting was more eagerly sought after than to them. They made war a very personal and individual matter. There are some remarkable accounts of incidents on these small craft among the letters quoted later.

Thus far we have discussed the Zeebrugge operation almost exclusively. Although it was obviously going to be more difficult than Ostend this did not mean that Ostend was considered to be of lesser importance. Fifty-nine ships were allotted to the Ostend operation, of which eleven were French. Unfortunately the Ostend operation failed both on the night of 23rd April and again on the night of 9th-10th May. The first attempt on Ostend, carried out simultaneously with the Zeebrugge raid, failed because of an ingenious piece of German deception. Although for the most part the Germans had removed marker buoys from the hazards around the Belgian coast, which was renowned for its drifting sandbanks, they had left a few in position at harbour entrances. However, at Ostend they had gone a step further and re-positioned a marker buoy, thereby creating an unsuspected hazard for any craft trying to enter the harbour without the knowledge and approval of the German command. The removal of the Stroom Bank buoy therefore completely deceived the two incoming blockships, *Sirius* and *Brilliant*, which both ran aground. Both ships were so damaged in the grounding that it was impossible to tow them off. The crews were evacuated by MLs and the two blockships blown up. As the Germans were well aware of what was happening and raked the whole area extensively with gunfire the task of the MLs may be imagined. The only gain from this was that for any future operation which might rely on enemy marker buoys there would be a careful aerial reconnaissance immediately to check that all buoys were where they might be expected to be.

The commanders of both *Brilliant* (Commander A. E. Godsal) and *Sirius* (Lieutenant-Commander H. N. M. Hardy), who had been rescued, begged to be allowed to make another attempt. This was permitted on the night of 9th May but was scarcely more successful. On the second occasion the much-battered *Vindictive* was allotted as one blockship and *Sappho* as another. On the night of the operation *Sappho* blew a hole in one of her boilers just when starting out and had to be left behind. *Vindictive*, now under command of Commander Godsal, reached the entrance to the harbour, although greatly hampered by thick fog. Eventually to disperse the fog one of the CMBs was instructed to light a million candle-power flare. This dispersed the fog but exposed *Vindictive* to all the firepower the Germans could muster. Godsal was killed with many others. Owing to the damage, *Vindictive* was not quite able to reach the position she wished, although the position she did reach caused the Germans considerable inconvenience. Again the smaller craft distinguished themselves in rescue operations.

After the end of the war it was discovered that submarines were unable to use the Bruges-Ostend canal as it was too shallow, although they used the harbour. The blocking of Ostend was therefore not as important as the blocking of Zeebrugge. A casualty of Ostend was Keyes' flagship, *Warwick*, which was damaged by a mine but managed to return to Dover.

As regards the effectiveness of the Zeebrugge blocking, it is interesting to note the observations of Captain Ion Hamilton Benn, who commanded the ML flotilla at Ostend on both occasions – at the age of 55. He was in Zeebrugge in charge of clearing the harbour the following October. He examined the Zeebrugge-Bruges canal and reported (in a private account) :

The two blockships that got into the canal on 23rd April completely blocked it and several German submarines that were inside fell into our hands when the Germans retreated from the area. The canal had been used as their base; several little docks had been cut in the side of the canal and roofed over with corrugated iron which was covered by a foot or two of turf, so as to be quite invisible from the air.

Unfortunately Captain Benn's account was only written for his family and circulated privately. Had the fact been published that he had seen German submarines trapped in the canal six months after the Zeebrugge raid, this would have put on record the fact that the raid was a complete success in its objectives and that those who believed otherwise were sadly and foolishly mistaken. Ironically the failure of the Ostend attempts made no difference to the achievement of Zeebrugge for the Bruges-Ostend canal was not navigable by submarines.

Captain Hamilton Benn, who died fifteen years ago, lived to the age of 99½. If he had had time to think of such matters as he stood off Ostend in a highly vulnerable ML in 1918, it seems unlikely that he would have rated his chances of reaching such an age very high.

2

Preparations and the Attack

In view of the number of German spies who must have been keeping an eye on the Dover area it is astonishing that the secret of the raid was so well kept. For two months beforehand, some very peculiar activities were going on. We have already noted the arrival of the two Merseyside ferry boats, which were now fitted with armour-plated sides. There was also extraordinary activity on the *Vindictive*, mainly designed to solve the problem that on arrival she would be considerably lower than the top of the 29ft. high Mole wall. For this the *Vindictive* needed to be fitted with steel gangways which would project at 45° from the side of the ship and rest on top of the wall. At the critical moment the assault parties would run up these gangways to the top of the wall, jump down four feet to the parapet path, and then descend a further sixteen feet to the floor level of the Mole where most of the German installations were. However, sixteen feet is a long way to jump, particularly if you are loaded down with weapons, grenades, flame-throwers and the like, so it would be necessary for the storming party to carry ladders as well for this part of their task.

All this required provision of the right equipment, and adequate training and rehearsal in its use. So too did the procedure of grappling the three ships, *Vindictive*, *Iris* and *Daffodil* to the wall of the Mole on which the Germans could scarcely be expected to have provided convenient bollards. This was not all. It was essential for the *Vindictive* to be able to fire down on the Mole and this necessitated the construction of a complicated superstructure on which heavy guns could be mounted. The crews of these exposed guns inevitably took a fearful pounding but as fast as one crew was killed another rushed to take its place.

Much of the special equipment, such as flame-throwers and flares, devices for creating smoke and artificial fog, among many other inventions and developments, stemmed from the brain of Wing-Commander F. A. Brock. Brock's family were the creators of the famous Brock's Fireworks, but Brock's knowledge extended well beyond pyrotechnics.

According to Captain A. F. B. Carpenter, Brock possessed 'an extra-ordinary knowledge of almost any subject. He was no mean authority on old prints and books, was also a keen philatelist, was a great shot and all-round sportsman . . . a Rugby footballer in one of the leading club fifteens.* His geniality and humour were hard to beat.'

Brock's inventive capacity was matched only by his industry. Admiral Lord Fisher wrote several letters telling him to stop working so hard. Brock doubtless appreciated the thought but carried on as before. Among Brock's numerous inventions were Very pistols, signal flares and distress flares of great power and, perhaps more important than anything, flame-less smoke screens. Prior to Brock the flames from smoke screen apparatus had made boats clearly conspicuous at night and thus an easy target. Many of these inventions were produced at the RN Experimental Station at Stratford which Brock had founded and commanded.

Brock had attended a demonstration of Zeppelins in 1914 in Germany, dressed up to look like an American tourist (nobody at that stage thought America would ever enter a European war). On the strength of his view of the Zeppelin he invented a special bullet for bringing it down. He held the rank of Lieutenant-Colonel in the Army, Wing-Commander in the Air Force and Lieutenant-Commander in the Navy, apparently concur-rently, which must be unique. Brock was far too valuable a man to risk in a hazardous venture such as Zeebrugge but he insisted that he must go partly to ensure that all his special apparatus worked, and partly so that he could have a close look at some new range-finding equipment which the Germans were suspected of using. It was when looking for that very equipment on the Mole that he was killed. His body was never found but there is a memorial plaque to him in the military cemetery at Zeebrugge.

In addition to the fitting-out of the ships for the raid there was the even more important problem of selecting the participants. Initially it had been thought that Army units should be used in the assault, rather than Marines or sailors, as they would have had experience of such work in trench warfare. This was not acceptable to Keyes and in consequence a battalion of Marines, the 4th, was formed from three companies, and put under the command of Lieutenant-Colonel B. N. Elliot. The Marine battalion totalled 740 officers and men and to it was added two hundred blue-jackets. A number of these had served in France in the trenches with the Naval Brigade and were no novices at close-quarter fighting. Fifty volunteers were taken from the Grand Fleet. They did not know what they were volunteering for but were merely given the reassurance that it was highly dangerous and they were unlikely to return alive! That

* Richmond.

satisfied them. Most of these were trained in demolition work. All the naval personnel involved in the actual attack (as apart from handling the ships) were under the command of Captain H. C. Halahan, of whom more later.

Even in wartime it is not possible to undertake training exercises involving nearly a thousand men without arousing some sort of interest locally, as well as in the men themselves. These were set to attack a replica of the Mole, marked out at Dover on a hillside. A rumour was circulated that the whole exercise was to capture some point behind the German lines in France. The rumour – like all rumours – travelled fast and was widely believed. The more fantastic the rumour, particularly in wartime, the greater its credibility.

As mentioned earlier, the first attack was planned for 11th/12th April and prior to this 61st Wing, RAF, stationed in France, had conducted numerous reconnaissance flights over the area. On the night of the 9th, 65th Wing bombed Zeebrugge from a low altitude in spite of intense anti-aircraft fire. A sudden change in the wind made the naval assault impossible and it was postponed. Unfortunately on the night of the 23rd mist and rain, valuable to assault forces, made it impossible for 65th Wing to repeat its former feat.

For the assault itself the attacking fleet needed to muster at sea where it was hoped its presence would not be observed and attract the attention and suspicion of any enemy reconnaissance aircraft. Before they set off orders had been given that the crews of the assault boats and the blockships should be reduced to the minimum. Once the ships were at sea, all surplus personnel were to be taken off and returned to Dover. But even without knowing what was ahead of them many men, including even some civilian workers, were determined to be in on it however hazardous. The result was that when the time came to disembark surplus personnel there were no surplus personnel to be found. Somewhere and somehow they had found out of the way corners in which to conceal themselves until it was too late for them to return. Then they boldly emerged and asked for rifles and ammunition. They received them. Many did excellent work in helping with the wounded.

At 5 p.m. on 22nd April Admiral Keyes sent out a battle-signal. It read simply 'St George for England'. His wife had reminded him just before he embarked that day that the following day was 'St George's Day'. Keyes felt this was an appropriate omen and thus came the signal. Carpenter, in command of *Vindictive*, promptly sent back a lively rejoinder, 'May we give the dragon's tail a damned good twist.' Thus came the inspiration for the Zeebrugge Association banner.

By 11.30 p.m. the fleet was closing on Zeebrugge under the benefit of a smoke screen laid by the MLs. The presence of twenty-four MLs and eight CMBs running very close to the Mole at high speed and laying smoke floats could hardly fail to attract German attention. Constant and accurate fire was directed at both the busy little craft and the smoke floats they were laying on the water; many of the latter were sunk, but enough remained to produce an effective screen. Much more serious was the fact that at 11.56 p.m. the wind suddenly changed from the north-east, which was exactly what was required to keep the smoke drifting towards the Mole and, instead, came from the south and began to blow it away. As the Germans were firing star shells as fast as they could manage, as well as using searchlights, the *Vindictive* was now proceeding to its destination in conditions of excellent visibility – especially for enemy gunners. Two people were probably more on tenterhooks than any others at that point, one was Captain A. F. B. Carpenter who was quite determined that while a single piece of the *Vindictive* was still afloat it should get to the Mole, and the other was Lieutenant-Commander Rosoman, who had been responsible for all the extra fittings on the ship and was equally determined to get there and prove they worked.

As the smoke cleared and *Vindictive* became clearly visible, the expected happened. Every German gun which could be trained on *Vindictive* opened fire at that moment and continued firing. Almost every German shell was a direct hit but as the salvos crashed into *Vindictive* she returned shot for shot from her own guns. The noise was indescribable and it seemed that under no circumstances could *Vindictive* survive, let alone reach the Mole. But Carpenter altered course slightly, increased speed and came in across the tide at 45° to the Mole. This had the effect of making the ship an even broader target for the German gunnery but as German shells and bullets ripped into her or ricocheted off her, she gradually closed that last vital 300 yards. In the last part of it, rifle fire was also added to the general din but with pieces of her superstructure falling away, and with men dying every minute, *Vindictive* surged on; at 00.01 on St George's Day, 23rd April, she came alongside the Mole.

But as one set of problems was solved another set appeared. Although neither steering nor engine room had been hit, many men and their guns had been reduced to twisted shambles. Among those killed were key figures such as Lieutenant-Colonel B. N. Elliot of the Royal Marines, and Captain Henry Halahan, leader of the Naval storming parties. Some of these casualties could have been avoided if senior officers had been ordered not to put themselves in exposed positions which, without orders to the contrary, they were certain to do.

Another unsuspected problem created by the five minute dash through the hail of German fire was that *Vindictive*'s speed and course had taken her 300 yards further along the Mole than originally intended. The consequence was that she was unable to use her larger guns to support her own assault parties. This fact reflects all the more credit on those parties for accomplishing so much without adequate covering fire.

As the *Vindictive* came alongside the Mole, the wash caused by her speedy arrival ground her against the wall damaging ramps not already ruined by enemy gunfire. Until *Daffodil* and *Iris* arrived to push *Vindictive* close to the Mole the special grappling anchors could not be used. The only benefit was that in that position the Germans could no longer bring their heavy guns to bear on her. Two ramps were usable and up these, thirty feet at forty-five degrees, went two parties, one Naval under Lieutenant-Commander Bryan Adams, the other of Marines under their Adjutant, the then Captain A. R. Chater, whose viewpoint of the raid appears later. Both came under short-range machine-gun fire.

Two more ramps were now worked into position and also a mole anchor fixed. The plan was for *Daffodil* to come alongside *Vindictive* and disembark its assault parties over the cruiser's side. In the event this was impossible and *Daffodil* had to disembark her men over her bows – in those conditions. *Iris* had planned to land her assault crews on the Mole with scaling ladders but the swell made this impossible and eventually *Iris* also had to land from over *Vindictive*.

Scenes of superhuman sacrifice and courage took place as the landing parties fought their way ashore. The top priority was not merely to land and kill enemy soldiers but to demolish the guns by which the blockships could be prevented from reaching their destinations. The assault parties therefore simply could not let themselves be pinned down. However their efforts to reach their objectives took an appalling toll.

Almost impossible risks were taken in securing the gangways to the Mole, for the rise and fall of the sea lifted them up and down a dozen feet. The same problem arose with the ferry boats. *Daffodil* was manoeuvred into position by Lieutenant H. G. Campbell who was already wounded in the head and unable to see out of one eye. *Iris* was in great trouble from the fact that the scaling ladders would not stay in position because of the heaving of the swell and several were broken. Fixing the Mole anchor cost several lives, including that of Lieutenant Commander G. Bradford who jumped on the Mole from a derrick carrying the anchor, which he secured. He was promptly shot and Petty Officer M. D. Hallihan, who attempted to recover his body, was also killed.

Other German guns had now ranged on the *Vindictive* and the whole of the ship's foremost 7.5 Howitzer crew were wiped out. A Naval crew promptly took their places and were also killed. The foretop was hit but Sergeant N. A. Finch, although knocked over backwards and severely wounded, kept the Lewis gun going and eventually, when that too was wrecked, carried a badly wounded shipmate down to the sick bay. He lived to receive his VC.

Among the first to land was Wing-Commander Brock. He ran quickly along the parapet wall towards the lighthouse (i.e. away from the shore). Here was a look-out point with a range-finder above it. A bomb was put inside the look-out post to make sure there were no occupants and as it was clear Brock went to examine the range-finder above. That was the last that was ever seen of him.

This detachment was commanded by Lieutenant-Commander Adams who led it with great verve and courage. Unfortunately for them when they moved beyond the look-out station they found themselves under fire from German destroyers anchored on the inside of the Mole and also German machine gun fire from further along. At this point there arrived on the scene Lieutenant-Commander A. L. Harrison who had been wounded on the *Vindictive*, and left there unconscious with a fractured jaw. On recovering consciousness, before having his wound dressed, Harrison had forced himself up the gangway on to the Mole. He promptly took control, sent Adams back for reinforcements, and then led a charge against the German machine gun post. Their objective was the German 4.1 but owing to the fact that the *Vindictive* had landed 300 yards further away than expected and the Mole was brilliantly lit they faced a near impossible task. Nevertheless, although they did not demolish this battery it never went into action against the blockships, so it seems that this storming party killed enough of the gun crews to neutralise the guns.

Inevitably the gallant Harrison was killed. He was an English Rugby football international and on many occasion had led English forwards with the same dash that he displayed on the Mole. He was a product of Dover College. How he managed to lead a charge with a head wound and a fractured jaw is a mystery. He was awarded a posthumous VC.

Meanwhile the Marine assault group had the double task of holding off reinforcements from the shore and also attacking the fortified zone 150 yards from the seaward end of the Mole. There was in fact insufficient time to do both before the blockships had passed the end of the Mole and the recall sounded. All this time, of course, while German attention on the Mole was being occupied, the blockships *Intrepid*,

Iphigenia and *Thetis*, were creeping nearer to round the edge of the Mole, pass through the harbour and sink themselves in the Bruges canal.

On the Mole No 5 Platoon, Royal Marines, under Lieutenant T. V. F. Cooke, led the attack, wiped out a sniper post, and covered the advance of the other Marine platoons. Cooke was twice wounded and was eventually carried back to *Vindictive* by Private J. D. L. Press, himself also wounded. Other platoons from the depleted A and B Companies were landed and took part in the battle here, but time ran out before they could complete their task. C Company had planned to demolish targets in this area but as it was crowded with our own men had to be content with hand-to-hand fighting and also throwing some bombs on to the decks of the German destroyers anchored alongside.

While all this was going on another surprise was being arranged for the Germans. The obsolete submarines *C1* and *C3* had been packed with explosive and towed towards the Mole by the destroyers *Trident* and *Mansfield*; after that they were to proceed under their own power. They were fitted with gyro-controls so that at the very end of their voyage the crews could be taken off and the submarines reach their suicidal destination empty of everything except high explosive.

By a strange mischance the tow rope of *C1* broke when it was still in mid-channel and *C3* arrived alone. That did not dismay her commander, Lieutenant R. D. Sandford, and disregarding the presence of the gyro equipment, which he did not feel could be entirely relied on, he steered *C3* into a viaduct arch with sufficient force to jam her there. Then he ordered his small crew into the skiff and himself lit the vital fuses. Losing no time at all he joined his comrades in the skiff on which, although they did not know it, the propeller shaft had just broken.

The Germans on the viaduct above, who at first had been amused by the antics of this stupid submarine which had presumably tried to pass under the viaduct and had jammed itself, now determined the crew should not escape and opened up on them with rifles and machine-guns. The skiff made slow headway being pulled against the current by oars, and with several men wounded their plight seems to have amused the Germans. A few seconds later there was a mammoth explosion and a great piece of viaduct went hurtling into the air. Unaware of what had happened, a company of German reinforcements, pedalling frantically towards the Mole, came to the point where the viaduct had just been blown and rode straight into the sea. All were drowned. The noise of the explosion was heard all over the Mole, but only just, as all on the Mole and the ships at the time are quite certain they had never before experienced such a general noise in their lives. Sandford, alas, who commanded *C3* so gallantly, died of typhoid six months later.

The blockships had been timed to pass the end of the Mole at twenty minutes past twelve. It was essential that the Germans should be kept occupied on the Mole while the blockships crossed the harbour, but once they were in then *Vindictive, Iris* and *Daffodil* must re-embark their storming parties and make their way back to Dover – if possible.

But retiring is not easy when you have roused a hornet's nest, particularly if you are determined to leave neither your wounded nor your dead behind. It was an awkward time, for the ships were under constant fire from the shore batteries. Yet men went back and forth for their comrades. Casualties were still being sustained, Carpenter was hit but not seriously, and Rosoman, his first lieutenant, was wounded in both legs. Finally it was done and the ships pulled away.

As they left, the shore batteries redoubled their efforts. One caught *Iris* on the bridge killing both Commander Gibbs and Major Eagles of the Royal Marines among others. As *Iris* lurched on, other shots crashed down on her and only a timely smoke screen from an ML enabled her to limp into obscurity. Even then she was not safe for another salvo caught her, setting her alight. The last explosion scattered her own bombs over the decks and Able Seaman F. E. M. Lake calmly but hastily picked them out of the debris and hurled them overboard. His hands were badly burned in the process, but if he had not continued the consequences would have been unimaginable. He received a well-earned CGM.

So many were the casualties on all three ships that the sick bays were crammed and the surgeons overwhelmed. They worked swiftly and without pause, surrounded by wounded and dying. Here was perhaps the greatest test of all. It is one thing to be cool and brave in the impending excitement of battle when all your limbs are intact, but quite another when battered, lacerated and close to death you wait your turn with the surgeons. Some of the wounded were past human aid and died where they lay. Those who lived bore their pain and discomfort stoically, even cheerfully.

3

The Blockships

The blockships, which were timed to round the Mole twenty minutes after the arrival of *Vindictive, Iris* and *Daffodil*, all had different tasks. *Thetis*, the leading ship, was to ram the lock gates, the other two were to ground themselves by the southern end of the piers. Breaking the lock gates would make it impossible to fill the canal and float any imprisoned craft, while the other two ships could be relied on to create a barrier of silt and complete the unnavigability of the canal.

Thetis duly rounded the Mole although under fairly heavy fire (though not as heavy as it would have been without the effects of the diversion) and promptly ran into anti-submarine nets at the harbour entrance. These she took with her. However she had been hit so often that both her engines went out of action and she began to sink. One engine was temporarily started and this was just sufficient to pull *Thetis* around into the dredged channel, where she would have the greatest nuisance value. Then orders were given to abandon ship. As *Thetis* settled down in the water, demolition charges blew out her bottom and she was there to stay.

Although not in the position originally intended she had done nearly as well. She was blocking a vital channel and in getting there she had gone through a wire net – at the cost of her own engines – leaving a clear passage for the other two blockships. Furthermore she had drawn the German fire on herself and enabled *Intrepid* to pass up the channel unscathed. But it should not be thought that *Thetis* took her pounding from the German guns impassively. Her own guns, though greatly outnumbered, fired till they were nearly red-hot. Needless to say there was an ML indifferent to its own risk ready at hand to rescue the crew of *Thetis*.

Intrepid had not missed her baptism of fire even though she was screened by *Thetis* in the harbour itself. She had had a smart welcome from German shrapnel just before she reached the Mole and when she forced her way into the canal, the Germans, aware now of what was afoot, launched all the high explosive they could muster at her.

The channel was slightly narrower than had been anticipated and when *Intrepid* came to her intended position she was not as squarely across the channel as she could have wished. Attempts to square her off had no effect and she was therefore sunk in the best position she could reach. Disembarking her crew was no easy task for there were eighty-seven men aboard – thirty-three more than there should have been. However, as nonchalantly as if taking part in some peacetime regatta, the MLs buzzed around unconcernedly and rescued the crews from Carley floats, skiffs and cutters. Only one man was lost and he was killed by a machine gun bullet when actually in the rescue ML.

Iphigenia was also overmanned owing to adroit concealment when surplus personnel should have been taken off. She too had been greeted by German shrapnel off the end of the Mole. She had an awkward moment when suddenly caught by flares and two searchlights but managed to elude these by disappearing into a smoke screen. She was helped greatly by a green light on the starboard side of *Thetis*. At the canal entrance she was hit twice by shells, one of which cut the siren steam pipe and surrounded her with clouds of steam.

Entering the canal she collided first with a barge and then with the port-bow of *Intrepid*. However the commander, Lieutenant E. Billyard-Leake, then swung her around, across the canal, blocking it perfectly. The crew embarked in the cutter and abandoned ship. The charges then blew out the bottom of *Iphigenia*. Most of the crew then transferred to *ML 282*, which, under the redoubtable Lieutenant Percy Dean, had already rescued the crew from *Intrepid*.

The courage and skill of junior officers on blockships and MLs was quite remarkable. No less remarkable was the complete understanding and trust between officers and all other ranks. Every man on every ship knew that at a moment of crisis his officer would be there calmly appraising the situation and utterly unconcerned for his own safety. Equally every officer knew that if he were wounded or killed one of his men would, at the first possible moment, carry his body back to the surgeons. This would not of course happen while the fight was continuing but it would certainly happen later.

Inevitably, public attention after the raid was concentrated on the main performers, *Vindictive, Iris, Daffodil, Thetis, Intrepid* and *Iphigenia*. But all told 1700 men were engaged in the Zeebrugge raid in various capacities, and some of the lesser known parts of the raid will perhaps emerge from the personal viewpoints which follow. Unfortunately for the historian the veterans of Zeebrugge tend to be unduly modest. They will speak of others glowingly but tend to obscure their own part. For example the destroyers cruised off the end of the Mole to protect the attacking ships from torpedo attack and also to assist the smoke-laying craft. One veteran the author spoke to had been eighteen at the time and described his part as being 'more or less an observer, not really taking much of a part'. (He had also fought in the Battle of Jutland when he was only sixteen.) In fact the destroyers were under constant fire from the shore batteries, and returning the fire with everything they had. Keyes' flagship, the *Warwick*, was heavily involved here. *North Star* was sunk.

Of the MLs and CMBs, Keyes wrote in his report : 'The zest of most of the young officers in the coastal motor boats, like that in the motor launches, compels one's admiration. He went on to quote one of many cases. Lieutenant E. Hill in a CMB had the misfortune to foul his propellers when only eighteen miles out from Dover on the night of 22nd April. He got a tow back to Dover from a drifter and arrived by 8 p.m. It took an hour and forty minutes to repair the damage and at 9.50 p.m. he set off once more. He covered the seventy-two miles to Zeebrugge in exactly two hours, took up position to lay smoke floats and stayed there doing his job calmly under heavy and continuous shell-fire. Some of the MLs, when not on other duties, amused themselves by moving close in to the shore, allowing themselves to be caught by searchlights, then moving away in a cloud of smoke just as the first salvo of German shells crashed into the sea where the ML had been a few seconds before.

When news of Zeebrugge came back to England one of the most awkward problems was to decide where the well-earned decorations should be bestowed. With so many acts of outstanding courage the list would be a long one but the difficulty with decorations is that if one unit receives a very large number of awards for an exploit which takes a short time – in this case little more than an hour – there are bound to be repercussions in other units where men are no less brave and would have been glad of such a chance. And thought had to be given to those who fought those endless grim battles in the trenches on the Western Front. As regards VCs which are inevitably the most prized decorations, it was decided to use the procedure laid down by Royal Warrant. This stipulates that when there are several men all equally deserving of a VC a ballot shall be made. Thus many Zeebrugge veterans received the satisfaction of knowing their names had been in the ballot as deserving VCs, though not, ultimately, receiving the coveted award. The ballot was not however a mere matter of drawing names out of a hat, but an election by all the men nominated as to which of their company was the most deserving. This procedure was applied to officers and men alike. Eventually eight

VCs were awarded, two of them posthumously. There were twenty-one
DSOs, twenty-nine DSCs, sixteen medals for conspicuous gallantry, one
hundred and forty-three distinguished service medals and two hundred
and eighty-three names mentioned in despatches (MID). For the Ostend
operation of 9th/10th May a further three VCs were awarded, ten
DSOs, eleven DSCs, two CGMs, sixty-three DSMs and one hundred and
one names mentioned in despatches.

PART TWO

I

HMS Vindictive and her Crew

HMS *Vindictive* was an old light cruiser of 5,600 tons. Originally that class of boat had been nicknamed the 'Fleet rams'. Her top speed was 17 knots, and she drew only 13 feet of water. She was old, expendable yet serviceable, and was therefore ideal for her allotted task.

For the Zeebrugge raid Captain A. F. B. Carpenter was appointed captain of the *Vindictive*, although at the time Captain Halahan was senior. However, this anomaly was settled by a strict definition of areas of responsibility. Carpenter was to navigate *Vindictive* but Halahan would be in charge of all the assault operations.

There is no doubt that Carpenter handled the ship with great skill and was also extremely lucky. Although grazed by passing bullets, his only real damage was a flesh wound in the shoulder. However, as the illustrations show, his clothing was not so fortunate.

Just as the entire force had great admiration for Sir Roger Keyes, so did the company of *Vindictive* think very highly of Captain Carpenter. The respect between officers and men was mutual. All were, of course, hand-picked from volunteers, and by any standards were of exceptionally high quality. Carpenter had a pleasing sense of humour. In his own book, written in 1921, his own part is, not surprisingly, put into the background, although he had been awarded the VC.

Carpenter was very conscious of the need for surprise. Zeebrugge was a suicidal mission but if the Germans could be caught napping – as they were – there was an excellent chance of success. Unfortunately a change of wind blew away the smoke screen and exposed *Vindictive* to point-blank fire but miraculously she was not hit in any place which would have rendered her helpless, i.e. waterline, steering or engine-room. One letter criticises the MLs for not reacting quickly enough to the change in the wind direction but E. Hilton Young, in his account (see page 64) notes that one did, and acted accordingly – at fearful risk to itself for it crossed the line of fire.

Perhaps the most remarkable feature of Zeebrugge was the morale of all those who took part. Rarely, if ever, can such a large yet closely knit band of brothers have worked so selflessly together. It was vital that they should, for the obstacles to success were so numerous, from mines to bad weather, from uncharted shoals to outlying submarines, that only the coolest and bravest could have thought success was possible. How cool and how brave those men were is disclosed in the following pages.

*

Contemporary letter from Engineer Commander W. A. Bury – this and the following two letters were sent in to me by Commander Rosoman's son.

Ever so many thanks for your much appreciated letter. It is indeed high time I answered it, but I have been postponing this in the hope that I would soon be able to sit up and write properly. They say this slow progress is quite normal. I had three halfcrowns in my trouser pocket and was struck at such close range (about 30-40 yards) that the bullet took one through with it, and so there was a great deal of tissue, etc., damaged inside the thigh, which has wasted considerably.

But to get on with something more interesting. When I joined up at Chatham nobody could give me any information as to the job, but I was told to report to Captain Davidson, *Hindustan*. On board there I found many Grand Fleet officers collected all looking very mysteriously at one another but not daring to ask what the job was, as we understood that all would be made clear by the Admiral, who was to come down to see us that afternoon. When he arrived, the Admiral saw us all in the captain's cabin, weeded out married men, told us all details, and filled us with enthusiasm in his extraordinary quiet way, told each officer off for his particular job, and left us with a strong sense of assurance. All the executive officers were carefully selected : Harrison, Godsal, Sneyd, Hardy, Bradford, Adams, etc., and a splendid lot they were, but I think all the engineers, like myself, were told off from ships where they could be spared. Being the senior EO of the lot, I got the *Vindictive,* and had most of the organization of the engine-room ratings of all ships, which made things interesting until we got into running order.

There was a considerable amount to be done in the *Vindictive* in the way of preparation and outfit, both below and on deck, and myself and her 1st Lieutenant (Rosoman) were the only officers attached to her for a considerable time. Meanwhile, the bluejacket landing party (about 260 strong), under Harrison, Adams, Bradford, etc., were daily trained up in the fields which the soldiers used. They were taught all the new tactics, including 'dirty work' at close quarters with rifles and bayonet, etc., by army experts. ER ratings were all put through rifle and bayonet exercises too. The Marine detachments did similar training elsewhere. They were about 730 strong.

Eventually all was got ready, smoke devices fitted, flame projectors fitted, precautionary measures taken in the way of special fire arrangements, splinter protection in the funnels and uptakes, brows fitted, ammunition stored for Stokes guns, Mills grenades, howitzers, machine-guns, etc., etc. A mess was started, and extra accommodation found for the Marine officers who would have to live on board during the period of waiting, so Rosoman's hands were full. We had two 7.5 howitzers, and one 11-inch ditto, two pom-poms in fore top, and three on port side. Many Stokes guns behind sandbags on boat deck, ammunition was everywhere, to say nothing of gas flasks, smoke flasks, oil flasks, etc., all on upper deck, so we quite expected to put up a good Brock's Benefit if hit.

Finally the squadron sailed for an isolated spot. *Hindustan* came with us to accommodate the surplus of marines and officers whom we couldn't stow. *Vindictive, Sirius, Thetis, Brilliant, Iphigenia, Intrepid, Iris* and *Daffodil*. It can be readily understood that as not only the success but the possibility of the enterprise depended almost entirely on the smoke screen and various jobs assigned to small craft, only certain weather conditions (direction of wind combined with state of sea and condition of tide during dark hours) would suit. Eventually such a favourable combination came along, and we started off with all our equipment.

All went well until we were within twelve to fourteen miles of Zeebrugge when the wind shifted and we had to retrace our steps. The two Ostend craft were only just recalled in time by a CMB. The Admiral in the *Warwick* made one letter, I believe, by wireless, and promptly got a reply in the shape of a 15-inch projectile in the vicinity, presumably by D.W. The 16-point turn was accomplished by large and small craft, without mishap, notwithstanding the close formation, etc. We saw no enemy craft, though we afterwards heard they were not far off with a destroyer patrol. Of course this nearly broke our hearts. Another attempt was made, but we had to return on account of the sea, after we had been under way only two hours.

The First Sea Lord and First Lord had come down before we sailed to wish us good luck and see the ship. After our first close attempt doubts were entertained as to the possibility of the success of the enterprise, and for an awful day we thought the show was to be quashed – fortunately the Admiral overrode their fears.

Then followed a weary waiting for the next period of tides, the first of which would serve on the night 22nd-23rd April. In the interval we had made certain improvements in the way of protection, etc. The Admiral came to see us again and put to flight any pessimistic rumours. All went like clock-work, and we made all our positions correctly. When we were about fifteen to twenty minutes off the Mole, the Huns fired a very bright starshell which lasted about half a minute, and showed up what there was to see, mostly smoke. I had been standing at the top of the ER hatch watching the effects of the monitors' bombardment, and as soon as the star-shell died out I went below. There were several shots fired then at us, from where I don't know, but of course we didn't reply. Before we got alongside several shells hit the forepart of the ship. Captain Halahan, RN, was killed at the top of the ER casing, and Colonel Elliot and Major Cordner, both of the RMA, on fore bridge.

While we were manoeuvring the engines alongside we were rather badly gassed down below, but the use of gas masks rendered it fairly innocuous. The torpedo netting in the uptakes arrested splinters, and no damage was done to the machinery. In the meantime a perfect bedlam of hell broke out all round, and the old ship shook all over. It was impossible to say which were Hun hits and which were our own explosions. Out pompoms barked away merrily for a while, and then stopped, all the crews being wiped out, as were also the crews of the 7.5 howitzers. Not so the 11-inch on the QD, however, which got off 36 healthy rounds into a battery ashore. Captain Carpenter conned the ship in from the foremost flame house, and had just left it when it was riddled with shrapnel. The *Daffodil* nosed us in against the wall and held us there, and discharged her marines into us. The *Iris* went ahead of us and tried to secure to the parapet with grapnels – almost an impossibility on account of the motion alongside. Bradford climbed the spar and, taking the grapnel in his hands, he jumped on to the parapet and secured it; all the time he was being shot at, the bullets striking the funnel behind him, and those below warning him to slide down. He took no notice, and was shot dead just as he reported 'secure' to Gibbs. The grapnel broke away with the motion, and Hawkings did exactly the same thing, and was also shot.

I had made a plasticine model of the Mole, harbour, forts and lock-gates, etc., for general guidance (from aerial photos and confidential plans), also a larger model of the portion of the Mole which we were to go alongside, showing supposed guns, etc., and so soon as the engines were finished with I meant to dash on to the Mole to see how it tallied. When I reached the upper deck I found the brows nearly all shot away, and the crowded marines falling down on their faces all round me, so that I was much too frightened to look for a ladder, but directed my attention to business on the upper deck (where there were by now practically no officers, all being forward, except one lieutenant).

The ship was enfiladed for a while by a destroyer, which came out round the point of the Mole astern of us, and she did a good deal of damage, but was sunk by a CMB, and our crews claimed some shots into her too. It did not matter much what portion of the Mole we went alongside, for the whole place bristled with guns. The hull of the ship, as long as we were alongside, was protected from batteries ashore by the curve of the Mole, but the upper deck and superstructures were at the mercy of the guns on the parapet, and the super-imposed (4-inch) guns at the end of the Mole (which is a regular fortress), so the fore bridge, funnels, boat-deck, etc., suffered severely.

The bluejackets were the first over the top, led by Harrison, who was shot through the face, but, however, kept on, until again shot through the neck. (Both Bradford and Harrison have since been awarded posthumous VCs.) They suffered badly from the machine-guns' cross-fire from Huns under cover. The marines followed, using scaling ladders to drop the 16 feet from parapet to Mole. They did good work bombing destroyers, etc., alongside, and the bluejackets on the parapet bagged most of the crews with their Lewis guns as they ran across the Mole to try to pull away the marines' ladders. Chamberlain walked down to the after flat unaided, with one of his lungs blown out through his back, but died almost at the foot of the ladder. Walker had his left arm blown off, and much shrapnel in his head and neck, but sat up and shouted encouragement to his men. Rosoman was shot in both ankles, but refused to quit the conning-tower. The men were splendid; no matter what condition they were in they always asked, 'Did the blockships get in, sir?' It was a most difficult job dealing with the casualties; the small hatches, steep ladders, and darkness made it so. Never again shall I believe yarns about people rushing about picking up wounded on their backs. I could hardly move some of them, and my chief stoker, a huge strong chap, couldn't lift them.

Once or twice we were violently pushed along the deck by some mysterious explosion, but got off without a scratch. In the meantime, the *Vindictive* and her landing party having drawn the fire, the *Iphigenia*, *Intrepid* and *Thetis*, guided towards the gate by Captain Collins in a ML, steamed into the inner harbour and sank in the narrow canal entrance. *Thetis*, leading, unfortunately fouled one of the submerged nets, and got out of position; she shook herself free, however, and gained quite an obstructive billet before sinking. Their three crews were taken off by two MLs, the other two having misfired.

I think I am correct in saying that no enemy craft attempted any action, except the destroyer before-mentioned. The *North Star* wandered inside and eased off all her fish at the wall where SMs and TBs were alongside, and we believed two craft were sunk. When we had been alongside fifty-five minutes, the retire sounded. Only one brow was left, and a number of wounded were rescued from the Mole. Palmer, a captain, RMLI, went back on the Mole to look for some missing, and refused to come off till he had found them. He was left behind. We had a big quarter boom rigged out as a propeller guard, and when they rang down 'full speed astern', this took the spring; her nose left the wall (against a sluicing tide) and then we crashed away at 16 knots, switched on the smoke and quickly worked up to 19 knots. There were two big shells which hit us getting away, both forward : in the issuing-room and canteen, above WL. These shells burst into very small fragments. Two men who were close to, had their clothes stripped right off, but there was not a mark on their bodies : killed stone dead. Most of the salvos which followed us out were short. All the time we were alongside nothing attempted to torpedo us.

The old 'C' boat, full of explosives, did a fine piece of work. She made her way into the butt end of the Mole, where the tide is allowed to pass through piles – the Huns had a searchlight on her and allowed her to come right in, thinking she had lost her way, and no doubt expecting to capture her intact. She got her nose between the piles; about 200 Huns collected right over her to jeer; Sandford set his fuse to five minutes, got away in his berthon boat; then they opened fire on him; he was shot through the thigh. In five minutes the old 'C' boat, ten tons of amatol, with about 20 Huns and thirty yards of the Mole, went sky high!

The *Iris* suffered very badly when getting away. Once she left the shelter of the wall ahead of us, they searched her with shell fire, and her casualties were a considerable proportion of the whole. The marines were so crowded on her decks. Poor Gibbs had his leg blown off and only lived a little while. Our doctors had a strenuous time, and did marvellously well; every cabin had at least three cases in it, and there was not a square inch of deck which had not a stretcher on it fore and aft. Many of the wounds were of a dreadful character, on account of the high explosive. The extraordinary feature which struck me was the length of time that several lived who had large pieces of their heads blown away. One man (quite paralysed) kept on asking me where he was hit, and what was happening, when would we be in, etc. he was quite clear when we got back : he had no back to his head. We had no room to separate out the dead from amongst the living, so thickly were they packed. At daybreak the upper deck was a dreadful sight; truncated remains, sand bags, blackened corpses, represented the howitzer and Stokes gun crews. All but one were blown to bits in the fore top, where they did such good work with their pom-poms. Yet the men gathered round and gave a hearty cheer when we sighted our squadron all complete, and out of danger.

When we got alongside at Dover the gruesome business of removing the wounded and dead was the first job. We made a beeline for the hotel and a bath, where we met the survivors from the other craft, and very glad we were to see them.

Next day we had forty Press representatives snapshotting and interviewing. Personally I was fortunate enough to avoid them. The Ostend ships were not so fortunate as we were. Had they gone on their dead reckoning they would have made the entrance, but they came across a certain buoy which was lighted and had been shifted one mile. This they, unfortunately, shaped their course by, and landed one mile adrift, where they got a hot reception from the shore batteries, and evident anti-landing preparations. The two captains, Commander Godsal and Lieutenant Commander Hardy, at once volunteered to take the *Vindictive* over with their crews the next night. Several of my people volunteered to stop on with me, and I kept four ERA's, having persuaded the Admiral that it was only fair to the new captain to have someone who knew the ship. There were several delays, however, due to unfavourable conditions, etc., and in the end we had to wait for the next tide period. Commander Godsal and myself had, without any difficulty, collected a new volunteer crew of stokers and a few seamen. We went round Dover harbour, visited the captain of each monitor and destroyer, who cleared lower deck for us and so we collected the volunteers.

During the time we were waiting we removed everything that could be of value to the Hun as far as possible; gave away fittings, furniture, etc., to various offices ashore, and patched up the holes in the sides and funnels, some of which were quite five feet across. When the favourable time came we pushed off quietly, the *Sappho* joining us later, with Hardy in command, who had the other Ostend ship before. They had bad luck; blew a boiler joint or something, and had to drop out at Dunkirk, where we dropped our surplus stokers, and proceeded with only the bare necessary numbers, about forty-five in all. There was keen competition amongst the stokers to go all the way, and they had to resort to cutting out who should remain behind.

It was a dull night, with just the right wind for the smoke. The entrance to Ostend is quite an insignificant one, and difficult to find. When we got quite close, a genuine sea fog came down and rather defeated us for a little time. We steamed up and down W. and E. past the entrance, without seeing it, but got it fair the third time. The Huns saw us through the fog three times, each time in a different place; hence their yarn about 'repelling two cruisers with "accurate gun-fire" '. Just then we seemed to steam into a barrage of shrapnel, and at the same moment our aircraft fairly bombed seven sorts of hell out of the place, which must have saved us sufficient shelling to sink us, for we got right in without anything penetrating engine-rooms or stokeholds. A little outside the entrance the preliminary message came down the telephone to clear the stokeholds; but as it was quite evident from down below that they were getting in a lot of direct hits on the upper deck and superstructure, I delayed sending the stokehold hands up till as late as possible.

The Captain's arrangements were to turn the ship with her starboard side out to seaward : our cutters were that side, and the men were told off for each of them. I was to use my discretion about sending the hands up. This preliminary warning was to give us an idea down below where we were; the final order 'Abandon engineroom' (which we had several alternative ways of transmitting), of course meant that the ship was in position, and having seen every one out, I was to proceed to touch off the after group of mines, this being the signal to those in the conning-tower that everyone was up, and they would then touch off their group forward. We had about 1500 lb of amatol in different places : there was a double charge in the port engine-room. The helm was put to starboard, and we felt the ship bump. This was the last order poor Godsal gave; undoubtedly he meant to port the helm immediately afterwards, but he stepped out of the conning tower to see better, and was killed.

A short while before we bumped, the man on the steering engine got a feeble message from the sub-lieutenant in the after steering control 'All out here.' They were on the top of the engine-room casing. Nothing was seen of this after control party again, as shortly after we had cleared the ER, the place where they were was blown over the side. Then we got the order 'abandon engineroom,' and the engines were left running full astern port, half ahead starboard.

Every one went up. I waited in the engineroom till each petty officer reported his part cleared, and then went up myself. There was a fearful din on the upper deck, as well as shrapnel; the machine-gun bullets were making a noise just like pneumatic caulkers. Several of our people never got further than the escape doors, and all made for the cutters, which were just touching the water. Seeing that the ship was not slewing (our port propeller had been damaged against Zeebrugge Mole), and also there was a danger of the falling funnels and things cutting the electric leads, I made my way aft, to the dynamo-exploders, and fired the after mines. Several portions of the port engine shot up into the air, and the poor old ship sat down on the mud with a loud crash, at an angle of about 30 degrees to the pier, where her bows touched, and on a fairly even keel.

Then I got down the sea gangway and into a cutter, which was all splintered by a pom-pom or something, and to my intense surprise and relief, saw there was a motor launch alongside, and scrambled over her bows somehow. She was in a sinking condition, and had very little free-board forward. Nearly all our people were already in her. Of course they switched machine-guns on to us; star-shells made the place bright, and many of us were hit. It is uncomfortable when you can see the bullets coming; they used tracers, red and green. They must have been 1870 gunners, because the launch passed fairly close to the pier, and none of us should have been missed getting over the ship's side. They followed us out into the smoke with various calibres, lots of spray and sparks, but no more hits. We closed the *Warwick* just in time, for we were on fire as well as sinking, and to make sure of her we blew up the ML. Not long after, we walked on a mine which badly damaged us aft, so we had to clear out and board *Velox*. These shifts did the badly wounded folk no good. Finally we were hoisted on board the *Liberty,* where the doctors had a field-day cutting up uniforms, doping with chloroform, etc. The captain of the ML (Drummond) was badly wounded before he came alongside the *Vindictive,* and had two of his people knocked out; notwithstanding which he remained standing on one leg, and holding on with one hand all the time till he was lifted out into the *Warwick.* He gets a VC.

Engineer Lieutenant-Commander William Bury was specially promoted for Zeebrugge for his work during the preparation of the expedition, not only in his own department but in every possible way in which he could assist. When *Vindictive* was alongside the Mole, he displayed great bravery in helping to bring in the wounded and in generally assisting the medical staff. He immediately volunteered for

Ostend, begging to be allowed to remain in charge of the engine-room department of *Vindictive*. He worked energetically to fit her out for Ostend, and on the night of 9th/10th May he again rendered invaluable service. He remained in the engine-room until the last possible moment, and when everyone was clear he blew the bottom out of the ship by firing the main and auxiliary after charges. He was very severely wounded, and was awarded the DSO.

Captain Carpenter, Lieutenant Sandford, Lieutenant-Commander Bradford, and *Lieutenant-Commander Harrison* were awarded VCs for their services on 23rd April (for their citations see page 205). *Lieutenant-Commander Drummond* (of ML 254) was specially promoted for the 1st Ostend operation for contributing to the success of the smoke screen 'by his skill and judgement', and was awarded the VC at Ostend on 9th/10th May.

Commander Godsal in *Brilliant* was promoted and awarded the DSO for leading the Ostend blockships on 23rd April; he stood in to the shore in the face of a tremendous barrage from the shore batteries, as the wind had shifted and driven back the smoke screen at a critical moment. He immediately volunteered for the second Ostend operation, where he was killed in *Vindictive*.

Lieutenant-Commander Hardy, in command of *Sirius* in the first operation, was specially promoted. After the ship was sunk and abandoned he returned to look for the engineer officer, who was thought to have been left behind. He immediately volunteered for the second operation. He and Godsal also received the Croix de Guerre.

Captain Ralph Collins, the Flag Captain to VADP, and commanding the Zeebrugge MLs, received the Croix de Guerre.

Lieutenant-Commander Bryan Adams was specially promoted; in command of A Company of the storming party, he was amongst the first to land on the Mole and remained there the whole time, behaving with great coolness and bravery. He was the senior surviving officer of the Grand Fleet contingent at Zeebrugge; there were 10 officers of whom 5 were killed, and 2 wounded.

Colonel Elliot DSO, Major Cordner and *Lt Hawkings* were killed, and mentioned in despatches.

Commander Ralph Sneyd, DSO, commanded the *Thetis,* and was the senior officer and leader of the blockships. He was awarded special promotion for Zeebrugge, and the Croix de Guerre. *Thetis* forced her way through the net obstruction protecting the inner harbour, by which both her engines were brought up. Her way carried her to the west side of the Channel where she sank from enemy fire. Commander Sneyd seeing it was impossible to take the ship further blew the charges to make salvage impracticable. While still under heavy fire, and wounded, Sneyd gave directions ensuring *Intrepid* and *Iphigenia's* positions for sinking, and did not abandon his own ship until he was satisfied he could be of no further assistance in attaining the objective.

Captain John Palmer, DSC, who remained behind on the Mole was made a prisoner of war.[1]

*

Contemporary letter from Commander R. Rosoman, First Lieutenant of Vindictive: it is a masterpiece of understatement.

You have asked me for my account of the exploit and what my part of the show was. It is very natural that you should take an interest in the proceedings, but you know I am more accustomed to handle ships and boats than pens and paper; therefore you will know you have invited me to do a job I don't like, and one at which I am not au fait.

I notice you inquire how I got into it, all questions which I must try to answer, so here goes. You know I was commanding *Canning,* and not pleased with her passive job, but naturally one serves where one is appointed. We were alongside a repair ship having oxygen bottling plant installed, and I was on leave prior to my knowledge of any new appointment. When I returned, my 1st lieutenant received me at the gangway and said how sorry he was that I was vacating my command. I had no knowledge of this, and asked him what he was talking about? He proceeded to explain; all of which was nothing to do with Zeebrugge or *Vindictive;* therefore I cut it out.

My relief arrived. I handed over the command and came down to London, with no orders whatever. My relief's appointment was vice me; but, at the expiration of a 14-days' balloon course at Roehampton, he turned up too early because he did roughly 48 hours there and came north, hence no news as to my disposal. No use going on with details. I arrived in London with no orders; therefore reported myself at the Admiralty. No news there owing to this gap which I have mentioned. I was invited to proceed on leave pending appointment, which I did, leaving address. First telegram was : Report to 1st Sea Lord's Office on a certain Monday, but cancelled before the Monday arrived. Second information : appointed to *Arrogant* additional.

Somewhat, or shall we say still puzzled, I proceeded to Dover and

* The above notes, and similar notes that follow, are based on the citations for the decorations received by the officers and men concerned. The citations for the eleven VCs awarded are given on pages 205-210.

went on board *Arrogant* about 8 p.m., where I met Ralph Collins, whom I think you know, 1st Lieutenant of *Kent,* I think, when I was out in China. He is Flag Captain now to Vice-Admiral Dover Patrol. I asked about my appointment; but he could give me no information, except that he had applied for a 1st Lieutenant, and imagined I was the answer to it. As I had been in command for two and a half years, naturally it did not seem the sort of thing that I should be appointed to. I mentioned it, asking why additional? Collins naturally suggested I should see VADP in the morning, and this was fixed. Being puzzled and worried, I went into the Admiral's office the next morning, feeling as if I was carrying about two bower anchors on my back; but when I came out it seemed to me there was at least two feet of air between my feet and the pavement.

I had never met the Admiral before, but, to save my poor old pen and paper in wartime, I will only tell you that I was very much impressed with his direct way in dealing with things. To cut it short, he told me he had no command for me, but wanted me to be 1st Lieutenant of *Vindictive,* and introduced me to Carpenter. We left for Chatham the same afternoon, never having met before. Carpenter was on VADP's staff at Dover, busy with many things; therefore, your old brother was left to fit *Vindictive* out. The engineer officers arrived from the Grand Fleet for *Vindictive* and block ships.

Bury I knew from China days, so naturally I hoped he would come to *Vindictive.* He did, so we worked hand in glove like a couple of thieves. Splendid chap, Bury. Weather was pretty good, but a bit warm for the time of year, and I found, after my lazy command, I was not as bright at dashing round a dockyard as I might have been, and wanted a smart young lieutenant to assist me. This was not forthcoming, but one Hilton Young, a lieutenant RNVR, turned up, who assisted me in training the guns' crews, and was full out to do all he could, but not being a lieutenant RN, or shall we say a sailor, could not do all he would have loved to do.*

In due course we were ready to leave Chatham, and then Carpenter joined up, and off we went down the Medway to a somewhat isolated anchorage, where I could get the landing brows rigged out, which I could not do in Chatham yard, owing to many eyes observing. As we passed out of the lock, we collected a lieutenant RN, Ferguson, which pleased me very much. The monotonous days in the isolated anchorage, I will pass over.

We were a well-prepared infernal machine by this time, with our

* See pages 64-86.

frightfulness on board : flame projectors, bombs of all descriptions, and our own ammunition all on deck; because shell-rooms and magazines were stuffed up with buoyancy. Before proceeding, I must tell you about our PMO [Principal Medical Officer], McCutcheon. He joined with no idea of what we were playing at, and asked me if I could tell him how many casualties he was to be prepared for. I asked him if he knew anything about the show. He did not, except that he understood he had joined a Suicide Club. I thought a bit, and told him I had no authority to tell him what it was. As he was coming along and must keep quiet, I decided to tell him. I told him. His reply was simply ripping : 'It is not a Suicide Club at all! No, I can do a lot of good work and save many lives.' And, by Jove, he did. His organization was magnificent.

Our stay at the isolated anchorage was very trying, but we had lots of work to do which, of course, was done by everybody. The accommodation for officers and men was never intended to house the quantity we shipped, because, you know, we had blue-jacket storming parties and Marine storming parties on board. I double-banked the cabins and did all I knew to make people as comfortable as possible. Bury and I camped out together, because we knew each other, and had so much to deal with together; also I knew he did not snore.

In due course, tide, time and weather favoured us, so we received orders to sail. The gunnery lieutenant, Bramble, serving in *Hindustan*, very full out to come along, joined up to help; and very glad I was. Osborne, Commander E. on VADP Staff, joined up to do G. duties, just a few days after leaving Chatham; also a valuable asset. The fact, the whole outfit was present, and off we fussed.

Very funny procession, we towing the two ferry boats, *Iris* and *Daffodil*, in command of, as you know, Gibbs and Campbell – both splendid seamen. I must not forget to add the Chaplain, Peshall – splendid fellow, who volunteered to blow along, and VADP fixed permission.

We proceeded down the Thames Estuary, followed by the block ships. Off the Kentish Knock we met all the light forces and received on board Brock, the Wing-Commander, who was the clever devil who invented the smoke-screen upon which the success of the venture hinged to a great extent.

The skipper, Carpenter, being an expert navigator, saw to the navigation, upon which the whole thing really depended.

We proceeded. Splendid conditions as far as we knew. At the eleventh hour luck was against us; a slight wind came off shore, which put the hat on carrying out the expedition, and the VADP turned us back. I

have often thought what a difficult decision it was to make, but he very
wisely made it, and back we turned our comic flotilla, which was somewhat of a bobbery pack. If I had not been present, I should never have
realized it possible to get within sixteen miles of a hostile port and
turn round, which, mark you, took some time, without being interfered
with by hostile patrols. It was a very sad return, because you may
realize when you are in for a sort of death-or-glory stunt, to have to
defer it is not an easy matter to deal with, certainly not from the
executive officers' point of view.

We returned, anchored and waited, coaled, etc., etc. Once more we
got under way, but I think several of us were convinced weather conditions were against us. They were, and we returned quite soon and
anchored. Another monotonous period occurred here, owing to having
to wait until the next favourable times of tides.

I gleaned that the Powers-that-be up London-side nearly put the hat
on the venture; but thanks to VADP and Carpenter knowing, among
other things, how miserably disappointed we should be if it did not
come off, kept it still a going concern. The very first day of the next
period, 22nd April, all seemed favourable, and we were ordered to
weigh. It was with a great sense of relief that I received this order
because, by this time, I was feeling that the difficult conditions under
which we were living could not last much longer. We proceeded, and
the bobbery pack formed up, as before. The night was a somewhat
bad one for observation purposes, owing to what is generally known as
a Scotch mist; hence, no aerial bombardment, which, by the way, I
have not mentioned before, but was in the complete organization. The
wetness caused by the said Scotch mist pleased me, because I was somewhat afraid of fire, owing to the large amount of wood in the ship –
assembling platforms, ramps, brows, etc., which I had drenched down
with some anti-fire mixture supplied by the RNAS, but of the value
of which I knew nothing. You also know that old ships have not the
same complete anti-fire arrangements that modern ships have.

All went well as we approached our objective. At a certain spot we
were to slip the ferry boats, ditto hawser, and other things had to
happen. They did. It was my duty to slip the ferry boats, and before
proceeding forward I went to my cabin for something, I don't remember
what, but why I mention it is because I met Halahan, and much to my
surprise he had a piece of gauze stuck over his left eye. I asked what
had happened? and he told me he had gone on the quarter-deck to
look round and had forgotten the towing hawser over which he had
tripped, and had come down, cutting his eyebrow, with the result it

had been mended by a few stitches put in by the medicos. I expressed regret at this, because it was rather a bad handicap for a man starting on a desperate bit of work.

I proceeded to the conning-tower, and the skipper went into the flame-projector house to con the ship. It had been made into a very nice little bullet-proof corner by the able hands of Hilton Young, whom I had detailed for the job because he was somewhat versed in defeating the busy bullet. Soon we observed the smoke-screens ably put up by the ML's, and then the Hun started putting up star-shells. If you have never seen a star-shell you cannot realize how brilliantly they light up their surroundings.

I was in the conning-tower, as I have mentioned, when the first went up, and my cox'n, of *Delphinium* and *Canning,* was at the helm, a man I knew I could thoroughly rely upon. The skipper was in the flame-house in direct communication with me by voice-pipe.

The cox'n remarked : 'We shall get it in the neck now, sir.'

I said : 'Yes, I expect so;' but we didn't. I wondered why.

Soon I realized that the smoke-screen was so good we could not see the star itself until it had climbed over the artificial fog-bank, and so realized the Hun could not see us. We sighted the Mole about 800 yards off.

Carpenter said, 'Can you see the Mole, No 1 ?'

I had just seen it, and said, 'Yes, sir,' when the Hun saw us, and we got it good and hearty. Fortunately the skipper was not hit, and soon we were tucked under the Mole, where the ship's vitals were very much protected. As we arrived alongside the skipper told me to nip down and stand by the anchor, which I did, and let go in accordance with orders, nipping up again to get the wall anchors in place.

I am going into too many details. *Daffodil* pushed us alongside; wall anchors were never placed on account of derricks for placing same being too short, but we had a great effort for it. Adams, commanding landing-party, jumped on jetty and with a few men struggled hard to haul the foremost one in place on the parapet, but it couldn't be done. *Daffodil,* wonderfully handled, held up to the wall, and the landing-parties went out, Adams going off to take charge of his men. I may mention here that I was on the fore-bridge during this stage, and well above the Mole parapet, looking upon the Mole, and saw a very different sight to what I expected. The machine-gun fire and shell-fire were terrific, but not a Hun to be seen, and I had expected to see crowds of the brutes. The landing of storming-party was difficult, owing to the rise and fall of ship about four feet. I had better tell you that there were many casualties among officers and men before we got alongside.

The only thing we had to hit back with, as we tucked up under the Mole, was the fore-top, which mounted two pom-poms, and some Lewis guns, manned very ably by Blue Marines. Osborne was up there looking after the shoot, ably assisted by Rigby, who, I regret to say, was killed – practically all gun-crews were killed. Sergeant Finch, although badly wounded, kept firing as long as he could. Splendid chap; got VC. Osborne, fortunately, came down before the fatal shell came into the top, otherwise it is likely he would have been done in.

The skipper went aft as soon as we were getting out the storming-party to loose off the rockets to guide the block-ships in, and the work was well and ably done. The explosion of the submarine was a fine affair, and did in many Huns; also prevented reinforcements coming on the Mole.

After the picnic had been going on for sometime and we knew the block-ships had gone in, I met the skipper on the fore-shelter deck. While we were discussing the advisability of shoving off, owing to the fact that the heavy shore batteries were getting on to us, something landed in amongst a heap of Stokes ammunition and caused a few explosions, also a small fire. My coxswain, Petty-Officer Youlton, who was doing coxswain to Carpenter, was in attendance, and at once got busy with it. I got a bit of something through my right knee which stung a bit, but I joined Youlton, who was trying to stamp it out, and threw what I thought was a sandbag on it. It wasn't, as I knew when I lifted it.

The skipper decided it was time the emergency recall was sounded; this was done by the ferry-boats' whistles, as *Vindictive*'s sirens were out of action, and steam shut off in consequence. The storming-parties came in, and after waiting for five minutes after the last man had come in, on account of great fear of leaving anybody behind, the Captain told me to go down and slip the cable. This was not easily done because, while lighting people in with an electric torch, I was hit again above my left ankle, which was not agreeable. It turned out this severed some tendons and splintered a bone.

The slipping was done, but cable would not run out, so I had to nip back to conning-tower to say so, and we steamed the cable out; ably assisted by *Daffodil*, who plucked us off the wall as previously arranged. When clear, we fussed off, *Daffodil* slipping the tow. Smoke was made to cover our departure, and we went up round Thornton Ridge and so home. The Captain was very anxious to get me out of the conning-tower when he knew I was wounded; but this I refused to do because it was my billet, and the medicos had many men to deal with who wanted help far more than I did. Aft there, I could not help them; sitting down in the conning-tower I could do my job. Compasses were badly upset, but we got a destroyer to lead us. After passing West Hinder, I went aft to off boot because my left foot had swollen up a good deal, and the thing was painful. Was helped aft, and I may tell you the decks were not a pleasant sight. Off boot, on dry sock, and bedroom slipper; back to conning-tower, which I left when Dover was sighted.

Great reception in Dover. *Warwick* flying VADP's flag, passed *Vindictive* as I was coming aft. Loud cheers; she looked very smart and splendid. Here I took no further active part in the proceedings. We were berthed and wounded taken out. Some of us proceeded to Chatham hospital, where we received very necessary attention.

I have only told you about *Vindictive* and myself, which I understand you want, but I will not conclude without drawing your attention to the splendid work of block-ships, which really did their job.

The failure of the Ostend block-ships to reach their objective was due to the Hun having shifted the Stroombank Buoy to the eastward. This, unfortunately, put them on the beach to the eastward of Ostend, which is rather a difficult place to find in times of peace, as many yachtsmen have told me when racing across there, and all being done to point out the finishing line after dark, the first yacht to find the finishing line generally being the winner, although, maybe, not the first to arrive.

Lieutenant-Commander Robert Rosoman received special promotion for Zeebrugge. In the absence of his captain he was mainly responsible for the complete preparation of the ship. He set a magnificent example during the action and refused to leave the conning position during the return voyage although shot through both legs.

The Reverend Charles Peshall, received a DSO for his cheerful encouragement and assistance to the wounded, calm demeanour during the battle, strength of character, and splendid comradeship which were most conspicuous to all with whom he came in contact. He showed great physical strength and did almost superhuman work in carrying the wounded from the Mole over the brows into *Vindictive*.

Petty Officer Edwin Youlton received a CGM. He steered *Vindictive* alongside the Mole at Zeebrugge, after which he remained with his CO throughout. When a bursting shell caused a fire in a pile of boxes containing fused Stokes bombs, he averted catastrophe by stamping on the burning parts. He repeated this brave action shortly afterwards when the fire restarted just before he was struck down and severely wounded by a shell.

Staff Surgeon James McCutcheon, and *Lieutenant-Commander Frank Bramble* were awarded special promotion. McCutcheon organised the medical arrangements excellently, and by his own personal skill and attention contributed to the saving of the lives of many gallant officers and men. He imbued his subordinates with a fine spirit, his citation said, and 'it would be difficult to exaggerate the splendid qualities displayed by this officer.' Lieutenant-Commander Bramble was 'of the greatest assistance in looking after the gunnery requirements of the squadron and had charge of the port battery of 6 inch guns in *Vindictive,* where he was wounded.'

Captain Halahan was killed in the attack and mentioned in despatches.

*

Contemporary letter from Commander E. S. Osborne : '*We went like Hades*'.

Well, as soon as I got down here, this business was going on, and I was given charge of gunnery outfits of *Vindictive* and five blocking ships and two ferry steamers. Then the VA was going to *Vindictive,* and I asked to be with him, and he consented. When he altered his plans and went in *Warwick,* I was left as 'G' of the expedition and second to Halahan and 3rd to Carpenter in *Vindictive.* Conceive the armament of the good ship *V,* who incidentally carried the *Conqueror's* old crest which I changed to last year; mind you, I am not one bit superstitious, but, when I saw the good crest and perceived that though not in *Conqueror* I was in her nearest affinity, I was bucked. Those who have left the good ship *Conqueror* and come up against it, have not fared too well, have they? Two 6 inch BL, two 6 inch QF, one 11 inch howitzer, two 7.5 inch howitzers, five $2\frac{1}{2}$-pdrs. pom-poms, 16 Stokes' mortars, 12 Lewis guns.

Well, early in April this collection left Chatham, and we proceeded to get squared up. We made two previous efforts, first cancelled owing to unfavourable wind, and lastly bad weather. In the first case we got within about an hour's run. Another wait for a week or so and we came to Monday, every one fearfully pleased that we should get it over and all very merry and bright. We started about 1 o'clock and gradually collected a multitude of craft : destroyers, towing submarines and CMBs, motor launches, and the old *V* finally towed the *Iris* and *Daffodil*. Some photos taken, some gin consumed, and then dinner. We sat down five in the Captain's fore cabin : Halahan, Colonel Elliot, Major Cordner, Lieutenant-Commander Brock, and myself : six hours later I was the only one left.

After dinner we closed up two foremost 6in, and at 11 p.m. 'Action Stations : Fall in the Landing Parties.' All tows had been slipped by now, and I was in fore-top with Rigby, a young RMA sub, 8 RMA's and my petty officer. An occasional B.F. loosed off a rifle, not greatly to the joy of the remainder.

About 11.45 the monitor started bombarding, and then the motor launches and CMB's streaked ahead and put up the most wonderful smoke screen. Suddenly there was a crash and a star-shell burst – *ma foi*, a goodly star-shell, which seemed to illuminate us all; but our smoke screen hid us. More bursts, more star-shells. When the real shell started, I am not quite sure; but suddenly the smoke cleared and we saw the Mole. Fore-top opening fire was the permissive to all guns. Each gun-layer on a model had been shown his target, 500 yards, half-way up wall and alter point of aim as necessary. Allow, my 'hereditary enemy' (he was a torpedoman, and I a gunner), that this was a simple and unbreakable control. We had decided not to fire till we were sure they had spotted us. Well, a shell burst close to fore-top when we were about 200 yards off, I should say, and pinked Rigby and self very slightly in the face; so turned to the guns' crews of the F. top (2 pom-poms, 6 Lewis guns) and told them to open on the enemy's battery. The port battery, I'm glad to say, had no delay in opening fire, possibly one-fifth of a second later. 'What electrical communications!' you will remark. Thank heavens we had no insts. or telephones.

Well, we now had about two or three hundred yards to go, and they knocked out a number; but our battery, I am told, silenced them. Owing to din in fore-top, and number of weapons being fired, I did not see. Alongside rather a swell, all but two of our landing brows smashed by gunfire; but, as soon as I had gone and *Daffodil* had shoved us in, over they went, and no easy matter with brow lifting about four feet clear of coping as ship rolled.

When men had started to go out, I left Rigby in F top, and told him only to fire when absolutely certain where our own men were. Rather a job getting the Marines over the brows and ladders passed out, owing to roll, as when on the Mole parapet there was another 15 ft. drop, at least, to get on to the Mole proper. On board shells were now bursting on the funnels, bridges, and showers of splinters coming on to the upper deck. We fired rockets to show blockers way in, and as soon as we saw they were in, the recall (emergency) was made, 'Ks' on siren, if we were compelled to leave earlier than expected. Twenty minutes later we had got all the men back and shoved off. *Daffodil* towed our bow off; we let off smoke boxes on bows and quarters and went like hell, 16½ knots, wonderful work by stokers. Sheets of flame coming out of the funnels. I can't describe the state of the ship; she was an absolute shambles.

A few minutes later leaving top, a direct hit came, and poor Rigby and five were killed, and two badly wounded. When alongside we bombarded Goeben battery with our 11 inch how [howitzer] and the dock gates with our midships 7.5 in., and I believe jotted Goeben some. The centre bow had her percussion gear shot away; whilst replacing it half crew were wiped out. The unfortunate forward how had two crews wiped out.

Well, we went like Hades, and the Huns kept on plastering the water 200 yds. astern of us, thank God! The poor old *Iris* ran up alongside the Mole; but the swell prevented her from landing her men; poor Bradford and Hawkings were killed trying to make her fast. The Conquerors were in *Iris*, and I hear the conduct of all hands when she got plastered with shell for only two or three minutes, and got 65 killed and 102 wounded, was wonderful! My luck was in, only three bruises, one on chest, one on left arm, and one on heel, and a small cut on face; but one shell burst in my face. My steel helmet was as near as a touch penetrated by the right temple; goggles shattered, gas apparatus shot away; one clean shell-hole in right lapel of coat, one clean shell-hole in left arm of coat, and right heel of boot shot.

Our casualties were high, almost all from shell-fire and machine-gun fire at close range. On the jetty F-top pumped pom-pom into two destroyers and two sheds and landing party bomber destroyers, some dug-outs and knocked out some guns; but abreast the ship there were not many Huns close to. We fired a lot of Stokes bombs, also the CMB's fired all they had on board at the air-sheds.

The behaviour of the men was wonderful; because, you must remember, that before we got alongside Halahan, Walker, Chamberlain (I believe), Edwards, and half the seamen landing party in *Vindictive* were already down; Colonel Elliott, Brigade-Major, and several Marine officers also down; only two brows left and a continuous stream of shell and a good deal of machine fire.

Enuff, old son. I've spun a long enough yarn. Give my love to all my old shipmates and remember me to Kelly and the ship's company, and tell them they may well be proud of their representatives. All during the training I kept asking Bradford how the Conquerors were doing, and he swore by them; not the smallest thing had he ever to say against one of them.

On the way back, rum, whisky, chicken broth, more rum, more whisky, etc., etc.

Commander Edward Osborne, Gunnery Officer on the Staff of VAD, was specially promoted and awarded the DSO. He was responsible for the fitting out of *Vindictive* with howitzers, mortars, pom-pom and machine guns. During the action he displayed an exceptional combination of knowledge, skill, courage and devotion to duty in circumstances of great difficulty and danger.

Lieutenant Chamberlain was killed, and *Lieutenant Walker* and *Commander P. H. Edwards* wounded. They were all mentioned in despatches.

*

Account by J. Keble Bell

Vindictive was fitted along the port side with a high false deck, whence ran the eighteen brows, or gang-ways, by which the storming and demolition parties were to land. The men were gathered in readiness on the main and lower decks, while Colonel Elliot, who was to lead the marines, waited on the false deck just abaft the bridge, and Captain H. C. Halahan, who commanded the bluejackets, was amidships. The gangways were lowered, and scraped and rebounded upon the high parapet of the Mole as *Vindictive* rolled; and the word for the assault had not yet been given when both leaders were killed, Colonel Elliot by a shell and Captain Halahan by the machine-gun fire which swept the decks. The same shell that killed Colonel Elliot also did fearful execution in the forward Stokes Mortar Battery.

'The men were magnificent.' Every officer bears the same testimony. The mere landing on the Mole was a perilous business; it involved a passage across the crashing, splintering gangways, a drop over the parapet into the field of fire of the German machine gun which swept its length, and a further drop of some sixteen feet to the surface of the Mole itself. Many were killed and more were wounded as they crowded up to the gangways; but nothing hindered the orderly and speedy landing by every gangway.

Lieutenant H. T. C. Walker had his arm carried away by a shell on the upper deck and lay in the darkness while the storming parties trod him under. He was recognised and dragged aside by the Commander. He raised his remaining arm in greeting. 'Good luck to you,' he called, and as the rest of the stormers hastened by, 'Good luck.'

The lower deck was a shambles as the Commander made the rounds of his ship; yet those wounded and dying raised themselves to cheer as he made his tour. The crew of the howitzer which was mounted forward had all been killed; a second crew was destroyed likewise; and even then a third crew was taking over the gun. In the stern cabin a firework expert, who had never been to sea before – one of Captain Brock's employees – was steadily firing great illuminating rockets out of a scuttle to show up the lighthouse on the end of the Mole to the block ship and their escort.

*

Account by E. Hilton Young, MP, Lieutenant Commander, RNVR
(later Lord Kennet, DSO, DSC)

The truck gun that I was to look after for a time – 'Mother' was her name – lived on a spur of the railway in a quiet meadow half-way between Coxyde and Furnes. She had had a stormy youth, but latterly she had fallen on very quiet days. In fact, when I went to take charge of her she had not been used for nearly a year, but now there was an idea that she might be wanted again. We had half a dozen railway trucks for living quarters and for ammunition and so on, a pigsty, and a fowl run. They had all been camouflaged in light green and white, which made them by far the most conspicuous objects in the countryside. It was that, no doubt, which accounted for the frequency with which we were bombed.

I was roused from sleep one night by the smacking and grunting of three big bombs falling in the field near by. There was a large truck quite full of cordite at the end of the train. When I turned out to see if any damage had been done, there was a thread of smoke coming from it, and I found that a splinter had gone through its side, and had set fire to some bits of sacking in a corner. We threw them out, and went to bed and thought no more about it; but a few days later, when we were turning out the boxes of cordite in order to rearrange them, we found that one of the boxes was blackened. Opening it, we found that it was empty, and that its inside was charred. The splinter of bomb, perhaps with some thermite on it, had penetrated the box and ignited the cordite; but the admirable stuff had burned gently away without upsetting the rest of the cordite in the van. There was enough to have blown the whole train to Ostend. It was a remarkable bit of luck.

One evening I was sitting on the steps of my van and wondering what was going to happen next. 'It is an uncertain outlook,' I pondered. 'In a few days we shall all be recalled. It is no good asking to be allowed to stay with Mother; she is no good. I wonder where I shall find myself a month hence – at sea in some torpid battle squadron, I suppose. I shall have to go and brave that dreadful ogres' den at the Admiralty. Why couldn't they leave us alone at Lewin?'

At this moment Bill, best of commanding officers and most dynamic of men, came strolling down the line to pass the news. He told me where everybody was going to. He himself was going to reconstruct labour in a government office, and Captain Halahan, who was in general command of the siege guns, was going on to the staff at Dover in order to help to organize some special show.

'What sort of a show, Bill? Will there be anything in it to suit a man out of a job?'

'It is something very pink,' said Bill. 'I dare say that they are going to have a shot at Zeebrugge.'

That was the first I heard of the Zeebrugge affair. I remembered then a plan of the Commodore's invention that I had heard about in the *Centaur* a year before – a plan for blocking Zeebrugge with old merchant ships – and I wondered idly if this affair was going to be anything of that sort. Next day among my official notices from Bill was an instruction to call for volunteers 'for an undertaking of real danger'. It came originally from Captain Halahan, and he wanted thirty men. He did not ask for any officers. 'That is rather comic,' I reflected, 'we are to ask the hands to volunteer for a dangerous service which we are not allowed to undertake ourselves.'

I fell in the crew of Mother that evening in order to read the notice to them. There were a number of pictures that during the next two months were stamped indelibly upon the retina of my inward eye, and the scene that evening was the first of them. Our train was set solitarily amongst the shining pools and ooze of the pasture. A row of sad, thin lindens, splintered and broken by shells and bombs, stood black against a sunset of pale wet silver. The khaki-clad sailormen were drawn up in a row along the duck-boards that served us for a causeway through the mud, while from the steps of a truck I read to them the curt notice about the undertaking of real danger.

I told them to go away and to think it over, hoping for their sakes that they would not volunteer. All of them had been for two years on this front, under continuous fire, and suffering heavy casualties. They had just been released, and were to go home for leave before re-employment. They had earned a rest, I thought, and they must have thought so too; but half of them gave in their names during the evening.

The first to come was our desperado gang, a club of seven fire-eaters who had joined together to make a corner in all the 'fierce' jobs. They came together first in the trenches by the Yser as the crew of a boat that was to row over a forlorn hope of a raid to land in the German trenches. The army had thought that since there were sailors on the spot it would be nice to have some of them to help in the aquatic part of their proceedings. Where the dauntless seven led others were eager to follow, and the number that Captain Halahan needed might have been had several times over. For all I could see, most of the men were quite indifferent whether after their long service they went home to their families or engaged in the new service of real danger; but at the back of their minds, no doubt, there was something more than indifference.

Usually the sailorman is reluctant to volunteer, and dislikes to be asked whether he will do so. It is due in part to his reluctance to make himself conspicuous before his mates; in part it is due also to a superstition. He thinks that if he volunteers he is 'asking for it', and tempting Providence to 'take it out of him'; but if he is 'told off' he is quite content, because it is then a question of common luck.

I sent in the names of my volunteers next day, and soon afterwards we heard that they had been accepted. Most of Barrington's crew had volunteered too. A few days later I was recalled to England, and said good-bye to Flanders. I went to see the ogres at the Admiralty, facing that grim ordeal on this occasion not once but twice, and from my second visit I came away with orders to report for a special service on board HMS *Hindustan* at Chatham dockyard. I knew no more about the service than that it was the same as that about which Bill had told me at Coxyde. The ogre told me little. 'It is very pink,' he said. 'There will be a fight; you will find the rest of the people already collected in the *Hindustan*.'

I was sure that the affair must have something to do with shutting up Zeebrugge, but how, or what part therein was to be mine, of that I had no idea. It seemed clear, however, that it was something particularly warlike; any operation against Zeebrugge must be, which was a place so tremendously defended with every sort of big and little gun, trench, rifle, and mine, and as I walked across the Horse Guards Parade to the Pelicans' Lake with my appointment to the *Hindustan* in my pocket my heart was in my boots. 'It is a bad world,' I reflected, 'and few abide in it;' and I thought of a lad at Harwich, and how he had argued that to avoid a dangerous duty for fear of death was mere nonsense, because it was to let one's self become half alive in order to avoid being dead. 'That seems rather too abstract and metaphysical an argument,' I thought, 'when one comes to the point. I seem to need some more concrete encouragement. How does the matter stand? I shall not in any case live for ever. Had I any prospect of doing so, these problems of active service would be much more difficult :

> Comrade, if to turn and fly
> Made a soldier never die,
> Fly I would, for who would not?
> 'Tis sure no pleasure to be shot.

But I have no prospect at all of living for ever. Ending is no doubt a troublesome business, and I would avoid it if I could; but I cannot. The question is 'when' and not 'if', and 'when' measured in years is not, after all, a very important question; at least it is not nearly so important as the question whether the English or the Germans are to win in the war.'

At this point a pelican by the rails of the pond lifted his bill and gave a sonorous grunt, with a derisive expression on his debauched and cynical countenance. It was easy to understand what he would say : 'A lot of difference to England and Germany you are going to make ! Run away and play, my lad ! England is not going under for the lack of your efforts.'

Shaken in my argument by the disconcertingly keen sense of humour of the bird, I walked on in great doubt, wondering whether it was all worth while. It mattered a lot to me, and, as the bird said, it didn't matter a pin to England. But then the thought came that the victory for which England asked was not, in the first place, a victory for her arms, it was a victory for her spirit in the hearts of her children, and that by a victory there her spirit triumphed more than by a victory in the field. On the whole that seemed to be a true and sufficient answer to the bird, and I snapped my fingers under its derisive bill, and stopped thinking about it.

I went to Chatham dockyard and tramped across the rails and amongst the sheds to the edge of the square basin of dirty water where lay that aged giant the *Hindustan*. In command of her was Captain Davidson, who was the nurse of the expedition. I still knew nothing of its object or of the plan of operations. The captain took me out on to his stern-walk and showed me an aged cruiser, the *Vindictive*, lying half hidden on the far side of his ship. The cruiser swarmed with dockyard hands, and rang with riveters' hammers.

'There is your ship,' he said. 'The look of her may tell you something of what she is for.'

Surely it did ! There were machine guns and short-range howitzers; there was an unnaturally large top with a short-range armament; there was a high platform or false deck of wood built all along one side of the ship, and there were wooden slopes to give ready access to the platform for men running from below. Here was a ship equipped for a landing, and for a landing in the face of the enemy. If to land, then where? The false deck was about the height of Zeebrugge Mole. 'We are to land parties on the Mole,' I thought, 'and they will fight their way to the lock gates and blow them up.'* It was not until some time later that I noticed the blockships lying in sequestered corners of the basin, and so came to understand the true purpose of the operation, and the part that the *Vindictive* was to play in it.

But that we were in for a landing in the face of the enemy was clear enough at the first glance; and troubled by anxious thoughts about the desperate nature of the undertaking which I had so suddenly discovered, I went to the wardroom of the *Hindustan*, to find in the company assembled there an atmosphere inimical to anxiety. There were many there whose names will not be forgotten; to have known them, for a few short weeks even, was as good a gift as life could give. There were strong Harrison, a quiet tower of confidence and security; dark, electric Chamberlain, and dark, smiling Bradford, whose manner had ever the graciousness and gentleness with which the true warrior spirit is wont to surround itself in order to save it from hurting other spirits less finely tempered than itself. These great fighting men were leaders of the landing-party of seamen, and all three of them fell in the *Vindictive* or on the Mole. There were many others in that wardroom who were to die gloriously, but these three, of those who died, took a leading part in the work beforehand, and live most vividly in my memory.

Even amongst ourselves we did not talk about the purpose of the expedition, and it was not until I had been a week in the *Vindictive* that Rosoman, her 1st lieutenant, took me into the locked cabin aft where the models and charts were kept, and told me what that purpose was. Three old light cruisers, *Iphigenia, Thetis* and *Intrepid*, full of concrete, were to run in and sink themselves in the Zeebrugge Canal. The *Vindictive*, meanwhile, was to attack the Mole that curves round in front of the mouth of the canal, in order to create a diversion in favour of the blockships. Unless the batteries at the end of the Mole could be captured, or their attention could be distracted, there was not much chance of the blockships getting past them. The *Vindictive* would carry

* This was the programme of the expedition to Ostend in 1798, under Captain H. R. Popham, R.N., which resulted in the successful landing of troops under Major-General Eyre Coote, who blew up the sluice gates of the Bruges Canal, but through stress of weather were unable to re-embark, and were forced to surrender.

parties of seamen and marines to land on the Mole in order to attack the batteries and to make havoc. The seamen were to be under the command of Captain Halahan, and the marines under that of Colonel Elliot, who had commanded the party of marines with our mission in Serbia. Two Liverpool ferry-boats, the *Iris* and the *Daffodil*, would accompany us with more landing parties. There was supposed to be a garrison of about a thousand men on the Mole, and photographs taken by our aircraft showed it to be strongly fortified with posts for machine guns, wire entanglements, and blockhouses.

An effort would be made to destroy the viaduct at the shoreward end of the Mole by ramming it with a couple of old submarines full of explosives and blowing them up; that would cut the Mole off from the shore and so prevent the enemy from hurrying out reinforcements in order to overwhelm our landing parties and perhaps to capture the ship. A fleet of motor launches and of fast coastal motor boats from Dover would come with us and make a smoke screen in order to conceal us during the approach. The Dover destroyers would stand by in order to help; the monitors would lie off and bombard the shore; there would be a great preliminary attack from the air just before we were due to arrive, and my old friends the heavy guns in Flanders would join in the uproar. There was to be a simultaneous attack on Ostend by two blockships similar to ours, and *Sirius* and the *Brilliant*.

When I heard the plan there were plenty of things that I wanted to ask about. Whatever chance we had depended on the attack being a complete surprise, and I should have liked to have asked what was going to happen if the numerous fleet that we should be, some sixty or seventy vessels, was seen by a German seaplane or patrol boat during the four daylight hours of our passage to Zeebrugge. I should have liked to have asked, too, how we were going to avoid the contact minefields, and what would happen if the enemy had laid observation mines round the Mole. But questions were out of fashion in the *Vindictive*, and I had to supply the answers out of my own imagination, which was not a very difficult thing to do.

For a fortnight the ship stayed in the dockyard basin while the work of equipping her and of training the hands was being finished. The seamen's landing parties went ashore daily for physical training under Harrison and Bryan Adams. A demolition party was being trained under Dickinson; its work was to burn, blow up, and tear down the structures on the Mole. Rosoman and I were, during that period, the only two officers of the ship, as distinguished from officers of the landing parties. Rosoman was busy all day preparing the special arrangements of the ship, the fenders that were to keep her off the Mole, the great hooks that were to hold her into it, the fourteen hinged brows (drawbridges) over which the men were to land, apparatus for making smoke, two giant flame throwers and their high pressure oil-supply, special slips for the cables, specially defended control positions, and a host of other arrangements. There was never a more overworked and harassed man, or one so highly gifted with the qualities of imperturbability and cheerfulness that are so inestimably valuable under such circumstances.

It fell to my share to train the crews of the ship's guns. She had four 6-inch guns left (the rest had been taken out of her), so that there were four crews to be exercised in 6-inch gun drill in general, and in our probable proceedings during the attack in particular. In addition to her own 6-inch guns, the ship had been specially equipped with an 11-inch short-range anti-submarine howitzer on the quarter-deck, and two similar 7.5-inch howitzers, one on the forecastle and one on the boat-deck abaft the funnels. The purpose of these was to shell the dock gates in the canal and the chief gun positions ashore. They were manned by detachments of the Royal Marine Artillery under Brooks,* as were three pompoms in the top and two more in the port battery between two of my 6-inch guns. The catalogue of the ship's armament was completed by sixteen Stokes mortars, also manned by marines, which were to be placed in groups along the port side. Their business, aided by the flame throwers, was to clear the Germans away from that part of the Mole on which our parties were to land.

The 6-inch gun crews did their training in the 'batteries' of the gunnery school at Chatham Naval Barracks. Like the rest of the company of the *Vindictive* (as distinguished from the landing parties), they came as a draft from the Chatham depot. They were a very young lot, and there were all too few trained gunnery ratings amongst them, but they were very willing and cheerful. I found fifteen of our thirty volunteers from the Siege Guns already in the ship when I arrived, pleasant and familiar faces; the other fifteen could not be spared in time from Flanders. Having arrived late, these fifteen had all to be put down below in the ammunition parties, and that outraged their feelings as war-worn veterans. One by one the swashbucklers came and asked whether they might not have a place in the guns' crews, and Rosoman gave me leave to bring some of them up. They all proved a tower of strength, wherever they were.

It was necessary for our attempt that there should be a certain relation between the dark hours and the times of the tide. We must make it on one of five or six consecutive nights of the month, and if we missed them

* See page 181.

we should have a long wait, with all its additional risks of discovery, before the next series of nights began on which the conditions would be suitable. We must also have an onshore wind for the smoke screen, but that was a matter of pure chance which could not be foreseen or controlled. When the time appointed by the moon was at hand the *Vindictive* and the blockships moved out of the docks to the Swin, a lonely and remote anchorage at the mouth of the Thames, where they were free from observation. The land was a gray line upon the horizon, and there was nothing to see but a steel beacon standing in a melancholy attitude with its thin legs in the waves that were breaking white over the sands. All the fortnight that we stayed there it rained hard and blew hard, and it was very cold. The appointments of the *Vindictive*, whose return, although it was desired, was not expected, were not, it will be understood, luxurious. Another officer, Ferguson, joined us for the work of the ship, but we were still short-handed; and all that fortnight we were cold, dirty, tired, and uncomfortable.

In the Swin the ship received the finishing touches to her equipment, victuals, and ammunition. The authorities expressed their warm interest in us by sending us some of everything that they had. We became a perfect museum of frightfulness, full to the brim with every sort of solid and liquid that could be offensive to the Germans. Even after we were as full as we could hold stuff kept on coming – cases, barrels, boxes, cylinders and sacks. Towards the end of the time the work of the officer of the watch became half a nightmare, half a joke. All day long tugs and lighters kept on arriving with fresh consignments of gear, some of it necessary, some of it 'just a few spares', duplicate of what we had already and for which there was no earthly room; some of it the happy thought of someone who thought it might come in useful.

It was as hard work to keep the unnecessary stuff off the ship as it was to get the necessary stuff on. While one was busy on the forecastle a lighter would slip alongside aft and deposit its unwanted load on the quarter-deck, and then the tired hands had to hoist it all back again. There were twelve vast and superfluous casks of oil that showed an ingenuity in stealing on board unobserved that was positively fiendish. Turn one's back for a minute and one found them slinking over the side, or one broke one's shins on them already hidden like stowaways in some secret place below. They must have been casks of exceptionally keen patriotic feeling and burning with zeal for the Service. We could not but admire their spirit; but they were not wanted, so after they had been repeatedly expelled in vain they were sent ashore to be put under arrest until the expedition had started.

In nightmares there is usually some dreadful Thing – some horror that lurks at the heart of the dream. The central horror of the nightmare part of those days was a certain beast of a salvage pump, a thing like a fire-engine that weighed a couple of tons, for which the engineers had a fancy in case they should have to pump out a flooded compartment. It was after dark; we had just cleared the last of a procession of craft that had been arriving since early morning, and the tired watch were crawling below, when this object turned up alongside on a tug and demanded to be taken on board. We had no derricks, and how to lift it was a mystery to me. I tried to persuade it to go away, but it would not be persuaded. Rosoman, who, like a spiritualist medium, could make heavy objects lift themselves, was too busy to attend to the affair. The engineers stood in the background and said that the pump was the apple of their eyes. I am not sure now how the thing did come on board. I believe that it was hanging for a long time from a davit supported chiefly by a complicated arrangement of spun-yarn, while the scandalized petty officer of the watch loudly took all to witness that he had no responsibility for the pro-ceedings, and I comforted myself with the thought that, if the spun-yard did break, after all the guns at Zeebrugge would probably save us the trouble of a court-martial.

The climax came when the davit 'took charge' and swung suddenly in-board. The pump waved itself in the air, leaped at the ship like a tiger, and then instead of breaking itself into pieces and knocking a hole in our side, as it ought to have done, it settled with a slide and as lightly as a feather at the exact spot on the deck at which it was wanted. What could I do but bow and smirk, like the conjuror when he has produced the rabbit? But the petty officer said darkly that it might happen like that once, but it wouldn't happen like that twice. With the pump safely on deck the worst was over, but there were still hours of work to be done in coaxing it down below, along a passage, and through countless doors to its home in some obscure corner near the engines. It rests there still, no doubt, beneath the waters of Ostend harbour, and I feel for any one who tries to raise it.

While we were waiting in the Swin we put a final polish on our train-ing in a series of full-dress rehearsals. The ship's company and the land-ing parties mustered at the stations which they would occupy when the ship was approaching the Mole, and did for exercise all that they would have to do in the action. Our proceedings were controlled by a series of signals on the whistle. My station was at the 6-inch guns on the port or Mole side. When we were alongside and could no longer shoot at the batteries on the end of the Mole the crews of the two port guns were to mount on to the landing deck over their heads and to make fast the retaining hooks that were to hold the ship to the Mole. There were two of these hooks, one fore and one aft – they were like gigantic fish-hooks about five feet long – and they were hung on to small davits with a wire hawser attached to each. We were to swing out the davits, to lower the hooks over the wall of the Mole, and we were then to make the hawsers fast. After that we were to help to secure the ends of the brows on the Mole, and finally we were to muster in the starboard battery for fire parties, repair parties, and for whatever else was required.

When leaving the Mole we were to recover the hooks, or if we could not do that we were to pay out the hawsers so that they should not foul the propellers, and we were then to stand by our guns again to engage the Mole batteries. But there was always something a little perfunctory about our orders for what we were to do when we were coming away.

We performed these motions again and again, clambering from station to station at the sound of the whistle, until we could have done it all in our sleep. Bury, our chief engineer, had made a clay model of the Mole, and we had it on deck and used it to teach the guns' crews what to expect during the approach. As the *Vindictive* turned to starboard in order to come alongside, we in the port battery should see the flashes from the batteries on the Mole appear on our port bow, coming from starboard. We might see also the black outline of the lighthouse at the end of the Mole. Those were to be our targets, but we were not to fire until our top had opened fire. The noise of the pom-poms up there, close above our heads, was to be our signal to begin.

Captain Carpenter, who was to command the *Vindictive*, and Captain Halahan had now arrived in the ship, and at conferences in the captain's cabin we went over all the chances and possibilities. The general opinion was that our worst time must inevitably be while we were turning to starboard across the front of the Mole batteries in order to come along-side. For three or four minutes then (if we got so far) we should be within four or five hundred yards of the batteries – so close that no smoke screen could hide us and no gun of theirs could miss. I remember Captain Halahan making a sardonic reckoning of how many hits competent gunners ought to make in the time which would be at their disposal, with the number of guns that we knew that they had on the Mole; and his reckoning turned out to be not far wrong.

The critical series of nights began for which the tide was in the right phase during the dark hours, and we were all in a state of expectation, anxious or eager according to our temperaments. People did not talk about their chance of coming through – people never do. I think that everybody was fairly sure that the ship would go down with a great many casualties, and that a certain number would get picked up by the small craft or struggle ashore and be made prisoner. At any rate there was some sort of a chance that one might come through, and since there was a chance it was unnecessary to confront too definitely an unwelcome possibility. It is a noticeable thing that if there is any chance at all that anybody will survive such an adventure one's inner self helps one with an automatic and confident assumption that one will be oneself amongst the lucky ones. That effects a great economy of heroism – the great and abused word should indeed be kept for those only who, for the sake of duty, face what they know to be certain death, as Harrison, Bradford, Hawkings, Rigby, and some others faced it when the time came.

It was, I think, on the third of the suitable days that the rumour spread in the morning that we were off. We took the marines' and seamen's parties on board and filed out of the Swin, the *Vindictive* leading and the blockships and the ferry-boats following her. The Dover contingent was waiting for us between the Goodwins and the South Falls. The sea was covered with craft – long lines of motor launches and coastal motor boats; the two old submarines, filled with explosives; a couple of transports to take off the surplus crews of the blockships when we got near to our destination; and many divisions of destroyers to tow the submarines and the coastal motor boats, and to protect us on the way. The ordered lines of them all waiting for us there at this wide rendezvous on the gray waters had an aspect of intense purpose and expectation. I looked at the craft and saw how they all moved together in perfect unanimity in answer to the fluttering hoists, as if they were one machine; and I thought of the men in the craft and of the immense diversity of motive and emotion that underlay the unanimity of the ships.

We steamed eastward without event through daylight into dark. At 10 p.m. I went on to the bridge. The expedition was then at the very gates of Zeebrugge, and in a few minutes we should be committed to the attack. We were all screwed up to the sticking point, and as I climbed up the ladder I said to myself, 'Now we are in for it!' Ferguson, whom I was relieving, turned round to me and said, 'It's off!'

The wind had failed us at the last moment; there were now light airs blowing off the shore, and the Admiral had just signalled to us to go home. Whether I was more glad or sorry I could not possibly say. My mind was a jumble of pleasure at the relief from sheer funk and of disgust at the disappointment of our plans. It is good to be relieved suddenly from the prospect that the next half-hour will be an unpleasant one, but it is bad when one has been braced up for a crisis to have suddenly to relax again with the crisis unfulfilled.

Everything else was in a jumble too. At sea and by night it is not an easy thing to change on the spur of the moment an elaborate scheme of operations that affects several score of craft, especially when most of those craft are small ones with a rudimentary signalling staff or none at all. Signalmen were sent to prominent positions about the *Vindictive* in order to wink at all and sundry the essence of the new order, 'Course west.' But some of the small craft which were far off could not see the signal, and some of those which were near at hand would not. No doubt they all did keep a pretty good formation in reality, or many in the throng would have been sunk; but for a time it seemed as if we had run into a block in the traffic of some Piccadilly of the high seas.

Motor craft when they are going slow make a loud buzzing noise. As the *Vindictive* turned she ran into a crowd of them all sculling round in circles and buzzing loudly like drowning beetles. The water all round about was like one of those horrible insect traps that are put in the dining-room in summer charged with sweet beer and soon become full of wasps and flies that swim about tipsy. A motor launch would lurch across our bows buzzing, and then when she saw us she would fall into a hypnotic state, and as we turned to avoid her she would turn with us and come across our bows again. So it seemed at least, but then in the company of ships at sea in any emergency the movements of every ship except one's own always seem to be inspired by sheer idiocy.

Every now and then a coastal motor boat would dash up out of the dark and shout at us some question which was quite inaudible above the din of her motors. Probably it was her position that she wanted to know, and we shouted that back at her. The answer must have been as inaudible as the question, but the boat did not seem to trouble about that; she dashed off into the dark again apparently much the better for her little chat. The dark was full of winking sparks and of the rattling and droning of the invisible motors, and the wakes of the speeding motor boats drew lines of glimmering white upon the black. Far away over Zeebrugge there was an exhibition of tiny fireworks. It was the air-raid that was meant to support our attack. Shrapnel sparkled in the sky there, and strings of fire-balls swung upwards with a waving serpentine motion. It was a pity to have to waste all that, but in a few minutes the *Vindictive* had drawn clear of the crowd, the expedition had re-formed behind her, and we were on our way home to wait for the next time.

We cast another once more in the Swin, and for the whole of the rest of the first series of suitable days it blew much too hard for the motor launches to leave Dover. On the last day of the series we formed up and started off on the bare chance of the weather improving, but it got worse, and we turned back again after an hour. There was nothing for it but to wait ten days for the next series. A rumour went round the ship that the attempt was to be abandoned. Some authority, it was said, thought that our abortive cruise must have let out the secret, and that it was all no good.

Next day we heard that the attempt was to be made at all costs. These climaxes and anti-climaxes were the most trying part of the whole business. It made things much better when Admiral Keyes came over from Dover and spoke to our ship's company assembled on the quarter-deck, telling us that we were certainly to try again when the right time came. We got through the ten days of waiting as best we could; the second series of suitable days began, and with the first of them came fairer weather.

We started off again, joined the Dover craft at the rendezvous, and steered a course for Zeebrugge. At 11 o'clock p.m. we arrived at the point from which we turned back the time before, and the wind was favourable. A few minutes later we took the critical step that committed us to the attack, wind or no wind, and we went to action stations. The night was overcast, but there was some star-shine, and also I think a low, young moon behind the clouds. Altogether there was a faint glimmer of light on the sea, and large objects could be seen dimly some five hundred yards away.

I left the bridge and went to my station in the port battery where my two 6-inch guns were, one forward and one aft, underneath the wooden platform or false deck where the leading companies of the landing parties were now mustered. The after gun was in the open battery; the forward gun was partly enclosed by the superstructure and stood in a dark bay or casemate approached from the battery deck aft by a narrow entry a few yards long. I took my station in this bay near a voice-pipe behind the gun. Inside the bay it was impossible to see more than some slight differences in the blackness of the shadows all round. When we had felt over the gear that was needed for the gun, the crew settled down around it to wait. Some illicit cigarette ends began to glow in the corners, but it seemed an occasion for a little relaxation in the rigour of the rules. Looking out down the battery deck I could see or rather feel that they were crowded with men, mostly of the marines' landing parties, and presently a lot more of them came tumbling into our bay through a door out on to the forecastle. They filled our cramped space so full that we could not move in the dark without treading on somebody, but the decks were so full also that there was nowhere else for them to go, and they had to stay. They crowded so closely round the gun that there was hardly room to load, and if we had to fire in a hurry they were in danger of injury from the recoil. All the time we had to be telling them to stand clear, and often to be feeling about in the dark in order to make sure that there was nobody in the way; and that was our chief external occupation and anxiety during the approach.

For half an hour we waited and smoked in the dark, and there was plenty of time for a short look forward and a long look back. There was a recompense then for our several failures in a keen sense of satisfaction and relief, born of our disappointments, that at last we were sure of an attempt of some sort if not of a successful attempt. After the repeated bathos of the failures and the dismal and nervous days of waiting, one could almost forget, in satisfaction that something was going to happen after all, the circumstances that the something would probably involve one's own extinction.

What else were men thinking about during that half-hour? What do men think about in the presence of death? Some think much; some do not think at all. Each must find the best thought that he can according to his capacity; for the mind, in that pass in which none is so strong that he can despise help, turns for help to whatever it loves best – not in longing or regret, but because in love there is confidence and security. If a man has loved common things best, the thought of common things will be all that he has to help him in the presence of death. If he has loved the face of nature and the good works of man, and above all good friends, then in that pass the beauty of the good things that he has loved comes back to him to be his strength, and the memory of his friends surrounds and fortifies him.

In times of waiting under great stress of anxiety the thoughts turn backwards and occupy themselves with memory; they do not busy themselves much with the future. Up till the very last moment that night it was impossible to realize with any vivid conviction that the great adventure was actually about to happen. The ship was stealing along in such profound silence, the sea all round was so completely tranquil, the darkness was so limitless and so empty, that it seemed as if we might go on thus for ever. So the minutes passed until now it was a quarter to twelve, and suddenly there came a shock of conviction – 'We must be within a mile or two of the Mole, and we are holding our course; in ten minutes we shall be into it.'

To ease strained nerves it was a good thing then to run over again with the guns' crews all that they were to expect and that they were to do.

In a few moments the ship would begin to turn towards the Mole under port helm. The Mole itself would probably be invisible in the dark. We should see the flashes of the guns in the battery at the end of the Mole appearing on the port bow. Those flashes were to be our target. If we could see the lighthouse on the end of the Mole we were to fire at that too. We were not to open fire before the top.

At this moment from behind us and far away to sea there came a dull thud! thud! It was the great monitors waking Zeebrugge with their enormous shells. The attack had begun. It was tremendously hearty and encouraging to hear our own big guns opening the dance, and to think that we were getting all the help in our adventure that could be given us. Still a minute or two ticked away, and nothing happened; still there might have been nothing but open sea ahead of us; but in fact the guns of Zeebrugge might be less than a mile away. It was incredible that nothing should be happening. Had they no patrols or searchlights at all? Fortune was favouring us beyond our dreams. This was the critical time; every second almost that passed now without our being observed much increased our chance of getting alongside. I stepped up to the projecting embrasure of the gun to have a look round. The foggy air was streaky with some thicker fumes than fog, and behind me I could just descry in the darkness a line of faint, gray plumes; it was the motor craft pouring out smoke in order to screen us.

Then far, far away on our left the brilliant light of a German star-shell appeared suddenly in the sky, then another nearer at hand, and then one right overhead, which, to our seeming, lit the whole ship and the surrounding sea with an illumination so brilliant that we must be visible for a hundred miles. One could see each individual face in the crowd on deck staring angrily up at the star in hard black shadows and white lights. But still the Germans did not open fire, and looking out from the embrasure I could guess the reason. The sky was now thick with a perfect rain of shell-stars; but clearly as they showed us to ourselves it did not follow that they showed us to the Germans.

As each star fell into the smoke screen that now covered the sea, unless it was within a very few hundred yards of us, it was eclipsed as a star and became a large, vague nebula. Although then there was plenty of light about, a few hundred yards from the ship everything was blotted out in wreaths, eddies, and whirls of glowing vapour. The German gunners, I imagine, were peering into the vapour, unable to perceive any definite object in the shifting, dazzling glow, and wondering what in the name of goodness was going to come out of it.

So we steamed on until we were some four hundred yards from the

Mole, and we had just begun to turn to starboard in order to run along-side when the storm broke. This was the beginning of the bad three minutes that we had expected.* A searchlight shone out from the end of the Mole, swung to left and right, and settled on the ship. At once the guns on the Mole opened fire. From our dark bay we could see their quick flashes on our port bow, and there was a faint popping in the sea all round the ship. More accustomed to the crash which a shell makes when it bursts ashore, I did not realize at the time that this was the noise of shells that had missed us and were bursting in the sea.

At the next instant they began to hit. 'When is the top going to begin?' I thought. 'Will it never begin?'

During the next few minutes we had by far the greater part of our heavy casualties. There were swift, shaking detonations close by, and one blinding flash of blue light right in our eyes. It was at this moment that Captain Halahan and Colonel Elliot were killed on the landing-deck a few feet away; but at the time my attention was so wholly fixed in listening impatiently for the first shot from the top, in order that the 6-inch guns might begin too, that I hardly noticed what was going on. It was afterwards that I remembered the eruptions of sparks where the shells struck, the crash of splintering steel, the cries, and that smell which must haunt the memory of any one who has been in a sea-fight – the smell of blood and burning.

Casting a glance out through the embrasure I saw a fine sight. The wind during the last few minutes had dropped, the smoke screen was no longer drifting ahead of us, and the sea and everything on it was lit up continuously by leaping flashes, so that we were plainly visible to the gunners on the Mole. Quick as thought one of the motor craft grasped the situation and dashed forward, leaping – almost flying – across the waves with furious haste, pouring out smoke as she came. She swung across our bows, right between us and the batteries and under the very muzzles of their guns, and vanished into her own smoke unharmed. It was a gallant act, and glorious to see.

For a time it was the last thing that I saw. Something went ponk! just behind me. A Titan blacksmith whirled a heavy sledge-hammer and hit me with all his might a blow on the right arm that sent me spinning down the narrow entry, to fall in the middle of a group of marines who were crouching on the battery deck.

'Why, whatever's the matter with you?' said one in a surprised voice, and stirred me tentatively with his foot.

* In fact, I believe the bigger guns ashore had already been firing at random into the smoke for nearly twenty minutes, but I was quite unaware of that at the time.

The universe became a black star which had its radiant point just below my right shoulder.

When things became reasonable again I found that I was in need of help, but that I could crawl. I remembered that there was a dressing-station at the foot of a ladder near by. The crash and flame of striking shells was still making an inferno of the upper deck. It was no good lying about where I was. I might as well do something, so I crawled to the hatch amongst bodies and wreckage, and climbed down the ladder. While I was climbing down a shell burst a little farther forward in the same space, and the concussion knocked me off the ladder, but I was not hit. The space below was crowded with ammunition-parties and wounded, amongst whom the dressers were busy. There was hardly a clear inch of space, but some one gave me a stool on which to sit and to wait, and presently a dresser came and bandaged me. He was a stout fellow, as busy, quiet, and collected in that dreadful place is if he had been in a hospital ward. I was very sick, and a minute or two after that I found myself recovered.

When I got up on deck again the *Vindictive* was alongside the Mole, and sheltered for the time from the fire of the Mole batteries, but she was still being hit occasionally by shots from the batteries ashore. There were sudden eruptions of din alternating with dead silence. The wet, jade-green curve of the wall was dimly visible sweeping up out of the dark, and back into it again. The last of the landing-parties was going over the brows, and there was an intermittent crackling and flashing of rifle and machine-gun fire up and down the Mole. From our top came bursts of the deafening uproar of the pom-poms, the most ear-splitting noise in the world. Every now and then there was a loud roar and a bright flash aft on the quarter-deck. I thought for a time that big shells were hitting us there, but it was our 11-inch howitzer which Brooks and his marines kept firing away steadily all the time in spite of every distraction.

Looking out on to the forecastle, I saw the dim bulk of the *Daffodil* nosing into our starboard bow, and kicking the water out behind her as hard as she could. It was her business to hold us into the side of the Mole. Ferguson and some of the crew were busy there making fast a wire hawser in order to help her to keep her difficult position. Rifle bullets from the Mole made little splashes of fire on the deck about them as they worked.

I had to find out how far my guns' crews had got in the procedure that we had so often rehearsed, and I climbed up to our forward hook in search of them. The davit was turned out, but the hook was gone. I went aft along the landing-deck to the second hook, and I found the crews working at it under the lee of the house of the flame-thrower. A lot of things seemed to be hitting the far side of the house; I suppose that it was a rifle-fire from down the Mole. The davit was turned out, but it did not reach the Mole, and the hook was dangling useless between the Mole and the ship. We tried again and again to get it into place, but we did not succeed. Rosoman came along and tried too, but ultimately he told us to leave it; the Captain was going to keep the *Daffodil* shoving against our bows, and we must trust to her to hold us in.

I went up one of the brows on to the Mole in order to see how they were resting. The swell, which had been very bad at first, was diminishing, and such of the brows as survived seemed to be resting comfortably enough. There was a lull in the firing close at hand just then, and a glance up and down the Mole showed nothing but a few rifle flashes, but I could hear in the comparative silence the steady thud! thud! of the guns ashore and of the monitors out at sea. That noise went on all the time as the background of the prevailing din; one heard them thumping, and then one of our pom-poms in the top, or some Lewis gunners or bombers near at hand, would break in and down everything else with their uproar.

I went back on board to rejoin the guns' crews at the prescribed meeting-place in the starboard battery. Whilst making my way thither across the dark and littered deck I stumbled over somebody at the foot of one of the wooden ramps that led to the landing-deck. As well as I could see in the dark, there was a platoon of marines still waiting there crouched on the deck. A marine officer looked down from the landing platform.

'Aren't these folks going over?' I asked.

'These are all gone,' he said.

I was sitting down for a minute on a mushroom head in the battery, when shells began to strike our upper works and the funnels and cowls which stuck up above the sheltering Mole. The German destroyers had seen them from inside the harbour, and were shooting at them from a few hundred yards away. When a shell struck a cowl or a funnel a spray of splinters from the thin steel structure dashed down into the battery and caused many casualties there. Our top also stuck up above the Mole just ahead of the funnels, and it was, no doubt, the uproar of its automatic guns that attracted the attention of the destroyers. But the fire thus directed on them at point-blank range did not affect the resolution of Rigby and his stout crew of six marine artillerymen in the top.

While the destroyers' shells were striking our upper works close beside them I heard the guns there still bursting out at regular intervals into their mad barking. But soon there came a crash and a shower of sparks, and silence followed it. They are all gone, I said to myself; but in a minute or two a single gun in the top broke out again, and barked and barked. Then there was another crash, and the silence of the top became unbroken. Words cannot tell with what a glow of pride and exultation one heard that last gun speak. It seemed impossible that there should be any one left alive in the top after the first shell struck it, and when the gun spoke again it seemed as if the very dead could not be driven from their duty.

We learned afterwards that the first shell killed Rigby and all his crew except the sergeant. The sergeant was severely wounded, but he managed to get a gun back into action before the second shell struck, wounding him again, and putting his gun out of action. Would that Rigby had lived to know how faithfully his trust was discharged by the last member of his crew !

We could not see from the deck what was going on above us on the Mole, but whenever for a moment the *Vindictive* was silent we listened to the firing ashore and tried to guess what was happening there. I more than half expected a few survivors of our parties to come tumbling down the brows, followed by a rush of Germans to board the ship. But the Germans never made any attempt at a counter-attack of any sort or kind. When the *Vindictive* jumped at the Mole, as it must have seemed to them, out of the smoke, with her batteries of big guns and little guns, mortars and machine guns, crashing and vomiting fire all together, they cleared away from the place at which she ran alongside, and contented themselves with holding strong points farther up and down the Mole.

The Marines established themselves some two hundred yards towards the beach and engaged the strong points ahead of them. Bryan Adams led all that was left of the seamen's landing-parties in a gallant attack on the batteries at the lighthouse end of the Mole. Those were the batteries that had to be silenced in order to help the blockships to get in. Nearly half of the seamen's parties were casualties before the ship got alongside, and owing to the heavy swell the reinforcing parties from the *Iris* and *Daffodil* could not get ashore.

With numbers that were all too few to start with, and that dwindled rapidly under the fire of the numerous machine guns opposed to him, Adams led rush after rush along the Mole, trying to get to the batteries and to destroy the guns. Harrison, who was in command of this party, was severely wounded during the approach. When his wounds had been bound he joined Adams and his men on the Mole, and was killed leading one of the rushes, a most glorious victor over pain and death.

The attack of this gallant band died away for sheer lack of men to carry it on; but it achieved its purpose. When the blockships passed they encountered a severe fire from the guns on the extension of the Mole, but the most dangerous battery, the big battery at the end of the Mole itself, was silent. I think that it is probable that all the gunners had left the battery in order to resist Harrison's and Adam's attack.

One reason, no doubt, for the absence of any attempt at a counter-attack by the enemy was the complete success of one of the old sub-marines – that in command of Sandford – in blowing up the viaduct at the landward end of the Mole. A big gap was made in the viaduct which cut the Mole off from the shore, so that the enemy could send out no reinforcements to help the defenders of the Mole. Those who saw the explosion say that it was the biggest ever seen; but I was busy at the moment with the *Iris*, and never even noticed it.

The *Iris* had appeared out of the dark and come alongside us at our starboard waist. Owing to the heavy swell she had found it impossible to carry out her intention of landing her men on the Mole ahead of us. The scaling ladders could not be made fast, and Bradford and Hawkings, the leaders of her landing-parties of seamen, who had climbed on to the Mole in order to try to secure the ladders, had both been killed in the attempt. Bradford climbed up a davit and jumped ashore; Hawkings, his second in command, climbed up by a line. The Mole at that point was swept by machine-gun and rifle fire, and was incessantly illuminated by star-shells and rockets. They must have known well that their under-taking was all but hopeless; there could not have been a more gallant act.

Now the *Iris* was going to try to land her parties over the *Vindictive*, which, thanks to the continual thrust of the *Daffodil* against her bow, was keeping her position fairly comfortably alongside. But beside the *Vindictive* the *Iris* still danced in the swell like a cork, and it was some time before we could get a hawser on board from her or secure it when we had got it. Twice the hawser carried away, but at last it was done, and the men in the *Iris*, watching their opportunity, began to jump into the *Vindictive*. But meanwhile time had fled. We seemed to have been alongside a few minutes only; we had been there an hour, and it was almost time to go. The order came that no more men were to land, that the *Iris* and the *Daffodil* were to blow their sirens (our own had been shot away) in order to recall the landing-parties, and that then the *Iris* was to go.

The sirens bellowed, we cast off the *Iris*'s hawser, and backing away from our side she turned and steamed out to sea on a course that took her right across the front of the Mole batteries at four or five hundred yards' distance. I watched her with a sinking heart, knowing how we had suffered on the same course coming in. She had not gone five hundred yards before the batteries began to crash and bang. It was a terrible thing to watch. At that short range the light fabric of the little ship was hulled through and through, flames and smoke spurting from her far side as the shells struck her. She disappeared from sight in the darkness enveloped in a thick cloud of smoke. I thought at the time that she had been sunk; in fact she survived, after suffering terribly heavy casualties.

Recalled by the bellowing sirens, the landing-parties poured back on board of us over the two remaining brows and streamed down below. For good or ill our part was done. The blockships were either past or sunk, we did not know which, and if we were to get away at all we must go now, or we should not be out of range of the enemy's big guns before dawn. The *Daffodil* gave a snort, expressive of relief at being released from her long, hard shove, and of satisfaction at its complete success, and backed away, giving our bow a pull out as she did so. Helped by the set of the tide, our bow began to swing away from the Mole, and in a minute we were clear, and our propellers were throbbing.

As soon as our guns were no longer masked by the Mole we were to be ready to engage the Mole batteries, and I established myself once more by my voice-pipe at the forward port 6-inch gun. Mr Cobby, our gunner (now lieutenant) came and helped me, and by shoving and hustling in the darkness managed to get everything ready at the gun, and to collect the emergency hands who were needed to replace casualties in the crew, so that I had plenty of time in which to think things over.

My first thoughts were, 'What luck we have had so far! We are actually leaving the Mole. A bit more luck, and really and truly we may pull through.' Then I thought, 'What has happened on the Mole? What has happened to the blockships? I wish that I knew!' And then I remembered what I had seen when the *Iris* passed the batteries, and I thought, 'In two minutes that will be happening to us.' My thoughts travelled no farther, and I waited for what was coming.

We stole on in deep silence. The din of firing had wholly ceased; all but the guns' crews were below, the decks were empty, and there was nothing to hear now but the wash of the waves alongside. The ship seemed to be waiting with her guns ready and her attention strained for the crash of a striking shell. But the minutes were passing. When was it going to begin?

Thick black fumes were eddying about the decks from our smoke apparatus. Once again, as on the approach, there came a faint popping from the sea. Each moment we expected the crash and the flame; but the moments passed, and still the silence of the ship's progress was unbroken. The moments passed, and astonishment crept into my mind. How much longer than I expected it was taking before the bad time began!

'I wish we could hurry up,' I thought, 'and get it over, one way or another.' And then I noticed that the popping in the sea had stopped. 'Whatever can be the matter with them?' I wondered; and then I realized with a flash that while I had been waiting and wondering a good ten minutes had passed, and that we must be past the front of the Mole batteries and leaving them fast behind.

I could hardly trust myself to believe it. Had we perhaps been making a detour inshore, and were the batteries yet to pass? Cobby was standing by the embrasure and could see out.

'What are we doing?' I called to him.

'We are well away,' he said. 'Here come our destroyers.'

So by the biggest wonder of that night of wonders we repassed the batteries not only unsunk but unhit. Confused by our smoke screen, and flurried, no doubt, by what had been happening on the Mole, the Germans dropped behind us every shot that they fired, in a furious and perfectly harmless bombardment of our wake.

We had pulled through, but we still had a race against time before us – to get out of range of the big guns ashore before we were revealed to them by the dawn that was about to break. With flames pouring from her battered funnels and burdened with triumph, death, and pain, the *Vindictive* sped away from Zeebrugge into the North Sea.

As soon as the destroyers met us we felt that we were all right, and finding myself now not so well as I had thought, I went and sat in the wardroom, where most of the wounded had been collected. McCutcheon, our senior medical officer, was busy amongst them, helping all with unhurried speed in that scene of anguish and extremity, and helping others to help by his quiet strength and undismayed hopefulness. Presently I found myself in a cabin on a bunk. People came in as they could spare time in order to pass the news. We were making straight out for Thornton Ridge, so as to get out of range of the shore as quickly as possible; we had altered course for Dover; we had passed the North Hinder; all was going well, and we should be at Dover before nine. Little by little I learned who was living and who was dead. The *Daffodil* and the *Iris* were safe, but there was no news yet of the blockships.

At last, and just before I drifted off into that vague indifference that is born of morphia, the Captain came round to tell us that the blockships had got in, and had been sunk in the canal. 'We have succeeded,' he said, and that was good news with which to drift away into a drowse that was for many days the end of all clear apprehension of realities.

Lieutenant Edward Hilton Young, MP, received special promotion for continuing to encourage and direct the men with indifference to suffering or danger despite being severely wounded in the right arm at the beginning of the action.

Lieutenant C. Dickinson in command of the demolition party, received the DSO for his splendid work on the Mole.

Gunner John H. Cobby received special promotion. He was employed in the most exposed positions, assisting in placing brows and Mole anchors, disembarking and re-embarking storming parties, securing *Daffodil* in place, and carrying the wounded below. He displayed throughout an entire disregard of personal danger and high qualities of initiative.

*

Account by W. W. Childs

During the latter part of the Great War, things were inclined to become monotonous in the Grand Fleet. The usual routine, gunnery drills, etc., which makes a ship efficient, intermingled with recreation became stale. The same old drills day in and day out got on one's nerves. Occasionally there was the usual order 'Raise Steam with all possible speed and report when ready', which meant the same old convoys to Norway which necessitated manning the guns all day and night in case of emergency, putting to sea in the worst weather possible with never a sign of a German ship, but the occasional rumours that there was 'something doing'.

This tedious life went on, and the only thing to look forward to being a few days' leave, only to return and once again settle down to a mere existence, which compelled us to keep watch at Scapa Flow.

About 12th February 1918, whilst serving on board HMS *Neptune*, after being 'strafed' for smoking in working hours, one of our officers (Lieutenant Chamberlain) sent for me. I went to his cabin, and he asked me if I would like to go with him on a secret 'stunt'. Before asking me, he wished to know if I was married, engaged, or if there was anyone dependent on me. To these I replied in the negative (not having contemplated 'suicide' just then). Of course, naturally I questioned him closely as to what kind of 'stunt' we were to be involved in, but being sworn to secrecy he could give me no information at all, except that if we came back alive we should be pretty lucky. (Very cheerful.) After careful thought, and with visions in my mind of 'convoys' (how I was beginning to dread them), I consented to go. He next asked me if I knew of six suitable seamen who would volunteer to accompany us. He already had sixteen names of men recommended to him, all refused, with the exception of Able Seamen J. Day, C. Reed, A. Everest, A. Hilling and F. Young. After interviewing a few more, we managed to secure Able Seaman McKenzie. These men were all good at some sport or other.

The following day we were taken on board HMS *Hercules* and found that, besides Lieutenant Chamberlain, myself and six able seamen, there were also others on the same mission, namly; a lieutenant, a petty officer, two leading seamen, and forty two seamen. Naturally we were all surprised, but still we could not find out what we had to do. Again different rumours went round such as : 'King's Messengers to France', 'Rounding up spies in Norway,' etc., etc. Whilst on board HMS *Hercules,* which was the flagship of the 4th Battle Squadron, we signed a paper to say that we were volunteers and that no claim could be made in the event of our failing to return. After signing our 'Death Warrants' we went back to the *Neptune* and were placed absolutely on our own, with nothing to do all day except to land on Flotta Isle for rifle and revolver practice. This did not prevent us doing our usual convoy duties, and we got the usual 'Raise Steam' signal and set out on one of our usual runs to Bergen. It was blowing a blizzard all the way over, and on the way back. After six days at sea, we arrived back at Scapa to refuel, etc., and within a week, we were off on another convoy. On our return to harbour we took in 1150 tons of coal, and during the midst of this 'pastime' the Master at Arms sent for me, telling me to collect my party, and proceed on four days' leave that same night.

Eventually this was postponed until the following morning when at 4 a.m. we left the *Neptune* for HMS *Imperieuse* to catch the mail steamer to Scrabster Pier, Thurso.

On board *Imperieuse* we found another collection of fifty men from each of the 1st and 2nd Battle Squadrons.

It was a happy crowd that travelled to London that day, and on reaching Kings Cross Station, people must have thought that the Navy had 'demobbed', seeing so many different ship's names on our cap ribbons. At King's Cross we dispersed to our various destinations.

After our leave, we duly returned to Chatham Barracks. The majority of the men arrived in good time, the very few who did not were sent back to their respective ships, there to undergo fourteen days C.B. On arrival at Chatham Barracks, we were all billeted on HMS *Hindustan* (an overflow ship since the breaking up of the 3rd Battle Squadron). Here we became a merry little party. All leave was stopped, no one being allowed outside the Dockyard Gates, but we were allowed to use the Dockyard Canteen. Needless to say, this privilege was taken full advantage of and the party very soon took charge. In no time we gained nicknames such as : 'The Suicide Club', 'Death or Glory Boys', 'Jellicoe's Light Horse', etc., etc. Some were very suitable for the party.

We were still without official news as to what we were going to do, although seeing the *Vindictive* and a few old cruisers being fitted out, gave us an idea what was in store for us, but for where, we did not know.

We now began to settle down to training, our first week consisting of a route march and swimming which went with a swing. The first week having passed, we now settled down to serious training, so on the Monday morning we joined up with the 5th Battalion Middlesex Regiment, stationed at Gillingham. We were still billeted on board the *Hindustan* so that it necessitated going backwards and forwards to Gillingham every night and morning. Within a very short space of time, soldiers and sailors were working as one. Our instructors were army sergeants and sergeant majors, who very soon won favour with the sailors; in fact, I know Sergeant Major Green used to turn blue in the face trying to drill Army discipline into us. (It was of no use, as Naval Discipline and Army Discipline are like chalk to cheese), but I must say that a finer set of instructors one could not wish to drill under. They taught us bayonet fighting, bombing, Lewis Gun drill, etc., and took us through a gas course; in fact they gave us a sample of modern day trench warfare. Doing this kind of instruction, gave us the impression that we were bound for France, but that was not to be. It was a bit too easy.

After a week of training on trench warfare, our battalion was divided up into four platoons and companies.

The Battle Cruisers forming A Company.

4th Battle Squadron forming B Company.

1st Battle Squadron forming C Company.

2nd Battle Squadron forming D Company.

Each company was split up into sections, our company (B) was detailed off as follows.

No 1 Section from HM Ships *Neptune* and *St Vincent*.

No 2 Section from HM Ships *Superb* and *Temeraire*.

No 3 Section from HM Ships *Hercules* and *Collingwood*.

No 4 Section from HM Ships *Colossus* and *Bellerophon*.

Each section was now told off for its own separate job. No 1 Section were detailed off for various jobs, such as :

Lewis Gun's Crew, Bomb Throwers, Rifle Grenadiers, Bengal Light Carriers, Wire Cutters and Parachute Light Firers.

No 2 Section formed No 1 Stokes Mortar Battery.

No 3 Section formed No 2 Stokes Battery.

No 4 Section formed No 3 Stokes Battery.

Each company was told off as follows :

A Company ....Infantry.

C Company ....Demolition Party.

B Company ....Infantry.

As stated before, No 1 Section of B Company supplied a Lewis Gun's Crew (as well as A Company).

B Company's Lewis Gun's Crew was comprised of the following :

No 1 AB McKenzie *Neptune*.

No 2 AB White *St Vincent*.

No 3 Myself (Spotting Officer) *Neptune*.

No 4 O. Sea. Ryan *St Vincent*.

During the training which lasted some six weeks, we carried out various night operations against the Middlesex Regiment at Raynham and Wouldham in Kent This was most enjoyable, and everybody went all out. During the last week, a model of the Mole had been constructed at Wouldham in an old disused chalk pit. Here we did the final assault using live ammunition. During this operation, we were allowed twenty-two 'casualties', i.e., allowing for twenty-two men to be either killed or wounded from stray bullets and shrapnel. As luck happened we did have two men wounded in reality, through too much elevation being put on a Stokes Gun, resulting in the shell going straight up in the air and coming down again to burst at the gun's crew's feet. This operation was witnessed by the Lords Commissioners of the Admiralty who came down from London for the occasion.

We next were fitted out with khaki from the Royal Marine Barracks at Chatham. This was very amusing, the sailors not being used to the 'Rig', invariably had yards of puttee trailing behind them just like 'Harry Tate's Navy'.

After six weeks of this splendid training, we left Chatham on board HMS *Hindustan* in company with *Dominion, Vindictive, Thetis, Iphigenia, Intrepid, Sirius* and *Brilliant*. The last five ships had been filled with concrete and were to be sunk, so as to block the Bruges

Canal, from which German submarines were operating against merchant shipping. We also had with us the two ferry boats *Iris* and *Daffodil*, two Liverpool ferry boats. We anchored at a place called The Swin, a few miles from Sheerness and you may guess we looked 'some' Fleet.

We were now told officially what we were going to do, and we were also told that any man who wished to back out, could do so with no fear of being punished. Not one man stepped out, so keen were the men on taking part in this 'Great Adventure'. During the time we remained on board the *Hindustan* our time was spent in practising landing men, and in sports and concerts which in every way made things an easy life. Occasionally the Lords of the Admiralty visited us and enquired how we were progressing. After a week we were transferred to different ships. A and B Companies going to *Vindictive*, C to *Daffodil* and D Company to the *Iris*. A few days after, the 4th Battalion of the Royal Marines arrived from Deal. This was the first intimation we had that any marines were taking part in the operation.

The 11th April came round and at noon we got up anchor and made a move for Zeebrugge. Misfortune seemed to dog us on this trip, for no sooner had we left the Swin, than a fire was discovered in the gunner's store, a bale of waste having caught fire. Needless to say, we got 'windy' for in this store were stowed 3,000 Mills Bombs and a goodly collection of Stokes Mortar Shells all ready for use, and our 'chummy ship' (the *Vanguard*) having blown up just recently, we had a good idea of the result in the event of an explosion. Anyhow, all hands soon made short work of transporting the bombs and shells to another stowage, and we breathed freely once again.

We jogged steadily along towing the *Iris* and*Daffodil*; we did this to save their fuel, for they would be needing it afterwards. When about mid-way across, we were met by Harry Tate's Navy, i.e. motor launches, coastal motor boats, and two destroyers, towing two submarines (*C1* and *C3*). These submarines had been fitted out in the form of two large torpedoes filled with high explosives. Their job was to force themselves between the piles of the viaduct leading on to the Mole and blow it up so as to prevent any enemy from trying to force the storming parties to retreat.

At 10.30 p.m. the main brace was spliced (ie an extra ration of rum was issued to each man). At 11 p.m. the order 'Stand To' was passed. We then went to our Action Stations, A and B Companies on the false deck that had been built, and the marines in the starboard battery. Things were now beginning to get exciting for we could see the guns on the Western Front blazing away, and we were witnesses of an air attack on

Zeebrugge; it was a fine sight. The *Iris* and *Daffodil* having been cast off were now following in our wake. The *Sirius* and *Brilliant* had been despatched to Ostend. The artificial smoke screen was started, and it was blowing towards the shore in our favour.

Just at this time, misfortune again came along, for the *Sirius* on leaving for Ostend, is thought to have wirelessed *Vindictive* a warning, for shortly afterwards a shell was sent over to us from the shore. The wind had changed completely, and now left us a clear target for the enemy. We were now about five miles from Zeebrugge. Just then a signal reached us, and we turned about and eventually arrived back at our base (The Swin).

On our way back, Leading Seaman Pearce, in charge of A Company's Lewis Gun, was accidentally shot through the thigh, the bullet cutting the main artery, causing his death within two days through loss of blood. This was rotten luck, as he had gone through the Siege of Ladysmith, and the Boer War. Through the regrettable death of Leading Seaman Pearce, A Company's Lewis Gun was placed under my charge, the crew being comprised of AB Lodwick, AB Turner and another able seaman.

On arrival at the base, we were greeted by Rear Admiral Sir Roger Keyes in HMS *Warwick*. He came on board *Vindictive*, and explained to us why we had not carried out the attack the previous night. He informed us that owing to the wind changing its direction, had we carried on and attempted it, very few of the men would have returned, and then only as prisoners of war after the armistice. Rather than allow that to happen (for the *Vindictive* would in all probability have been sunk by shore batteries), he said he would prefer to pack the job up and not attempt it. Of course we were all disappointed that we had not carried out the attack, but the Admiral knew best.

We were now transferred to HMS *Dominion* temporarily owing to there being insufficient room in the *Vindictive* for all hands, but the marines and ship's company remained on board.

From now on, all letters were stopped, and the Field Cards (as used in France) were issued, so as to prevent information from leaking out.

On 13th April, back we went again to the *Vindictive* and once again set out on our little 'jaunt', but we did not go far, as once again the wind changed, so again we turned back to the base, and transferred to the *Dominion*.

Nothing of note happened until the following Sunday morning when during the Church Service, the Captain told us to prepare to move on the next day. We did not, however, and on that evening the officers entertained us with a concert. During the concert, we were told that we should be transferring back to the *Vindictive* on the morrow (Tuesday). We did, and arrived on board about 10 a.m. and at noon we once again left amidst much cheering from the *Hindustan* and *Dominion* (left behind).

On our way over this time, I built a sandbag emplacement for our Lewis Guns which without a doubt saved our lives. To separate these, I had placed a 3/8th inch Zinc Plate between the guns, so that in the event of a shell bursting and putting one gun's crew out of action, the other gun's crew may be able to carry on.

Half way across, we again picked up Harry Tate's Navy who had come from Dover. There were about a hundred of these small craft, so one can imagine the terrible noise which was kicked up by their exhausts. Still, we were all merry and bright, and looking forward to the 'stunt' being successful, and the 'Zero Hour' (midnight).

At 10.30 p.m the main brace was again spliced which warmed us up a bit, for the night was beginning to get a bit chilly. We then went on deck and were witnesses of another air attack on Zeebrugge by our planes from Dunkirk. Our monitors were shelling the place from the sea, and marine field batteries were 'putting them over' from Flanders.

We were now beginning to draw close to the Belgian Coast, for we could see the guns firing on shore. Things were getting exciting again, but there was no panic. At 11 p.m. the order was passed to put on equipment and at 11.15 p.m. 'Action stations' was passed along, no bugle being sounded or it would have given the whole show away. The *Sirius* and *Brilliant* had been despatched to Ostend and the *Iris* and *Daffodil* had cast off tow. Not a light was to be seen from the ships and silence reigned. Onboard 'Chums' were saying goodbye in case they did not survive the action. The only noise to be heard was the throbbing of the motor launches' engines. The artificial smoke screen had been started, and one could scarcely see two yards ahead. The smoke screen was splendid, due to the efforts of Wing Commander Brock, of firework fame. We had on board about 18 RAF, and the only Army man was a lieutenant of the Royal Engineers, whose job was to work the flame throwers, fitted on the port side of the bridges.

At 11.55 p.m. the Germans evidently smelt a rat for suddenly a star shell lit up the sky, followed by others shortly after. No sooner had the second burst, the enemy scored a direct hit on our after funnel, practically blowing it to pieces. It seemed like hell let loose. The shrapnel and pieces of funnel caused havoc among the men, and the air was full of the cries of the wounded and dying. The Huns were hitting us every round they fired. At this time my sandbag dugout was demolished by two shells that hit us, taking away both sides, but not touching the front. These two shells wounded seven of us (myself only slightly), the only one of our crew not being wounded being AB Lodwick of A Company's Lewis Gun.

Having put an improvised tourniquet on Ordinary seaman Ryan (my No 4), I looked round and found ourselves alongside the Mole. What a huge wall it looked. At this time, I was knocked silly by a 303 bullet, which struck my tin hat and cutting its way through the rim, parted one of my putties. A lucky escape. I soon came to my senses again through hearing someone shout 'Over the Top'. Having lost AB Lodwick in the struggle, McKenzie and myself, the only two remaining of our crew, made our way towards the landing brows but we were greatly hampered by the weight we were carrying. The weights were as follows :

McKenzie. Lewis Gun and eight trays of ammunition (47 rounds in each tray), a revolver and 100 rounds, spare parts of the gun, gas mask, and shrapnel helmet, being roughly about 100 lbs.

Myself. 16 trays of Lewis Gun ammunition, a rifle and two bandoliers of 50 rounds each, two Mills Bombs, electric torch, wire nippers, gas mask and helmet. About 142 lbs. With this weight, you can guess we could only struggle along.

The *Vindictive* was rolling pretty heavily, owing to the swell. She was fitted with sixteen landing brows, but in going alongside the Mole all but two were smashed up, either by shell fire or the heavy seas.

Over these two we clambered, 'waiting for the roll' to hop on to the Mole. Having landed, McKenzie and I advanced towards the end of the Mole, our object being to fire upon some 5.5 guns about half way along. After about 50 yards we dropped down and opened fire. Here misfortune dropped in again for the Germans scored a direct hit on our Lewis Gun, blowing it out of our hands. This was bad luck, as at the time it was doing glorious work. McKenzie was severely wounded again. The Lewis Gun ammunition now being of no use without the gun, we threw the trays into the sea, thereby relieving us of some of the weight and we reverted to secondary armament, McKenzie his revolver, myself my rifle. This was better than nothing, so we opened fire on some Germans who were escaping from shelters underneath us, and were trying to reach the destroyers on the opposite side of the Mole. Had these Germans remained where they were they would in all probability be alive now, but panic reigned amongst them, and they were shot down or bayoneted.

We now advanced further, and came across a concrete sentry box. In here were some Germans who made a rush for it. In making a point with my bayonet at one of them, my blade finished up like a corkscrew. All of a sudden there was a terrific explosion which we surmised was the submarine *C3* blowing up. We guessed right. It seemed as though the flames would never stop going upwards. We then saw our blockships go steaming in to block the canal, and great cheers were given.

Shortly after, a succession of 'Ks' in the Morse Code was sounded on *Daffodil's* siren. This was the signal to recall all men on board again. This signal should have been sounded by the *Vindictive*, but owing to her siren being blown away, she was unable to do so.

Our senior officers, Captain Halahan and Lieutenant Commander Harrison having previously been killed, Lieutenant Commander Adams took charge and gave the order to retire, each man, as far as possible helping a wounded man back.

On our way back, we were passed by the marines who were charging down the Mole. We shouted to them that the 'Retire' had been sounded, but unfortunately they mistook our yells for shouts of encouragement and continued on eventually being taken prisoners.

After a great struggle we managed to get back on board, and saw the great damage caused by the terrific fire which she had been subjected to. I went down below decks and took off my equipment. Having got rid of that, the next thing to do was to attend to the more severely wounded. With the assistance of AB Day of B Company we went along to the sick bay to obtain some field dressings. When we got there we found a disastrous state of affairs. A shell had come through the ship's side and burst in the sick bay, wrecking it. We searched amidst the wreckage, and eventually found some dressings. We then went along the battery and found an old Marine Bugler with his leg smashed, and only hanging by the sinew. We could do practically nothing, except put a tourniquet on above the knee and cut his leg off with a knife. It was a rather unpleasant job – but what else could we do? We placed him under cover and next proceeded to where Lieutenant Commander Bramble was directing the port after gun (6 inch). He eventually collapsed but would not be attended to until someone relieved him. We got a Captain of Marines to relieve him. Lieutenant Commander Bramble was badly wounded in the calf of the leg, so we bandaged him up and gave him a 6 inch 'projjy'* for a pillow, The next thing we did was to assist Commander Osborne in getting down Sergeant Finch of the Royal Marines out of the Fore Top.

By now we had left the Mole, and the Germans were letting us have it with gas shells. Through having left my gas mask down below decks,

* Projectile (Shell).

I caught up a 'section' of it, though not a great deal, sufficient to keep me continually coughing. I fancied a drink so I went down below to get one but received a rude shock, as the fresh water tanks had been hit by shell and the water had run to waste, the only water remaining being 100 waterbottles which had been filled before the action. These were given to the wounded, and very shortly there was no water at all, not even for the remaining wounded. Someone had a brainwave, and suggested serving out rum. This was done, even the wounded having as much as they could get and very soon were forgetting their wounds. Everywhere one moved, so there were men 'laid out', and the only place for the men who had escaped serious wounds was on deck. After having drunk my rum, I went round searching for my section, No 1 B Company. The only one I could not account for was AB Everest. AB McKenzie I found to be seriously wounded. His right foot was smashed, and he had several pieecs of shrapnel in his back. The others of my section were more or less badly wounded, AB Orman had his arm blown off, AB White shrapnel in the head, Ordinary Seaman Ryan badly punctured, and another with his jaw smashed by a bullet.

The majority of the others were only slightly wounded but quite enough to get on with.

I also found that Lieutenant Chamberlain had been killed, Lieutenant Walker had had his arm blown off, Petty Officer Joyce was wounded in the arm, Leading Seaman Merryweather had his ear taken off by a bullet, Leading Seaman Day was unwounded though suffering from shock. These were all of B Company. One could not sleep, so the best thing that one could do was to wait for dawn. As it got light, we searched around for curious bits of shrapnel, etc. I managed to get a piece of the Mole which was blown on board by a shell, a fine relic. Whilst still searching, I came across the body of AB Everest, who had been killed by a bullet through the head. It upset us quite a lot as he was one of the best, and we much regretted his death.

We were not out of danger yet, for at 5.30 a.m. we nearly hit a floating mine. By altering course, we avoided it, and fired a couple of shells at it but could not explode it. Eventually one of our motor launches sunk it by rifle fire.

At 8 a.m we found ourselves entering Dover Harbour amidst great cheering from the ships in the harbour It upset us a bit for we were all beginning to feel the reaction of the night's work. We secured alongside the Prince of Wales Pier and the forenoon was spent in discharging the dead and wounded. Having only slight flesh wounds I did not go, for I had visions of 14 days' leave. After dining on 'Admiralty Ham' (Corned

Beef) and biscuits we proceeded out to No 3 Buoy. Here we all fell in on the quarter deck, and Captain Carpenter asked us if we wished to remain on board the *Vindictive* or go to the *Sir John Moore*, a monitor. Seeing that the *Vindictive* offered little comfort to us, through her being smashed about so much, we decided we would go to the monitor. We went, but found that the *Sir John Moore* had received orders to proceed to sea, so we shifted billets to the monitor *Erebus*, but failed to settle down to any sleep that night.

Next morning, all the survivors mustered on the pier and were checked.

All that remained of B Company were thirteen men unwounded out of fifty-two, and only sixty-two out of the battalion. We now entrained for Chatham being cheered all along the line, for the word had been passed that we were coming along. When we steamed into the dockyard at Chatham, everyone had stopped work to give us a rousing reception. The barracks band marched us into barracks and after a speech by the Commander in Chief, Admiral Sturdee, we proceeded to the canteen, where a 'Spread' had been provided. Many congratulations were sent to us, and on the whole we were treated very well. At 1.30 p.m. we proceeded out to the *Hindustan* at Sheerness to collect our bags and hammocks, and send them back to the Fleet.

We returned to barracks, and were sent on four days' leave with orders to return to my old ship the *Neptune*. On arrival on board the ship after leave, we had a few weeks on the 'Sick List' to recuperate.

On 22nd July 1918 I had to go on board the *Queen Elizabeth* to be presented with the DSM by H.M. The King who was visiting the Fleet. In the afternoon, the survivors proceeded on twenty-four days' leave, which was a happy termination to my experiences at Zeebrugge.

Of my Lewis Gun's Crew, the following decorations were received: Able Seaman McKenzie, VC, myself, DSM, Able Seaman White, DSM, Ordinary Seaman Ryan, Mentioned in Despatches. Able Seaman McKenzie later died from influenza, following septic poisoning of his smashed foot.

In addition *Sergeant Norman Finch* received the VC (see page 206). *Able Seaman Lodwick* and *Petty Officer Joyce* received the DSM.

*

From J. Antell: First on the Mole

My uncle Petty Officer George Antell took part, being one of the landing party on the *Vindictive*. I have heard it said that he was the first man who landed on the Mole, his officer being shot down in front

Admiral Lord Keyes; detail from the
portrait painted by de Lazlo

The approach to Zeebrugge. On the left is the *Warwick*, with the Admiral's flag, from the
painting by Bernard Gribble

Submarine shelters at Bruges

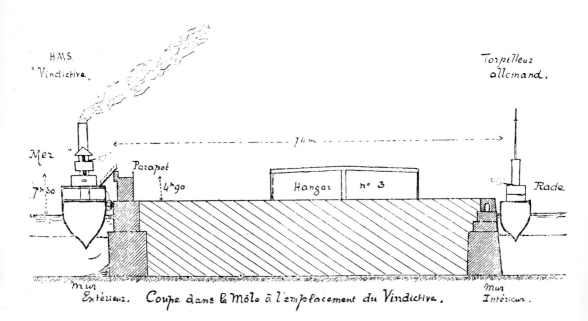

Cross section of the Mole at the point where *Vindictive* was positioned

The German Commander of the Mole batteries and his officers

One of the Mole batteries and its German crew — formidable enough opponents for anyone

Gun captured on the Mole

Artist's impression of Percy Dean in *ML282* rescuing the crews of the blockships *Iphigenia* and *Intrepid*

(Opposite) Storming the Mole: drawn by Charles de Lacey from details supplied by Captain Carpenter

The funnel of *Vindictive* after the attack

Wreckage on the *Vindictive*

Vindictive after her return from Zeebrugge : note the brows for landing on the Mole

Commander F. A. Brock

Engineer Lieutenant Commander W. A. Bury

Captain H. C. Halahan

Commander Valentine F. Gibbs

Lieutenant George N. Bradford   Lieutenant Claude E. K. Hawkings

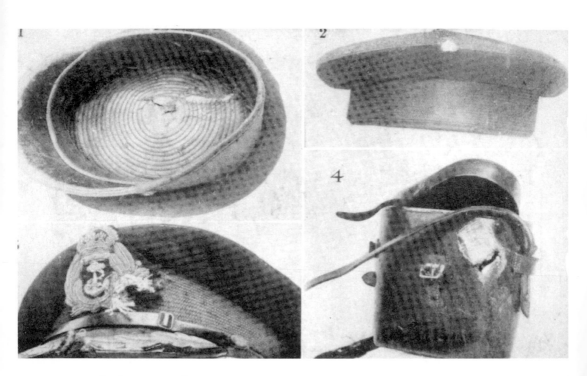

Lucky escapes – Captain Carpenter's cap and binoculars' case after the battle

The bridge of *Iris* after the battle

The viaduct after *C3* had blown up

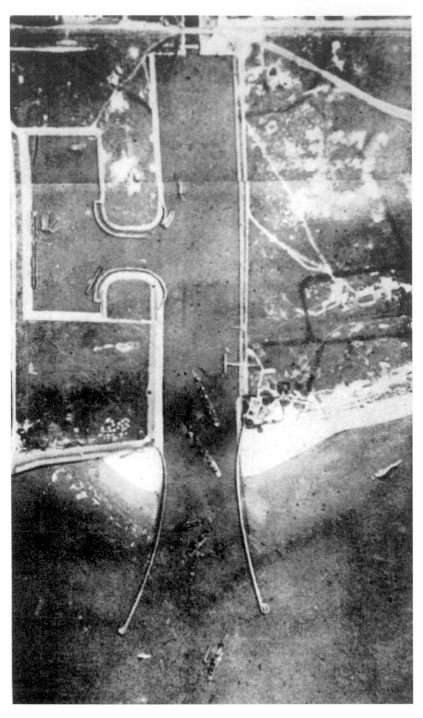

An official seaplane photograph of the blockships sunk in the canal at Zeebrugge

A German air photo of the blockships

The blockships *Intrepid* and *Iphigenia*

A later photograph of *Intrepid* and *Iphigenia*

(Opposite) Leaflet dropped by the British over Germany to show the Germans how successful the Zeebrugge raid had been

Thetis blocking the entrance to the canal

Photographie von Zeebrügge von einem englischen Flugzeug aufgenommen.

Die englischen Kriegsschiffe, die den Kanal verstopft haben.

1. „Intrepid.“ 2. „Iphigenie.“ 3. „Thetis.“ 4. Der Hafendammbruch.

Captain Ion Hamilton Benn

Lieutenant R. D. Sandford

Commander A. E. Godsal

Lieutenant Sir John Alleyne Bt.

Motor launches making a smoke screen to hide a Monitor

Some of the men who returned from the raid

of him on the gangway. He got forward with his Lewis gun team, but was wounded and was forced to return to his ship where I believe he was found later in a heap of dead comrades. He was awarded the DSM. He volunteered whilst serving on HMS *Lion*. In 1941, having rejoined the reserve, he was accidentally killed in a railway accident at Slough.

*

From J. de Boudrey-Falls: a front seat in the battle!

My brother-in-law Commander H. G. A Woolley, DSC, RN, was in that battle serving then as a midshipman. During the whole of the battle he sat out on a gun turret cleaning the glass outlook – never fearing about his own safety. Some years afterwards he became for many years secretary to the famous Admiral Sir Roger Keyes; he later left the navy, married an American and became Senior Security Officer to the Bank of New York in Washington; he came back in the Great War as SOI Bermuda.

Acting Paymaster Herbert Woolley was mentioned in despatches for his part at Zeebrugge and later at Ostend for his role in attending the wounded and the transportation of the wounded.

*

From G. H. Elliot Bailey: lost souvenirs

This year will commemorate the 60th anniversary of the raid so that anybody who took part in it and who was twenty years of age at that time will now be eighty and consequently the number of survivors will be few.

The majority of those who contact you will therefore be either relatives of survivors or of those who lost their lives. I was a lad of 13 at the time but well remember being told that my uncle Lieutenant Colonel B. N. Elliot DSO, who commanded the 4th Battalion Royal Marines, had been killed : apparently standing on the bridge of HMS *Vindictive* at the time when the wind suddenly changed direction exposing the raiding force to the German defences on the Mole.

Unfortunately, I lost all my possessions as a result of the 1939-45 war and cannot contribute much towards your book. Among the things I lost was a rather twisted electric lightguard from the *Vindictive*, a framed photograph and names of all the officers of the 4th Battalion taken when H.M. King George V inspected the battalion probably in March 1918, a framed photograph of the *Vindictive* at Dover after her return from Zeebrugge and copies of the Chatham newspapers reporting on the public funeral of those who lost their lives. All of these passed into

my hands on the death of my mother who was Lieutenant Colonel
Elliot's sister.

*

From C. W. J. Spicer: Commander Brock; smoke screens

In response to your letter in today's *Daily Telegraph*, I enclose a photograph of Wing Commander F. A. Brock, RN who, until Zeebrugge,
was Officer Commanding RN Experimental Base, Dover.

On the morning of 22nd April 1918, I saw Commander Brock wearing
khaki uniform and armed with a cutlass and two revolvers on his way to
board HMS *Vindictive*. He was last seen alive, punching the heads of
German gunners on the Mole. I am sure that his presence at the scene
was entirely voluntary.

Commander Brock was a member of the Brock firework family. He
was responsible for the development of floating flares, which when
dropped into the sea from fast coastal motor boats ignited spontane-
ously and lit a wide area with great brilliance. But his finest achievement
was the creation of smoke screens. This consisted of injecting a stream
of chloro-sulphuric acid under pressure to impinge on the hot surface
of the interior of funnels of destroyers or the exhaust of CMB's. The
smoke hung low on the water effectively hiding ships. Men from the RN
Experimental Base served on board the ships so fitted to operate the
primitive gear and some were present at the Zeebrugge operation.

About thirty years later, I lunched with senior RN officers at Portsmouth Dockyard and was intensely interested to learn that the same
method of forming smoke screens was still used.

*

From L. M. Gilroy: Not entirely accurate but interesting

My late father, Frederick Leighton Gilroy, served on the *Vindictive* in
the action at Zeebrugge on St George's Day (23rd April) 1918. My
mother said he was one of three survivors – one lived in Portsmouth, and
I don't know where the other lived.

From the account my mother gave me, the old destroyer *Vindictive* was
to be taken between the two moles at Zeebrugge, under cover of darkness, and then scuttled to block the entrance to the harbour. The crew
were to abandon ship the best way they could, and I believe the *Daffodil*
and *Iris* were standing by to pick them up. Unfortunately, the enemy saw
the ship and fired, blowing her up prematurely. My father was picked
up and transferred to a hospital ship, which was torpedoed, and then
picked up by another ship, and this too was either bombed or torpedoed.

My father was very young at the time, and was Stoker 1st Class. He was awarded the Distinguished Service Medal and was Mentioned in Despatches. He had received injuries – a bullet wound through his shoulder and some shrapnel in his jaw and body; he also swallowed a lot of oil as he was in the water for some time, and it is thought that this contributed to his comparatively early death, in his forties, during the last war. The DSM was presented to him by Admiral Keyes who, I believe, master-minded the mission, or part of it.

I read an account of the action not too long ago in one of the news-papers – I believe, the *Sunday Express* – which implied that the exercise was a failure, but I do not believe my father considered it a failure, though I may be wrong on this point.

My grandfather was an officer in the RNVR during the Great War 1916-18, and was also for many years Secretary of the Seamen's Union, being Havelock Wilson's right hand man in South Shields, and it was his remarks about 'doing his duty' which stung my father into volunteer-ing for this mission, which they were warned was a dangerous one.

I hope the above may be of some interest to you – I am sorry it is rather vague, but the information was given to me second-hand.

The account in this letter appears to mix the Zeebrugge operation and the second Ostend operation, in which *Vindictive* was sunk.

Stoker Gilroy was awarded the DSM, for the Ostend operation.

*

From H. F. Brock Griggs: the last of Commander Brock

My cousin Commander Frank Brock RN in partnership with Com-mander Roger Keyes RN (later Admiral Lord Keyes) planned the raid which, as you know, had a dual purpose objective (a) to blockade Zeebrugge harbour and so 'bottle up' the U-boat base and (b) to obtain at all costs, a sample of the devastatingly accurate Goertz range finder with which the German coastal batteries were equipped. To that end my cousin was last seen attacking one of these gun crews, singlehanded and was never heard of again.

*

From L. W. Deer: scaling ladders

I was in the Navy in the early 30's in the Shipwright Branch and there was a legend on that branch of the three young shipwrights who were on HMS *Vindictive* in that attack. Their names were Arthur Lambkin and 'Nuts' Newton and Cochrane. The first two if my memory serves me right were responsible for the scaling ladders and Cochrane on the fo'c'sle for the anchors but he was killed early in the attack. Lambkin was severely wounded and Newton unscathed.

Lambkin and Newton are still alive.

Able Seaman Cochrane was mentioned in despatches.

2

HMS Iris II and Daffodil

Readers will probably take particular pleasure from the fact that two of the ships used in this daunting task were not originally warships at all but humble ferryboats. There was no time to build special boats so a naval officer was sent around the ports to find something approximately suitable. They were not ideal, for their steaming qualities were poor, and their decks were too low. However they had a small draught, would probably ride over mines and they could stand bumps as ferryboats learn to do.

Keyes states : '*Daffodil* arrived three minutes after *Vindictive*, closely followed by *Iris II*. As already stated, *Daffodil's* primary duty was to rush *Vindictive* bodily on to the Mole, to enable her to be secured after which *Daffodil* was to come alongside and land her parties over that ship. In the end her men had to disembark from her bows on to *Vindictive* as it was found essential to continue to push *Vindictive* on to the Mole throughout the action. This duty was magnificently carried out by her commanding officer, Lieutenant Harold Campbell.

'The landing from *Iris II* was even more trying. The second alongside made her bump heavily and rendered the use of the scaling ladders very difficult, many having broken up. In the end, so impossible was it to get the Mole anchors to hold, that the cable was slipped and *Iris II* went alongside *Vindictive* to enable D Company and her Royal Marines to land across her, but only a few men had got to the *Vindictive* when the withdrawal signal was sounded.'

*

From J. Gillison: after the raid

You might be interested to know that I as a boy of 15 witnessed the return to Liverpool of the two Liverpool ferries *Iris* and *Daffodil* after the Raid. I was at that time a trainee on board the training ship *Indefatigable*, which was moored in the Mersey off New Ferry Pier and the news of the arrival of these vessels was passed round the ship and we all lined the upper deck to await their passage through the harbour. They passed quite close to our ship and we could see distinctly the jagged holes through the funnels and upperworks of the ferries. There was a continuous blare of sirens from the ships and tugs in the port and we boys cheered loudly as the ferries passed by us. We also visited the ships later as they lay alongside. It was an unforgettable day for me and, as I was expecting to go to sea myself soon afterwards, it was my first glimpse of what war at sea might mean to someone in active participation.

*

Extract from 'The Shields Gazette', 30th April 1918: sent by L. M. Gilroy

HAND-TO-HAND FIGHT

LOCAL MAN'S STORY OF ZEEBRUGGE RAID

Bernard Devlin, formerly a barman in Wallsend, of 5 Grey Street, Wallsend, Thomas Ball, of 48 Laburnum Avenue, Wallsend, both ABs as well as Private Frank Henderson, Royal Marines, whose mother, a widow resides at 45 Laburnum Avenue, Wallsend, took part in the raid on Zeebrugge. Devlin and Ball have reached home on leave, but Henderson is missing, and his brother has since received intimation that he had been killed. He was serving on the *Iris*, was 19 years of age, and before the war he was an apprentice with Messrs Walkers, Wallsend and with a shipping firm in Newcastle.

Ball has a souvenir of the raid, a piece of shrapnel which passed through his body belt and glanced along his body.

Devlin, who served on the *Daffodil*, was one of the demolition party and in speaking of the raid, he said the men could scarcely be held back while *Vindictive* and *Daffodil* were being made fast. He added that, in selecting the men from all who volunteered, preference was given to those who liked tennis and sport. The part to which he was attached crept towards the shore to silence the guns, and one of the men dashed up the steps to the lighthouse and smashed the lantern with a bomb. Three destroyers which were lying alongside the Mole were deluged with bombs and then boarded. There was some desperate hand-to-hand fighting, in which the British seamen were always on top. He saw a German jump overboard rather than fight! It was a hot time and feet and fists were freely used. When the submarine blew up, the men went wild with delight and fought harder than ever. On receiving the signal from the *Vindictive*, the survivors returned, and the vessels cast off amid a rain of shell fire. Devlin later became distinguished in another way. The *Daffodil*, he states, caught fire and he volunteered to go below and hand up the ammunition to be thrown overboard. Ultimately, the ship was taken in tow by a destroyer.

Devlin speaks in the highest praise of all the officers and men, and referring to Lieutenant Campbell of the *Daffodil*, he speaks of him as a man with six hearts. After the fight, Lieutenant Campbell, with blood streaming from him, smoked a cigarette and sang 'The End of a Perfect Day'.

*

From M. Anson:

My grandfather, Captain Sir Harold Campbell RN, took part in the Zeebrugge attack. As a lieutenant he was in command of T.S.S. *Daffodil*. After the action, in which he was awarded the DSO, he was presented with a beautifully made 4 foot long model of the ship by Palmers Ship-building & Iron Co. Ltd. We inherited this model when he died four years ago and it now stands in a part of our house which has become known as the 'Daffodil Room'.

Some years ago I visited the Museum at Zeebrugge and found that his photograph hangs there alongside some wreckage from the *Daffodil* herself which must have been blown off during the action.

Lieutenant Harold Campbell was specially promoted and awarded the DSO for handling his ship magnificently under extremely heavy and unceasing fire; but for his skill and devotion the storming parties from *Vindictive* could neither have landed, nor having been landed, recovered. During the greater part of the time he was suffering from a wound in the eye.

*

From H. A. Davies: quite wrong about the medical staff, who worked like Trojans, but interesting in showing how rumours arise

Before the raid on Zeebrugge several of my chums were transferred to Dover in order to disembark the casualties from the *Iris* and *Daffodil* on the return to England.

In April 1919 a hospital ship was at the Liverpool landing stage and one of my friends who had volunteered to stay in the Army for another two years sought me out and asked me to take him on one of the ferry boats – the *Daffodil* as it happened. He showed me how he and the others had carried the men off the boat.

It was grim and dreadful, as I take it that no medical staff went over

the Channel so the wounded did not have any treatment until they came
back to this country.

*

From G. Warrington: Aboard the 'Iris' and personal account

I was Petty-Officer i/c of the Forward Mole *Flammenwerfer* party,
to land in support of the Landing Party on HMS *Iris II*.

Iris crept out from under the German guns with, to quote the first
message 'Number One' got away, 'For God's sake send some doctors, I
have a shipload of dead and dying.'

Personal account

Two attempts were made to carry out the operation against Zeebrugge
in early April 1918. The first was called off, just before the final 'run
in' – a change of wind would have rendered the important smoke screen
useless. The second – also abandoned a few days later – the sea was
rough for the mosquito craft (who were to lay the smoke screen).

It was a beautiful morning on 22nd April, when *Iris* laid alongside
the old battleship, *Dominion*, to pick up the landing party. We decided
to leave the ship's cat, and dog on board *Dominion*! – no need for them
to be involved. Shortly before we pushed off, the cat and dog returned
to *Iris*, and were received with a terrific cheer. The betting was 10-1
against the return of the landing party, therefore the return of the
ship's pets was the greatest morale booster.

Sometime in the morning, No 1, Lieutenant Henderson, said to me,
'PO get your men together and cover the top deck with sand.' I asked
him why, and he gave me a look of pity, and said, 'Lad – it is to soak up
the blood.' (I was 19 years old, a Cheshire farmer's son.) Thick as the
sand was, it was only partially successful. There were eighty-odd dead,
and two hundred and sixty wounded.

There were 60 craft in that odd flotilla. An aircraft flew over – thankfully it was one of ours.

Late in the afternoon, when I went on the top deck I found everyone
looking to westward, and saying nothing. Tapping Sergeant Marines
(Stripey) on the shoulder, asked him what it was all about. I got the
same look from him I had had from Lieutenant Henderson. They were
watching for sunset. We all wondered if we'd see it rise in the morning.
Nothing further until we lay off the Blankenberge Buoy, where the squadron split up. During the afternoon we had been joined by two columns
of destroyers, the port column, led by Vice-Admiral Sir Roger Keyes
(GOC) and the starboard by Rear-Admiral Cecil Dampier, in the light

cruiser *Attentive*. (It may have been Commander Boyle, I'm not sure.)

The starboard column, accompanied by all the necessary craft, plus two blockships, *Sirius* and *Brilliant*, left for Ostend operation. The port column left for Zeebrugge; the bulk of the destroyers were to form a protecting screen to the north, in case of enemy surprise in that quarter. The flagship, *Warwick* (Vice-Admiral on board) plus destroyers, *Phoebe*, and *North Star*, were to patrol inside the harbour, to protect landing party ships, from intervention from enemy destroyers tied up therein. It was 11.30 p.m. We were due alongside the Mole at midnight.

We were on our own now. *Vindictive*, leading, looked like a great beetle with fourteen legs on one side (the landing brows).

We in *Iris* were followed by *Daffodil* and then the three blockships, *Thetis*, *Intrepid*, and *Iphigenia*.

Somewhere, a gun barked and a star shell burst high in the sky – this was *it*. 11.40 p.m. Another star shell, and then we could see the smoke screen. I don't know how long it was, but it was perfect Then the search-lights, trying to penetrate, a few at first, eventually twenty-three. The enemy realized it was not local, and the answer was behind the smoke screen. Shortly all his guns were firing – it was just plain hell. I was very frightened. An old marine shouted to me, 'Keep yer bloody yed down lad, or one of these b – shells will whip it off. I'll tell thee summat else – this is four landing parties for me, – the others were in the Dardanelles – they were bad enough, but this is *it*.'

I check my gun to see if the cylinders are spinning all right. Another voice breaks out, 'If any of you young bastards have prayers – now's your chance – we're right on top of the b – s.' Everything was a joke to this man – he had survived half a dozen naval actions. This time his luck ran out, a machine gun bullet between the eyes. He fell on the deck, it did not take the smile off his face – not even eternity will do that.

That night we received a signal from the Admiral – 'St George for England', to which the *Vindictive* Captain, Carpenter replied, 'May we give the dragon's tail a damned good twist.' We'll be alongside in three minutes – three hours, or days, time means nothing under these conditions. Gunfire of all sorts is now terrific. How we made it I do not know. There was a great cheer from a thousand men: 'The Mole' – then a silence, except for gunfire, each man weighing up his chances. A six gun battery, on top of us. A salvo of 5.9 hit *Vindictive*, smashing her bridge and upper works. The flashes seemed in the wrong place – the Germans had shifted their guns from the Mole to the pier. This was frightening, as *Vindictive* had practised how fast she could go and stop, right on the guns. Therefore she had to go past and pull up where the plan said she should have been. The salvo that hit *Vindictive* had immunised three howitzers and their giant *Flammenwerfer* effort was hopeless. Of the fourteen landing-brows, only two were serviceable. Captain Henry Halahan, (leading the seamen) was killed, along with Colonel Elliot (commanding Marines), also badly wounding Commander Patrick Edwards. I should mention the Padre of Marines. I only met him once and don't remember his name. He was a very great man, and the men worshipped him.

Leaving *Vindictive*, being pushed against the Mole by *Daffodil*, whose job it was to hold her there the whole time, *Iris* brushed along the wall some 200 yards near No 2 shed, which was her resting place. There was an almighty bang – everything stopped – even the German guns. I think everybody had forgotten it was necessary to isolate the Mole from the mainland, to prevent the enemy from reinforcing their troops already there. To this end, a 'C class' submarine (Lieutenant Sandford) had to ram his sub under the wooden pier at the shore end, and blow her up. She had been specially prepared with explosive charges, to go off a few minutes after Sandford and his skeleton crew had been evacuated from her, by his brother Commander Sandford.

As we in *Iris* passed along the Mole, we heard *Vindictive's* landing party sorting themselves out – so some had got ashore. Clearing the wall by machine gun fire, we ran alongside. The starboard anchor was dropped, we went astern on it, to bring us close in. There was an 8 knot current running along the wall, and the great hook fixed to the derrick was not strong enough to hold *Iris* in position. By now, the enemy was sweeping the wall with heavy machine gun fire. The effort was hopeless. In an effort to improve the position, Lieutenant-Commander Bradford slowly climbed up the derrick, to see if anything could be done from the wall itself. He hadn't a hope in hell's chance – machine gun fire was so intense but he kept on climbing – he was killed as he stepped on the wall. His second in command also tried, but suffered the same fate. We were getting casualties from stray ricocheting bullets. It was decided to abandon that position and retreat to *Vindictive* and land over her deck.

I was amazed at the resistance put up by men on *Vindictive* – its light armament was also lost. One Lewis gun was firing – although its operator was wounded.

We were getting in position to run along *Vindictive* – someone shouted, 'Go like hell – the wind has changed – blowing the smoke off shore.' We remained until the official retreat was sounded – from *Daffodil's* syren. Twenty minutes were allowed for those ashore to return. Then we backed off, and headed for home. The order came, 'All seamen and marines below.' Being neither, the three of us stayed wondering what it was all about. In a moment, *Iris* was raked with machine-gun fire, so we quickly got below.

A star-shell burst overhead, and caused almost panic conditions. 'Steady the blues, stand by to abandon ship if necessary.' Leaving my two men, I made way to some stacked timber, and divested myself of cutlass, revolver, and gas mask, and gave my life-belt a look over. I stayed there, and that is why I am here today. We came under fire from the Goeben battery, on the left of the canal. Fourteen times the 5.9s struck *Iris*, and somebody threw in two 11 inch for good measure. One 11 inch went through the funnel, before bursting on the bridge, killing and wounding all hands, including Captain, and Major of Marines.

The other 11 inch burst on the main deck, about 10 yards away, killing about 100 men. I had to remain under this pile of dead and wounded. I don't remember how long. When I came to, I moved to the wood stack again to join the others.

I knew my two men were dead – someone struck a match, and a voice barked, 'Put that bloody light out, we are sitting ducks. Speed has dropped to six knots. There will be no lights for an hour.' It was a long hour. Why the enemy never found us, you probably know, so I won't comment.

Eventually a light sprang up, someone had a torch and we surveyed the shambles. Coming from a farm, and I had done first aid at medical school, before leaving University, I could in a small way help. We had only one doctor. I helped one man who had a 6 inch nail embedded in his back, where it came from God knows. I went on the top deck in the half-light, and found ourselves looking in to the muzzles of a pair of 15 inch guns. Thank God, it was HMS *Erebus*. We had made contact again. They sent us help for our wounded and I thankfully ceased my administrations.

Later, I met the coxwain who yelled at me, 'Where in hell have you been, boy – report to No 1 on the Bridge.' Shaking hands, Mr Henderson said 'I'm glad to see you boy, I thought you had bought it.' He asked about the men, and I said, 'Not so bad, considering.'

Four destroyers arrived on the scene, and escorted us to Dover Harbour. It was a misty morning, but the White Cliffs of Dover were the most wonderful sight to us all.

Arrived at Dover about 2 p.m. to be given a big 'Chuck up' by all the boats in the harbour. It was a memorable experience, in which I was proud to participate.

G. Warrington,
Petty Officer on *Iris*

Lieutenant Oscar Henderson was awarded the DSO and the Croix de Guerre. When a shell carried away the port side of the bridge of his ship and caused a serious fire amongst the ammunition and bombs, he led a volunteer fire party with a hose on to the upper deck to quench the fire. He took over the command of the ship after Commander Gibbs had been killed.

*

From P. Watson: HMS Daffodil

My stepfather, Captain H. V. Rogers RNR, took part in the Zeebrugge Raid as navigator of HMS *Daffodil*. He got the DSC for this and also some nasty leg wounds which made it embarrassing for him to wear shorts later on when we were all in Burma. I would take issue with him about this, God bless him, and point out that these were honourable scars of war and that I was proud of them if he wasn't and he used to reply that he felt a bloody fool with hairless knees. There was also a pension of 16/- (yes *Shillings*) a week which was a source of wry amusement to him until the depression when he wrote to the Admiralty renouncing it since he was lucky enough to be bounding forward satisfactorily in his career and did not need it. He got a charming letter back – their Lordships seemed stunned, after all it can't be a thing that often happens – offering to start paying it again if ever in future years he felt inclined to change his mind. Had he lived on till these inflationary days he might well have been tempted, but alas he died in 1956 aged 68.

I inherited the engraved sword presented to him by his home town, Wrexham, North Wales and the gold cigarette case, also engraved, from the city of Liverpool, and *Daffodil's* log book. I have also a photograph of his reception by the Lord Mayor and his lady (much more frightening than the Germans, he said) and, I think, a snap of *Daffodil*.

Acting Lieutenant Harold Rogers was the navigating officer on *Daffodil*. His citation for the DSC read: 'Throughout the operations was of the greatest assistance, performing any duty required of him with promptness and fearlessness in an exposed position, and at times under very heavy fire. When his commanding officer was temporarily incapacitated by wounds he took command of the ship and did everything possible to ensure the safety of the ship and crew.'

*

Extracts from log of HMS Daffodil – Preparing for Action

SIGNAL LOG of HIS MAJESTY'S SHIP *DAFFODIL IV*
Sunday 7th April
4.30: from Vindictive to Daffodil
Have you a box of rockets and some sticks for me? Reply : we have 90 rocket sticks but can trace no rockets.

5.43: from Vindictive to Daffodil
Look out for the police trap.

6.00: from Daffodil to Iris
My cable has parted but slip has jambed in hawse pipe. I propose to go by that. Give us more cable. Please veer more cable. Reply: Veering. Please let me know when you have veered to the limit.

6.5: from Iris to Daffodil
You have full length of wire now.

Tuesday 9th April
8.0 from Daffodil to Iris
Request carpenter rating may be sent as soon as possible.

10.15: from Iris to Daffodil
If you want a carpenter you must apply for one from *Hindustan,* our carpenter is employed.

10.35: from Iris to Daffodil
I have sent a message in Picket boat asking for a carpenter to be sent to you.

12.0: from Daffodil to C.O. Daffodil and Hindustan
Can we be allowed to carry another 12 tons of coal in after end of boiler room when bunkers are full? Approved.

12.5: from SO: General
Weather forecast from London. Wind N.W. to N.E. 3 to 5. Some rain and mist.

12.15: from SO: General
A buoy showing a red light will be placed at the N.E. end of Gap.

1.40: from Daffodil to Hindustan
Request a boat may be sent for two carpenters.

3.10: from SO: General
Time table for operation memo 001-1 of sixteenth April was issued by
an oversight. It will not come into force till specially ordered by V.A.

5.15: from SO: General
Latest weather report on Belgium coast. Wind N.E. by E. 4. Visibility
half a mile.

5.35: from Iris to Daffodil
After dark tonight I propose to burn lights in compass, engine room tele-
graphs, shaded stern navigation lights, and to try my shaded flashing
lamp. Will you please report to me if any of these show up too much outside the ship? Reply : I will do the same.

6.30: from SO: General
The buoy in position B is showing a white occulating light.

9.5: from SO: General by lamp
How are my lights. Does this shaded lamp appear satisfactory?
Reply : Yes. I can see a green light and bright white light at masthead.
Reply : Can you see anything of our wheel house light and light in
compass? Reply : No. Can you see ours? Reply : I can see your stern
light reflecting on the water and a great deal of light coming from
Wheelhouse.

9.30: from Vindictive to Daffodil by lamp
Do you require any pistols, cutlasses, or Winchester rifles? If so how
many? I will send them over by boat. Reply : We have three defective
pistols and want three more rifles besides, also we have no ammunition
for same.

12.0: from SO: General by lamp
Raise steam for 12 knots at 4 hours notice by 0900 tomorrow acknowledge.

12.30: from SO: General by lamp
Latest weather report from Belgium coast. Wind N.E. visibility one mile.

Thursday 11th April
Place: Swin, Sheerness
11.27: from SO: General
Gunfleet reports some very heavy gunfire to the eastward.

12.45: from SO: General
Operation ordered will take place Codeword No ——— .

14.25: from Hindustan to Daffodil
You are to follow *Iris* out who will slip at 2.45.

14.45: from Daffodil to Hindustan
Au Revoir. Many thanks for all you have done for us.

15.00: from Hindustan: General
Captain, Officers and Ship's Company wish every success to Expedition and take off their hats to you.

18.38: from Vindictive to Daffodil by flag
Stop.

18.30: from Vindictive: General by semaphore
General Recall. Should the necessity arrive for withdrawing the force before the appointed time. Recall signals consisting of a succession of flashes from *Vindictive* together with the flashing of *Vindictive*'s searchlight up the Mole from the vertical.

Friday 12th April
Place: at Sea
9.5: from Thetis to Daffodil
Are you going on or shall I pass you? Reply : Please pass me. I can do no more.

9.40: from Vindictive to Daffodil
Daffodil close.

10.00: from Vindictive to Daffodil
Brilliant and *Sirius* went through the gate and could not find their way out again.

10.10: from Daffodil to Vindictive
I regret that my steaming is most unsatisfactory. I have had great trouble
in keeping 80 lbs of steam.

11.57 from V.A. Warwick to Daffodil
I am sorry for the postponement but it would have been folly to attempt
to attack with an offshore wind. Is your ship all right? Reply : Submitted.
Structure is quite all right, steaming capabilities very bad.

Wednesday 17th April
Place: Swin

12.00: from SO: General
Any ship having bags marked G. W. Greening E.R.A., J. Radford
Stoker, F. Shard Stoker, W. Edwards Ldg Seaman, W. Potter L.S.,
W. Snow AB communicate with *Hindustan.*

12.05: from SO: General
Field Service letters and cards are to be sent to *Hindustan* censored and
unsealed by a Commissioned Officer. No message is to be sent. No
address is to be given. Packets and bags are to be clearly named of
contents. Other letters are to be censored and sealed down and forwarded
to *Hindustan* in packets signed by a Commissioned Officer. Letters are
to be onboard *Hindustan* by 1100 BST Daily.

6.20: from SO: General
In case of German naval offensive ships must be prepared to slip at
short notice and withdraw to Mouse L.V. If attacked at long range
Vindictive and *Thetis* class making smoke screens steam on one engine
for slow speed at 1 hour's notice and on other engine at 4 hours' notice.
Dominion and *Hindustan* at 1 and 2 hours' notice. Officers and men may
be used as requisite to make up guns crews in emergency. Acknowledge.
Reply : your 1745 received.

Saturday 20th April
Place: Swin
9.40: from SO: General
Captains of blockships and ferry-ships are to repair onboard *Vindictive*
at 2 p.m. *Dominion's* steamboat will collect Captains of *Thetis, Iphigenia*
and Captain Halahan. *Hindustan's* picket boat will collect the remainder.
All Captains are to bring their charts.

10.45: from CO Intrepid to COs Thetis and Daffodil
Rayne wants us to lunch with him onboard *Dominion* today. He will send a boat for me about 11.30. He will put us onboard *Vindictive* after.

12.30: from SO: General
Following received from *Dominion:* We are holding a Boxing contest at 15.30 and would be pleased to see any officers or crew who care to come.

19.15: from Daffodil to Vindictive 1st Lieut. Lt Hewitt RNAS
Can you please tell me any information regarding Hammock belonging to R. G. Goodwin AM2. It was left by mistake when Goodwin joined *Daffodil.*

Monday 22nd April
Place: Swin and at sea
7.15: from C in C: General
British light forces operating in the Heligoland Bight Saturday April 20th obtained touch with enemy light forces who retired behind minefields. A few shots were exchanged at extreme range. One enemy destroyer was observed to be hit. All our ships returned. We have no casualties.

8.15: from SO: General
No orders yet. Preparations are to be made for getting up and serving out ammunition with minimum delay. *Iris* and *Daffodil* to bank fires at 45 minutes notice. If Nascent is signalled raise steam at once.

9.05: from SO: General by Semaphore
Weather Report Belgian Coast N.E.11. Visibility very good.

1015: from Hindustan to Iris and Daffodil
No orders yet but as time for preparations is short Notice Steam at 20 minutes' Notice.

10.45: from SO: General by flags
NASCENT.

10.53: Anchor away

11.12: Secured

11.20: from SO: General by Semaphore
Ships are warned that Chloro Sulphuric gas is dangerous. Smoke apparatus is to be carefully handled. Lt Cohen was gassed this forenoon.

11.35: from Iris to Daffodil by Semaphore
Be ready to leave at 1200.

11.35: from SO: General by Semaphore
Time ball will be dropped again at 11.15.

11.43: Hindustan left

11.50: Secured Vindictive

12.8: Left

12.15: from SO: General by flags
Good luck. God Speed.

12.20: from Intrepid to Daffodil by Semaphore
Better luck this time. Reply: Same to you and hope to see you first thing St George's Day. Reply: I've got a few for tomorrow night.

12.45: from SO: General
V.A. Dover reports weather likely to be temporary. Prepare to return if Code Word is made.

15.30: from Iris to Daffodil by Semaphore
What speed do you calculate from Mouse Light Vessel to here. Reply: About 10'4 Knots without tide. Reply: Some speed.

15.32: from Daffodil to Iris by Semaphore
Subt Have trouble with feed pump am waiting report whether serious or not.

15.40: from Iris to Daffodil by Semaphore
Is your Feed-Pump all right? Reply: Yes.

16.05: Securely in tow of Iris

16.05: from Vindictive: General by flags
Proceed.

16.10: from Vindictive to Iris and Daffodil by Semaphore
I am going 7 knots.

16.12: from Vindictive to Iris and Daffodil by Semaphore
I am going 9 knots.

16.19: from Vindictive: General by flags
Speed 10 knots.

Action Stations

7th May 1918
Place: Portsmouth
10 a.m. open to visitors till 7 p.m.
5.40: from C in C to Iris
Two steel chests from *Iris* have been brought to C in C's office by an official from N.S.O.'s Department. They are said to contain Confidential Books. A report is to be forwarded as to whence they were received and if information is available as to what they contain and disposal of the keys.

5.50: from Iris to C in C
Submit re your 1722 of today. I do not definitely know what the steel chests contain other than orders of operation. Keys of both chests cannot be traced and no doubt were lost in action. Most of confidential books were burnt prior to reaching Zeebrugge.

3

The Royal Marines

The 4th Battalion of the Royal Marines had been formed at Dover from a Company brought from Chatham, a Company from Plymouth and a Company from Portsmouth. The commanding officer, Lieutenant-Commander Elliot, DSO, who was killed at Zeebrugge, came of a family who had been serving with the Marines since 1716. The high standards and versatility of the Royal Marines need no special commendation here; they are well enough known.

*

Extracts from diary of RMLI private (from Lieutenant-Colonel C. E. J. Eagles). The anonymous writer was Irish, an avid reader, and blessed with a keen though cynical sense of humour. Colonel Eagles' father, Major C. E. C. Eagles DSO, was killed in the battle and was mentioned in despatches.

19th March
Volunteered for 4th Battalion at Deal. There were thirty volunteers out of M14, but there were only eleven taken. There were McDowell, Burgess, Whitley, Goodwin, Lightbown, Morris, Mitchell, Wilson, Poole and myself, and last, but not least, Smullen.

20th March
Passed the colonel for 4th Battalion, but, much to our surprise, we were told that we are to go to France in fourteen days, and we cannot get draft leave until we are two months there. We expressed our opinions on this move in no uncertain terms.

21st March (Sunday)
Went to Battalion Quarters El Room, North Barracks. Lightbown, McDowell, Malpas and I are all together in one room. There are a couple of other decent chaps as well, and several ex-drummers. Parade

in full marching order at 9.30 a.m. Inspected by Chatham major. All
the battalion are off on draft leave, and we volunteers are stuck for drill
and forced marches.

22nd March
Physical jerks and bayonet fighting are the leading lines in the training,
besides long marches. Lieutenant Claudet, our platoon commander (7th
Platoon), brought us out to Freedown and showed us a model of the
canal that we are to mop up in France. He says it will be only for two
and a half hours. It appears to be two miles long, and seems full of
trenches, dug-outs, pill-boxes, and ammunition dumps. We can plainly
see that there is an air of mystery about this whole stunt. What the devil
do they want going to the expense of sending 950 marines over to France
for two and a half hours' work, when they have millions of men there
already, is what puzzles some of us.

23rd March
Battalion back from leave. We pick up our place in Portsmouth section,
and train with them. Tons of work and training until eleven at night.

24th March
Same old thing. Gas-mask training and strangle-holds. Fed up with work,
and can't make out where this canal is.

25th March
Night training with star-shells, smoke-screen, and gas-masks. I don't like
the idea of fighting with gas-masks on in darkness. I got lost completely in
the smoke-screen. War must be a lot more than inconvenient.

26th March
Our captain brought us for a twelve-mile march before dinner. Looks like
as if we shall have a lot of marching in France. No prayers said for
captain.

27th March (Sunday)
A day of rest and letter-writing.

28th to 31st March
Routine training, marching, bayonet fighting.

1st April – Ditto

2nd April
Full rehearsal of stunt in Freedown at 9 p.m. Smoke-screen, gas, star-shells, fireworks, etc. Very solemn and dreadful, but most uncomfortable lying half an hour under the rain in wet grass.

3rd April
We are to leave here on Saturday, 6th April. Have been to the pictures twice this week.

4th April
Getting ready to leave.

5th April
Marching order, with gas-mask, barbed-wire pliers, sixty rounds ammunition, rug and waterproof sheet, muffler and gloves. Rather a heavy marching order.

6th April
Reveille sounded for us at 4.30 a.m. We are out sharp, and it seemed to me that everything I did had an added significance that morning. After breakfast we took what food was left with us in case we were hungry, and were in full marching order, with overcoats loose on us. It was the most uncomfortable hour or two I ever spent in my life from the time I put on these things until I got them off on the ship at Dover. We fell in opposite D Block in South Barracks, and marched to North Parade, where the Chatham and Plymouth sections were already assembled. The band played us up to the station. The airs were 'Auld Lang Syne', 'The Girl I Left Behind Me,' and 'Britons Never Shall Be Slaves'.

I never got a bit sentimental about this move up to the march to the railway-station, until I saw a young, fair-haired woman run up to her husband and kiss him passionately. She was standing on the side of the road as I passed on. I saw her left hand clenched hard over her handkerchief, and the wedding-ring looked new enough. She was biting her lip to try to hold the tension. It flung me back completely on myself, and I was thinking of my own wife and baby for a while, and that tune seemed to be completely out of place ('The Girl I Left Behind Me'). After a while I thought that it was just as well that the people at home knew so little. We poor devils have soft spots in our hearts just the same as anyone else, no matter what people say to the contrary; but we manage to conceal them very well.

Left Deal by 7 a.m. train, and we don't know where we are going to be sent from. I took off my gear the minute I could do so conveniently in the carriage. What a luxury it felt! And I had a fine novel from the library, that I should have returned, called *God's Clay*, which lasted me a few days' reading afterwards. I had settled down about ten minutes, when we arrived at Dover, and we were told to get out, and, when we did so, we marched on board a ship and were sent down below.

We were set guessing again. We had been below about three hours at sea, when we were ordered up, and were transferred to another boat. This left us in a knot. We could not follow the mysterious working of the mind of the Admiralty. We went down below again, and were four hours in this, when we came up to be landed on a battleship, which we got on about half-past four in the evening. Some of the old marines told me we were anchored at the mouth of the estuary of the Thames. We were put in Mess 50, a most comfortable position on the ship; but we are to sleep in hammocks, and I don't know how we shall all fit. However, I am sure we shall all sleep, as it so tires one with all the gear we have to carry with us. Lightbown and I sleep on the mess deck, the first night in our hammocks. Whitley and Poole slung theirs over our heads. We don't know what to think about this stunt.

7th April (Sunday)
Service on board for Church of England. Parade in the morning and evening. We have been informed today for the first time that we are to land on the Mole of Zeebrugge from the *Vindictive*, under a smoke-screen from the motorboats, same as the smoke-screen at Freedown. We are to land on the Mole and destroy all we can in the space of time that the wind and tide allow, and whilst the concrete ships are being sunk. The general opinion here at the moment is that it will be either completely successful or we shall be all wiped out.

8th April
Mess 50. Number of men, twenty-eight. No room. Don't like ship life. No room to even change your mind. Can't do anything but lose things. Got cigarettes and tobacco free. Food good, but bread is scarce. We had a bit of a concert for a short time last night.

9th April
Routine: Rise at 6.30 a.m.; Hammock stowed, and washed by 7.30 a.m.; breakfast to 8.30 a.m.; parade, 8.45 a.m.; physical drill at 10.30 a.m. to 11 a.m.; dinner, 12 noon; tea, 4 p.m.; supper, 7 p.m.; pipe down, 10 p.m. (concerts from 8 p.m. to 10 p.m.); went on board

Vindictive to see where we take up our positions. Spent about one hour on her, and came back to the ship.

10th April
The attack is to come off to-night. Hammocks stowed. Packs handed in, and we go on board *Vindictive*. We set sail for two hours, and the wind becomes unfavourable to work the smoke-screen, so we turn back again to the *Vindictive*. This tension is very bad for the nerves. Wish it was over.

11th April
Up at 6.30 a.m. First thought in my mind was, 'What way is the wind?' After breakfast and parade, the company sergeant-major announced the joyful tidings that the wind was 'it', if it would only remain so. We went once more through that routine of stowing packs and hammocks, and went on board the *Vindictive* at 3 p.m. At all our transhipping operations it was one of the Liverpool ferry-boats that acted as go-between. All the crew of the ship gave us a very hearty send-off, cheer after cheer echoing over the sunlit sea. I never could make out what were the sentiments that inspired such enthusiasm. I found afterwards that the crew collared all the rations we left, and they had considerably more room without our company. The *Vindictive* gave us a very warm welcome. They sent a spray of liquid fire over the quarter-deck and I should not care for an embrace of that kind. There was something horribly fascinating about the long flames curling and twisting in the air like luminous serpents. We took up our stations on the deck next to the pom-pom on the port side, and I left my equipment and gas-mask on top of an iron cylinder of some kind.

Lightbown and I went up to the upper-deck and stood over the engine-room, as it warmed the place all round. We had some songs and some gambling going on all the time. We found the ship was the better hotel and the *Vindictive* more liberal in refreshments. The landing is to take place at 2 a.m.

11th April
About 6 p.m. we fall in at our stations, and we got bombs and fireworks, and we are to hold in readiness now to fall in, in five minutes. Time seems ages, waiting. I cleaned my rifle, gas-mask, and ground my bayonet on the much-used stone on the ship. We got plenty of cigarettes and tobacco free, and also soup at 8 p.m., and rum at 12. We fell in on the deck ready at 1 a.m., and could see the searchlight on the Mole, and

star-shells going up, and shrapnel bursting. It was weirdly beautiful; but one felt that life hung on a very slender cord at that hour.

We got very tense and anxious from this vigil on deck, and I was sick of waiting. When we were told it was all a wash-out as the wind had changed, I can honestly say that I would have much preferred it came off then, as we had ourselves schooled up to facing the music, and now we found it was all to be done over again.

12th April

Tired and lazy. No news from home for a week, and no word from me. The officers promised that they would get some kind of a field letter for us to send home to ease the tension, as we were to stay on board for ten more days, until the tide would be favourable, and the change of the wind being equally so. Admiral Keyes came on board at dinner-time (about 12 noon) and explained the reason that we retired last night without firing a shot. He said without a smoke-screen that would be effective we would not have a dog's chance, and last night, the wind changed and the smoke-screen would be useless; hence his order to return. It takes a very self-reliant man to give an order like that in the last few minutes.

Routine as usual. Reading is my principal pastime. We had a concert on board to-night from 8 p.m. until 10 p.m. The colonel always attends, and nearly all the officers sing. Some of the songs are very sentimental, some are comic, and a big 'some' have a strong flavour which seems to be the exact taste of the majority of the audience.

13th April

The stunt is on again today, and we are all sincerely hoping it will come off tonight, as the suspense is chronic. We went on board the *Vindictive* at 3 p.m. and had tea. Then the wind changed, and we came back once more to the ship. We arrived about 10 p.m. We are completely fed up with this going and coming back again. We take all the spare provisions that are in the mess with us, in case we come back. As to the poor crew of the ship, they must be properly sick of giving us send-offs and seeing us come back again in a few hours.

14th April (Sunday)

No RC service on board. We shan't make another attempt before ten days. I expect to be balmy by then, for want of something to interest me. All my speculations are in the future. Am I to be, or not to be, after the landing? Went to evening prayers at the Seamen's Mess Deck, con-

ducted by the chaplain (Church of England). He is a real fine type of
a man's man. His mind is as broad as the sea. I should like to have had
a talk with him on some knotty points that he glided over quite easily.
One thing that surprised me was his asking for all our prayers for a dead
shipmate. I thought that they did not believe in praying for the dead.
That man was judged by his own works. I shall hear him again if
feasible.*

15th April

Oh, ye munition-workers, of big wages and little or no patriotism! Laugh
not at the delights of a simple marine! I nearly got a stroke of apoplexy
when I was told I was to get a week's wages today, so, after a desperate
struggle to hide my delight, I held out my hand in quite a cool fashion,
and received the sum of 4s., with three or four notices, which told me
to buy War Bonds and not waste paper. When my pulse got steadied a
bit after these transports of avarice, I bethought myself how shall I
invest this magnificent sum that a grateful country gives without a word
of protest. I had a flutter on the Crown and Anchor. I was lucky. I
worn 25s. But I don't think I could stop the war with that sum, so I did
not cable to the Kaiser that I had cornered the silver of a quarter of a
century of bobs. We got tapioca for dessert to-day. Must really admit
that we are really well fed, and the cooking is excellent. There is a quiet
modesty about the sailors that is very becoming and manly. When you
see how polite the cooks in the galleys here are, and remember the auto-
cratic rulers of cookhouses in the depot, you wonder how the one God
made them; but of course He meant to show how East and West can
meet.

The marines are great believers in Socialism. Everybody seems to take
what he wants and somebody else owns. Possession seems to be the only
form of ownership here. I have lost my rug, rifle, two novels, and en-
trenching tool, and have got someone else's. But you never hear anybody
complain about losing anything. It's bad form to say you lost anything,
as it seems to imply someone took it, and it lets others know that you are
anxious to acquire a substitute for what you have lost, which makes
them stand guard over their gear for a time.

16th April

No physical jerks this morning. Cold rain for a few hours. Gun-loading
competition between gun-crews of nine marines each, which lasted all
day. Terrible sameness about the game. I looked on for an hour and then

---

* Chaplain Peshall, awarded the DSO. See page 59.

got a book from the library of short stories by H. G. Wells. I have been very glad that this library is opened to us.

The battalion commenced to keep watches on the decks from to-day. The privilege of smoking on the mess-deck, which we enjoyed since the 6th inst, has been withdrawn on account of a fire at 3 a.m. on Sunday morning last. Strange how these fires originate. There was one on board the *Vindictive* whilst we were on board last Thursday.

At last we got the stereotyped letters to send home. It is the most scrupulously economical string of words that ever were connected together with the object of concealing affection or love, and the author, whoever he was, succeeded in making it read like a pawn-ticket.

We get daily papers all the week. Ireland, my country, is still in the limelight. How difficult it is to the imaginative dreamer of a Celt to explain to the slow, calm, level-headed, but conceited Saxon what he wants and why he wants it. I am very low in tobacco, and I lost all my money on the Crown and Anchor. I can't see where the next supply is to come from. I wish I could do the lonely soldier stunt on the *Daily Mail* – something like this : 'Lonely Marine, one of 950, sixteen miles from land, would be glad to correspond with any lady – young, or even very young – with more money than good taste; object, tobacco. In exchange he will give her full particulars of all the religious rites and ceremonies of this spick-and-span and beautifully pipe-clayed and polished body of men.'

22nd April
Stunt to come off to-night. Stowed hammock, packed up our packs, and went on board the *Vindictive*. We brought our dinners with us, cooked in the mess-tins; also all the bread, sugar and tea we had in the mess. We are doubtful that it will come off, but we all hope that it will. We have taken up our stations and had tea, and we are on the way to the Mole. Everything seems certain as the wind is holding favourable. I do wish that it comes off as the suspense is awful. We do not seem to realise what we are about, card-playing, singing, gambling and a gramophone going, all whiling away the last few hours on earth for some of us.

Glorious sunset at 6 p.m. after a perfect day. The sea is dotted with the steel walls of Britain – anything from a Dreadnought to a motor-boat – and all as silent as the grave. I wonder what kind of a racket they will knock up in a few hours hence.

At 7 p.m. I can count 57 vessels all going the same way home. We got tea at 8 p.m., and are to get our usual rum ration at 10 o'clock. If the wind is right at half-past ten we are to see it through to-night, no matter what happens. Going down now for a short sleep before the landing starts. I hope it won't be my last short one on this planet. All the boys are quite pleased now that it is to take place to-night. I hope we make a good show and have a decent slice of luck. It would be rotten to strike a mine, or have a collision with another of our ships. This finishes before the 'scrap'. I hope I shall be able to finish about the battle.

April 23rd

After the landing on the Mole I came back without a scratch. Corporal Smith was killed, also Rolfe of our platoon; Whitley and Corporal Regan are badly wounded. Haly, Poole and Taylor are slightly wounded. When we came in sight of the Mole the searchlight was working around in arcs of circles, and we stood outside its focus about three times. We were experiencing a bit of luck so far, not a shot had been fired up to the time we were about two ships' lengths from the Mole or breakwater. Then the searchlight got on us properly; we were lit up like daylight.

Then there was a noise when our guns opened fire, and a German destroyer about 200 yards from us replied. I had cotton-wool in my ears, and it sounded as if someone pulled the props from under the sky and it fell down. I dropped on the deck, and kept as low as I could. I often heard of people feeling small. I never felt so uncomfortably big in my life before. These thundering and banging and ear-splitting sounds continued for nearly ten minutes, and even then we could hear the wails of anguish of the dying and wounded.

Sergeant Braby came along, and said we were not to be alarmed as it was only our guns. Well, ours were some guns. How they managed to knock lumps off our own funnels I had not time to investigate, but I took the sergeant's word for it. Eventually we got alongside, and we were told to get ready to land. We got down two gangways and Plymouth section went over before us. The sailors were going over individually before that. Sergeant Braby gave us the order to go up and over. The fire-main had been perforated by shrapnel, and we had to pass under it. We got something to keep us cool; down my back I got a shower. The sergeant stood very near it. He was trying to hide the bodies of three of the pom-pom gun's crew from us when we got on a level with the hinge of our gangway. The battalion sergeant-major and the adjutant were superintending the getting over of the ladders.

Well, it was not like anything I ever saw on parade, except that these two were just as cool. I offered to give a hand with the ladders when I was passing up the gangway, but sergeant-major told me to go over.

Well, I walked up very carefully, and in the anxiety to keep my balance on the see-saw of the gangway, I forgot about the rain of lead, and I really felt comfortable when I put my foot on the concrete.

The sea-face of it stands about twenty-five feet over high-water, the outer face, for about four feet deep, is three feet higher than the inside. When I got off the outer face, and stepped down on the promenade portion, I thought it was the Mole proper; but when we moved over to a three-foot railing and looked down, we could see what appeared to be a very wide street about twenty feet below. Then I knew what the ladders were for. We had some trouble here. I was ten minutes before I got a ladder to go down by.

Sergeant Besant got on the ladder, and shouted for No 1 Section. As we were No 2 we did not go. We waited for Corporal Smith, but as things seemed a bit mixed, I asked McDowell to come along, and we went. Captain Bamford came up just then from the left side of us and we went down immediately after him. I had arranged with Lightbown that we would stick together, but in the confusion of getting over on to the ladders I lost him, so McDowell and I hung on together.

There was a group of bodies at the foot of the ladders – all Germans – who tried to knock the ladders, and amongst them three men in white ducks. The light during the landing was wonderful. I don't believe there was ever such a firework display. The German star shells, that light up the sea and land for miles, were terrible in their effective grandeur.

I ran across to the dump-house opposite the ship, and took cover by lying on the ground. The ground floor of the dump-house was raised about two-and-a-half feet over the roadway, and had a pathway like as if carts were loaded there, like at a railway goods store. We had a grand chance of chucking bombs in the doors of this dump-house, as we had splendid cover. Whilst amusing myself here, a portion of concrete was removed out of the Mole by the explosion of the submarine that was stuck in the piles. I could not attempt to describe what this operation sounded like. It was about the very last word in noise.

When we got back we were told that the dump-house was to be blown up now, so we went away to the left, and I could see no one to fire at. I felt rotten to hear the rattle of the shells striking the funnels, and could do nothing just then. Captain Bamford came up, and said, quite cool, 'Fall in, B Company'. I fell in with McDowell, and Sergeant Braby took charge of us. There were only sixteen there, and Captain Bamford was leading us along, when he looked back to see how many he had, and apparently he thought we were insufficient, as he told the sergeant to retire to the ship. The sirens had gone over ten minutes then, and we retired in two's to the ladders; it was running the gauntlet over that fire-swept zone. I went with McDowell, and we got up together on the two ladders.

*

From Lieutenant-Colonel C. S. V. Cooke: Major T. F. V. Cooke

My brother Major T. F. V. Cooke DSO – Croix-de-Guerre and palm was leading one of the Royal Marine detachments which landed on the Mole from HMS *Vindictive*. He was one of the first to set foot on the Mole, and was awarded the DSO and Croix-de-Guerre. Following the exploit, he was badly wounded in the head and eventually invalided out of the Service, but he lived for many years afterwards in Jersey.

Lieutenant Theodore Cooke's citation for the DSO and special promotion read : 'By his personal bravery under fire set a magnificent example to his men, and led them forward with the greatest courage and dash in spite of being wounded. He was wounded a second time whilst endeavouring to carry a wounded man back to the ship.

*

Account by Major General A. R. Chater, then Captain Chater

The most authentic account of the Zeebrugge Operation is that given, in Admiral Keyes' Despatch in the 2nd Supplement to the *London Gazette* of 19th February 1919. That was written at the time by people who had taken part in the operation. The account in the *Official War History* was written 13 years later when few of those who had taken part could be contacted.

I enclose for what it may be worth an extract from my personal narrative. This was written some fifty years ago.

ZEEBRUGGE OPERATION
22nd/23rd APRIL 1918
Extract from the personal narrative of Captain A. R. Chater
Adjutant, 4th Battalion Royal Marines

At 11 p.m. the Battalion went to action stations. As the result of experience on 11th April, very careful precautions were taken to see that no man got more than his own ration of rum. In spite of this, one old soldier must have borrowed someone else's tot, for when I went round the mess decks with the Sergeant Major as the men were closing-up, he shouted at us, 'We are just going over the top. We are all equal now'.

I remember catching sight of the same man some three hours later, and thinking what a changed and sober man he looked.

On the way up to my station beside the Battalion Commander on the bridge, I met Major Cordner, the Second in Command. We stopped and talked for a minute or two on the built up deck. Although I cannot remember the matter having been previously discussed, I had always assumed that Major Cordner's station would be somewhere near the after end of the built-up deck. At the end of our talk I remarked, 'And now you are going aft?' To my surprise he replied, 'No, I must be with the CO until the ship is alongside and then I will go aft.' Since then I have often regretted that I did not put more forcibly my point that the CO and Second in Command should not have been together. We went up to the bridge and joined the CO. The three of us stood together on the port side of the bridge. The remainder of Battalion Headquarters were below us on the lower bridge. I hung my fleece lined Burberry on the chart house door, where I later found it badly torn by shell splinters.

As the ship approached the harbour we heard the sound of shell fire ahead. Star shell started coming over us and we realised how well we were being concealed by our smoke. Then the wind changed, and the smoke suddenly drifted away and on the port bow we saw the Mole, about which, for the past two months and more, we had thought so much. A moment later there was a burst of shell fire and shells came whistling around us.

Breast-high splinter-proof mattresses had been placed around the bridge. Although only twenty-two years old, I probably had a far more intimate experience of shell fire than either the CO or the second in command. At Antwerp in 1914 I had quite unnecessarily put my head up over the parapet of a trench and been wounded for my stupidity. At Gallipoli I had been hit in the back by a shrapnel ball. We were still some distance from the Mole and now instinct told me to keep my head down. I suggested that my two seniors should do the same, but they either did not hear me or they did not agree with me. Anyhow they took no notice. A moment later, a shell appeared to hit the front part of the lower bridge beneath us. My two seniors dropped to the deck on either side of me. I grasped hold of them and spoke to them in turn, but neither of them answered me. I then made my way across the bridge and down the starboard ladder to the starboard waist, and called out for Major Weller, Commander of C Company and the next senior officer in the Battalion.

By the time I had found Major Weller and told him that the battalion

commander and second in command were casualties, the ship was alongside the Mole and the seamen storming party was landing.

B Company, stationed in the port waist, had to some extent been
protected from the shell fire whilst the ship was approaching the Mole –
by the built-up deck. C Company, in the starboard waist, had little protection and suffered considerable casualties before the ship was placed
alongside. The plan was for No 10 and 11 Platoons of C Company to
land first, but when the moment for this arrived, both platoon officers
and most of the men were already casualties, and the platoons as such,
appeared no longer to exist. Standing on the built-up deck, I therefore
called down to Lieutenant Cooke, Commanding No 5 Platoon of B
Company, to bring his platoon up to the port bridge ladder, which,
although narrow, was a much shorter route than the wide ramps which
led from the starboard side to the built-up deck. No 5 Platoon rushed up
the ladder, over the three remaining serviceable brows, and, turning to
the right advanced along the pathway on top of the sea wall.

I accompanied Lieutenant Cooke's platoon ashore to investigate the
height of the sea wall, of which conflicting reports had been received,
and the best means of getting down on to the Mole, and up again. I
found that there were no steps near to where the ship had been berthed,
and that the height was too great to jump down. Returning on board, I
gave instructions for hook ropes to be taken ashore to enable the men
to get down on to the Mole, and I made Sergeant-Major Thatcher personally responsible that, after the men had landed, scaling ladders were
taken ashore and placed and maintained in position. Without these
ladders, no man who got down on to the Mole, would have been able
to get back on to the ship. Having given these orders, I returned to the
sea wall, slid down a hook rope, and crossed over to No 3 shed on the
far side of the Mole. My impression is that the sea wall abreast of the
ship was not under rifle or MG fire at this time, but that the defenders
were shelling the Mole and their shells were striking the sea wall and the
sheds. Only the funnels and foretop of *Vindictive* were visible over the
sea wall. The pom-pom in the foretop was firing over our heads, and this
gave great encouragement. It was later found that Lieutenant Rigby
and the whole guns' crew had been killed with the exception of Sergeant
Finch, and he, although badly wounded, was firing the gun. For this
action, he was subsequently voted by the Battalion to receive a representa-
tive Victoria Cross.

A number of men collected by No 3 shed. Some units passed round
the inshore end of the shed to attack craft lying alongside the Mole.
Other units started preparing the sheds for demolition, but it was soon

realised that the defenders were doing more damage with their own shell-fire than we were likely to be able to do. I met Captain Bamford, B Company Commander, whose totally unperturbed manner had the most reassuring effect on all who came in contact with him that night. Together we discussed the situation. Our battalion plan had been based on the assumption that *Vindictive* would be put alongside some four hundred yards from the end of the Mole. All those men who belonged to units which were to have attacked the fortified zone, therefore, now found themselves at No 3 shed. No attack on the fortified zone had yet been made. As this was our principal objective, we decided to organize an attack on the fortified zone along the Mole. This entailed attacking a prepared position across some two hundred yards of flat pavement devoid of any form of cover. Led by Captain Bamford, the units started to move forward. They were well out in the open, when the ship's siren was heard making what was taken to be the emergency recall signal. Captain Bamford, therefore, gave the order to withdraw.

The signal arranged for the emergency recall was the sounding of the morse letter 'K' on the ship's siren. Although the siren was blowing, it was not making this signal. We had expected to be ashore for one and a quarter hours, but we had been ashore only forty-five minutes. As I was not convinced that the recall was intended, I returned to the ship and went to the conning tower, where I found Captain Carpenter, and asked him if we were to withdraw. Having been told that the recall was ordered, I returned to the sea wall and passed the order to all those whom I could reach by voice or signal. Units returned steadily to the ship, bringing wounded men with them. Several men who passed me thought I was wounded and wanted to carry me on board. The enemy were still shelling the sea wall, and those who had to cross the Mole and climb the ladders had the most hazardous time. Fortunately, some of the ladders remained intact until the end. When I could see no more men approaching, I returned on board and reported to that effect. A few moments later the ship left the Mole.

As the ship withdrew, we expected to be heavily shelled. Clouds of smoke were released aft, which, although almost asphyxiating to those of us who were on deck, hid us from the enemy, and to our surprise we were not hit.

As the danger from the enemy diminished I began to realise that my right knee was very painful. What had hit it I never knew, but it probably happened when the CO and Second in Command were killed.

Captain Arthur Chater was awarded the DSO and was specially promoted. His citation read: 'Was of the greatest assistance in keeping up communications between the various units of the battalion and carried out his duties in a calm manner which greatly contributed to the success of the operations. Gave great assistance in the preparation of the plan for the assault.

Captain Edward Bamford received the VC (see page 206).

Sergeant-Major Charles Thatcher received the DSC. He was mainly instrumental in conveying the heavy scaling ladders from the ship to the Mole, and throughout the operation displayed great coolness and devotion to duty.

*

From N. Wheeler: the Zeebrugge spirit

I am writing on behalf of my husband. He was one of the Royal Marines who took part on St George's Day Raid at Zeebrugge 22nd/23rd April and was wounded in that raid. He still belongs to the Zeebrugge Association (1918). I am sorry to say he has had to have both of his legs amputated 3 years ago and he is also 80 years old. Why I am writing to you is because he had a slight stroke and is unable to write.

*

From P. S. Beer: a record of long and varied service

I was at Deal in 1918 aged 18 years as a private in the RMSG when the Royal Marines were training for a secret mission which was well kept. It was only when the marines returned that we learned they had been on the Zeebrugge raid on 23rd April 1918. I have a photograph 11in. x 8in. of my M14 squad RMSG and all 39 men are named, they were short service men (duration of war). Five of these men volunteered for the secret mission; they all returned and one died of wounds at Deal.

I remember seeing the *Vindictive* in Dover harbour after the raid.

I was demobbed from the RMSG after the war and rejoined the Army for four years, half of which I spent in Ireland. When the 1939 war started I was on the reserve of the RASC, I went to France with 2nd Division, B.E., returning home via Dunkirk. In 1942 I went to India and Burma with 2nd Division.

*

From F. F. Jenks: a marine in HMS Centaur

I was serving on HMS *Concord* based at Harwich belonging to the 5th Light Cruiser Squadron and our Admiral was Sir Reginald York

Tyrwhitt whose flagship was HMS *Centaur*. I was in the Royal Marines and we manned the after 6 inch guns on the centre line. I myself was sight setter on our gun. The firing was controlled by the Warrant Officer and was called Directed firing. We were more or less covering the blockships which were to be sunk inside Zeebrugge to stop the U-boats from coming out in the Channel and the raiding parties of marines had to do as much damage as they could before being called back to their ships or any ships they could get back on board. Apart from the casualties there were either 11 or 12 marines and a marine officer was captured; one of them was my shipmate, Tommy Middleton, whose home was at Okehampton in Devon and when the war was ended and he was sent home he reported to the Marine Barracks; being a time serving marine he was sent back to the *Concord*. When the raid was over we were nearing Harwich when the flagship *Centaur* struck a mine but good fortune favoured her and she did not sink. The 5th Light Cruiser Squadron did quite a lot of sea time in those days.

I am 79 now and I had a lot of happy days in the North Sea and also attached to the Dover Patrol.

I left the *Concord* when we arrived at Constantinople after serving in the Black Sea; that was in 1919. I do hope you get a lot more information than I have given you but every little helps.

*

From J. M. Kirk: The Leicester RM Association

The Leicester Branch of the Royal Marines Association used to meet, and annually hold a dinner at the Fosse Hotel, Fosse Road, Leicester, to commemorate the Zeebrugge raid. The mainstay of the association was an old lady; I believe the name was Elliot (I have trouble remembering names) but her husband a Royal Marine Colonel led the raid and was killed, as I believe it was a suicide mission. At that time I think she lived on West Walk in Leicester, and her flat was a veritable museum of the Marine Corps. They had no children so I would not know what happened to all of the material, etc., that she possessed but I'm sure it would be important. Perhaps she left it to the Marine Association or Imperial War Museum.*

I wish you luck with your book; I am a patriot. Perhaps if more people read of the sacrifices that were made we would have a more peaceful world today.

*

* See also page 97.

From J. D. Davidson: Chatham Marine

As I was only twenty-three years old at the time of the Raid I was younger than most men who took part. I was a Royal Marine and the ship I was on was the *Iris*. The main ships involved were the *Vindictive Iris* and *Daffodil* at the Mole, itself, and the blocking ships who went inside the harbour to block the entrance to the Brugge canal U-boat base.

I was 81 last August the first and I believe there are only three of us of Chatham Division left alive, who took part in the Raid.

There were only 75 of us who came back to Chatham Barracks out of 1,000. Many were either killed or wounded.

One of the three of us is now at Victoria, B.C. Canada. He was in Commando, like me. I was in liaison with the Belgium Resistance before the raid as a courier and received the Honourable Order of the Knights of Brugge. Must dry up now as I am getting cramp in my fingers.

*

From H. J. Camfield and account by ex Colour Sergeant H. H. R. Camfield. Note that Colour Sergeant Camfield carried on with the raid with part of his jaw missing and a shoulder wound but was on parade the next day (before 15 months in hospital).

My father, ex Colour Sergeant H. H. R. Camfield Royal Marines, M.S.M. Croix de Guerre, now aged 90 years, took part in this raid on Zeebrugge on 23.4.18.

He was in company with Sergeant Finch VC in the fore-top and took part in the ballot for the VC, which was eventually awarded to Sergeant Finch.

Having celebrated his 90th birthday on 1st March 1977, he is still in full command of his faculties. He still digs and plants in his allotment and goes dancing every week with his wife at his club.

I am sure he will not only assist you, but would be delighted to do so.

Incidentally I served 18 years in the Royal Marines, concluding my service as a Bandmaster.

Account by H. H. R. Camfield

Regarding myself I think I'd better commence with the formation of the Battalion. One company from each RM Division plus one from the RMA at Eastney and the volunteers from the Fleet, converged at Deal, Kent. Naturally, all was work and lectures, till the time came when we were embarked in steamers bound for Clacton-on-Sea where we were transferred to the battleship HMS *Hindustan*. We were then introduced to an exact model of the Mole, which of course, prior to Clacton, we knew nothing about, but after seeing the model, all the training at Deal fell into place. We were there for 3 days, and very busy ones they were too, but it was not all work. We enjoyed games and fun plus a concert. On 22nd April after sundown we embarked in *Vindictive, Iris* and *Daffodil* and made our way out to sea, accompanied by submarines and various motor craft.

As we drew near Zeebrugge we saw star shells, searchlights, bursting shells, etc., and knew the RAF had been doing their softening up. Soon the 'pipe' called us into action stations. My position was starboard side of the funnel casing, amidships. As we went alongside the Mole a shell exploded on the bridge, killing our OC Lieutenant-Colonel Elliot and the second in command. Our two flame throwers were wrecked, a shell hit the after funnel and ricocheted down to where my section were waiting. I was hit in the jaw, taking my lower teeth and jaw bone with it and tearing my chin down, and then wounded my right shoulder. It also took Nos 1 and 2 Lewis guns' head right off. Then the order came for action. My platoon, under the command of Lieutenant Cooke, with Sergeant Burt* in my place, rushed down the gangway (there were only a few as the others were shot away). Before the action I asked my section to bring Lieutenant Cooke aboard dead or alive. He was badly wounded in the head and was brought on board by his batman, who was subsequently awarded the CGM. Lieutenant Cooke was promoted to Battalion Major, as soon as the 'Retire' was sounded. Two seamen planted the Union Jack on the end of the Mole.

There was also difficulty in releasing the wire from the bollard on shore, and a RM was detailed to chop the wire off, which he did. We then went astern to clear from the Mole. Tables and stools were lowered down to the stokehold to burn and increase steam in order to get away quickly. As we were leaving we received a hail of shells, which did a lot of harm to *Iris* and *Daffodil*.

During the action, Sergeant (later Lieutenant) Finch kept up his firing on to the Mole, although his crew were either wounded or killed. He was awarded the VC; Captain Bamford, OC No 1 Company also received the VC.

We reached Dover the next morning, and after being tied up, the 'pipe' went 'all walking wounded fall in on the jetty'. Admiral Sir Roger Keyes was on the jetty and shook hands with all of us before entraining for Gillingham Hospital at which place I was interned for 15 months

* He received the DSM.

then transferred to Haslar Hospital at Gosport, and after a sojourn there, was sent to duty. Naturally I could not carry out my duties as a Gunnery Instructor, as shouting was just not what I could do. I returned to pensions in 1926 after serving over 21 years. Well, God is good, as I am now in my 91st year, still working my allotment and go dancing every Saturday evening with my wife.

I do hope the foregoing will be of some assistance to you, and I wish you every success in your labours.

*

From R. Minnis: the death of a private soldier

My uncle (my mother's brother), CH21203 Private Roy Manfred Adams RMLI, was killed in the raid. His body was brought back to Dover on HMS *Vindictive* and then taken to his parents' house at Lydd, Kent. He had a military funeral and is buried in the local cemetery.

I am in possession of a brass collar badge and identity tag which were removed from his body; his two war medals and a large brass medallion, the like of which, I understand, was presented to the relatives of all who died in the war.

My mother, who is 75 years old, has only a vague recollection of what happened, so I cannot give you any further details. In any case, the death of a private soldier in the Royal Marines Light Infantry is unlikely to be of much interest in the account you are writing, but if you think I can be of any further assistance, please feel free to contact me.

*

Account by Marine A. R. Gordon: recommended for VC

Alexander Robert Gordon:

Enlisted in the Royal Marines Light Infantry 3rd April 1916 aged 19. Discharged 3rd May 1919 aged 22. Headquarters Deal; training there and at Chatham. First ship HMS *Inflexible*. Duties Convoys in North Sea and base at Scapa Flow. Rumours went around the ship that volunteers were required for a special engagement, and I was one of them. With others I took part in special training at Chatham Barracks.

When told of the mission, the storming of the Mole at Zeebrugge and blocking the harbour, we all shouted and were delighted to start this wonderful exploit as we had been on edge for weeks and waiting so long.

As you may know from Admiral Keyes the first attempt on 11th April would have been doomed to failure owing to change of wind and the smoke screen would have been useless; also, the second attempt two days later. The Admiralty decided to cancel the operation, but Vice-Admiral Keyes 'with the words of Haig's Order of the Day ringing in his ears, had set his heart on fighting on to the end'. However, the order to cancel was rescinded and at 5 p.m. on 22nd April 1918 the Armada of 140 ships sailed.

Earlier in the afternoon walking down to the harbour with her husband to see him off, Eva Keyes, outwardly unperturbed, had reminded him that the next morning would be St George's Day and begged him to use 'St George for England' as his Battle Cry. 'It is sure to be the best day for our enterprise,' she said, 'St George can be trusted to bring good fortune to England'. Remembering these words, Keyes made his famous signal, by semaphore, as soon as the Armada had started on its way.

The centre column of the attack led by *Vindictive* had *Iris* in tow. This was my vessel. Of the three vessels *Vindictive*, *Daffodil* and *Iris*, *Iris* alone throughout the operation had met with nothing but misfortune. After more than forty minutes vain endeavour to secure his ship to the wall, Commander Gibbs had decided to drop back alongside *Vindictive* to enable his landing parties to get ashore across the latter's deck. On arrival alongside, however, he found that the blockships had already entered the harbour and that the main object of the Mole diversion had consequently come to an end. *Vindictive*'s landing parties had been ordered to re-embark immediately, and *Iris*'s contingent would not be required to land. *Iris* instead was ordered to return to the rendezvous, where *Vindictive* and *Daffodil* would join her as soon as all her men had been withdrawn.

Iris was obliged to change her position and fall in astern of *Vindictive* and suffered very heavily from fire. A single big shell plunged through the upper deck and burst below at a point where 56 marines were waiting the order to go up the gangway. 49 were killed and the remaining seven were wounded. I was among the seven wounded.

On my Service Certificate: *London Gazette* 23rd July 1918. Participation in ballot for the award of the Victoria Cross for operation against Zeebrugge and Ostend 22nd/23rd April 1918. I was unlucky in the draw.

Wounds: amputation of left leg below the knee. Right ankle shattered, but, after many operations the surgeon succeeded in saving leg.

Sir Roger Keyes (afterwards Lord Keyes) kept in touch with me and I have many letters from him. Through Sir Roger's personal efforts a job was found for me at the Howard Pneumatic Engineering Co. Ltd.,

Fort Road, Eastbourne, where I worked for 22 years. My son is named Roger after the famous Admiral.

The bow of the *Vindictive* is preserved as a memorial at Ostend.

As the attack progressed the thunder of the German guns was terrific and their star shells lit up the amazing scene.

*

From S. A. Bamford: One of the first marines to land. He is now 84. Both his brothers were killed in the Somme battles. The letter included details of the annual re-unions.

I was one of the first to land off the HMS *Vindictive*. I was a member of the 4th Royal Marines Battalion.

*

From E. Head: a bomb thrower on the Vindictive

My husband Private Ernest J. Head RMLI was at that battle, and took part in the storming of the Mole. Sorry to say he died two years ago and being a very peace loving man said little about his war experiences, but I do know he was a bomb thrower. They evidently went in pairs and his companion got killed; he, luckily, came out without a scratch. He was on the *Vindictive* which I think got badly damaged. I have a silver top cane which he won as a first prize for bomb throwing so I think he must have been very good. I hope this little information might be of some help but I'm afraid it's very little.

*

From E. F. Tracey in Canada: ex-Colour Sergeant

How I came to be there! Towards the end of 1917, we of No 89 Squad had finished our Headquarters training in Naval Gunnery and Field Service and were ready for draft. My pal 'Timber' Woods of Newcastle and myself decided to celebrate, and out we went in Chatham to the Long Bar in the High Street.

Beer was at its very best in those days at 2d a glass, 4d a pint. We had 3 glasses I think, and felt like jumping over the moon. At that time casualties in France were very high and reinforcements were going over every few days for the 1st and 2nd Royal Marine battalions in France. 'Timber' Woods and myself decided to volunteer, and asked the barmaid for two pieces of paper, and wrote out our request to volunteer for service in France, went back to barracks and put our requests on the Company File.

Eventually we were put into a unit which was later to become part of the 4th Battalion Royal Marines with a Company (about 200) each from Chatham, Portsmouth and Plymouth Headquarters, and some of the Royal Marine Artillery from Eastney, plus Naval Medical units.

These formations were drafted to the Royal Marine Depot at Deal, to become the 4th Battalion for Special Service.

We engaged in strenuous training of a close combat nature, particularly at night, to attack various targets marked out in canvas, this was an aid towards seeing and knowing a target when we got there.

We were mustered one day in the Globe Theatre and our battalion commander, Lieutenant-Colonel Elliot, gave us the story that the objective was somewhere around Calais (this was a blind!) where at that time the German offensive was forcing the Allied troops back towards the coast.

The Colonel had a family history in the Corps and pledged himself towards the battalion and stuck to his words. At times, he and some of the officers would come to the canteen and join in with a toast to the 4th Battalion, etc.

Right now, in front of me I have a photograph of No 1 Platoon (A Company Chatham) and in the front centre is Major Eagles, Company Commander, and flanked by Captain Del Strother second in command, and our Platoon Commander Lieutenant Inskip.

They were of the very best, and word soon got around that other units were similar, as though the officers had been picked for a team job. They bought mouth organs for use on the march, and they made themselves interested in a man with his affairs at home, etc. On parade, it was On Parade, but even so at times when on the march the officers would move along the unit and come out with a cheery 'Everybody happy' or something like it.

Off parade, it was Off Parade; Lieutenant Inskip would often come out with something like : 'How are you today, are you short in any way, can I help you at all?'

I would say every man was 100% content within his unit, and would not want to leave that high degree of contentment.

Up at the top of the photograph with his forage cap tilted over to the left is 'Peter Jackson', and seated on the ground in front is his witty pal 'Jenny Wren'. What a couple they were! Never knew what they'd come out with on the march or in the canteen, but it would certainly create laughter and maybe a cheer. In the canteen, one of them, or both, would stand on the table, glass in hand, and call out : 'To the 4th, to Lieutenant Inskip, to Major Eagles', or somebody else from another unit, and – 'To your feet and up glasses!'

Over to the right in the front rank is 'Barge' Hefferman, Lance Corporal Bugler, and possibly the senior bugler in the Corps at that time. He handled the bugle as clear as a nightingale in the woods. If the call was, 'We've finished for the day' and a wind blowing, he'd sound the bugle at other locations so that nobody missed it.

Early in the month of March, Mr Churchill who at the time was First Lord of the Admiralty, came down to Deal to review the 4th Battalion. He did not rush, and spoke to as many as possible, sometimes two, three or four at a time. He wanted to get his message across and he did.

I was in No 1 Platoon and an early customer. He stood in front of me and put questions : 'What is your age, my lad ?'

I replied 18 years and 3 months (actually I was 12 months younger).

'You sure ?'

'Yes, Sir.'

'You don't look it.'

'But I am, Sir.'

'Do you want to go ?'

'Yes, Sir.'

'Good luck to you, and good luck to you and you.'

That's how he went around the Battalion, taking 1½ hours or more, and I think it fair to say that on getting back to the Admiralty he may have reported to Vice-Admiral Roger Keyes (who, unknown to us, was to be our leader), the morale of the 4th Battalion is at a very high pitch, and they're ready to go.

After the inspection we were 'closed in', in tight square formation towards the centre of the parade, with Mr Churchill standing on top of gymnasium horse boxes as he addressed us, and these are more or less his words : 'You are going on a daring and arduous stunt from which none of you may return, but every endeavour will be made to get as many as possible back; if any of you for any reason at all, mothers, wives or anything else, do not want to go, on dismissal of this parade, you may go to your Company Office and say so, and not a word will be said against you.'

After that, the toasts in the canteen were more frequent with Major Eagles saying, 'I'm proud to lead you, etc., etc.' and the same with Lieutenant Inskip and other officers. It was the spirit of – let's get in and do the job.

A few days later HM King George V visited the RM depot at Deal and while there he took the salute of the 4th Battalion. In appreciation the King directed that the best all round recruit should in future wear the

Royal Cypher as 'King's Badgeman' (and he still does) and that no future unit would bear the title 4th Battalion.

On 6th April the 4th Battalion marched out of the RM Depot for the Railway Station to the tune of : 'Just break the news to Mother, and tell her how I love her, just kiss her dear sweet lips for me, for I'm not coming home, etc., etc.' A roar went up and the band switched to another tune !

Arriving Dover we went aboard the Cross Channel trooper and with all onboard the skipper shouted (what he'd been doing many times), 'Let go the lines for France' and there was a great cheer, followed by the order, 'Everybody below deck.'

On clearing Dover, the skipper opened his sealed orders and found he had to alter course to the left, away from France. (We were wondering.) After a couple of hours or so we arrived off the Thames estuary with no land in sight and to remain in secrecy until after the job was done, and came to a stop alongside the battleship HMS *Hindustan*, and while going aboard we spotted other ships in the vicinity which later we heard were the *Vindictive, Iris, Daffodil* and five cruisers, and like them we were to remain in secrecy.

Shortly after getting aboard *Hindustan* we were assembled on the quarter-deck, and Lieutenant-Colonel Elliot with a smile gave us the 'change in plan'.

Zeebrugge was to be our objective, we were to land on the Mole to give the impression a general landing was being made and to draw the fire of the shore batteries to allow three blockships to go unhindered as much as possible to the canal entrance. Motor launches and coastal motor boats would put up a smoke screen and do rescue work, and a submarine filled with explosive would blow up the viaduct to prevent reinforcements coming on to the Mole. The Colonel finished as usual, 'I'm proud to lead you, etc.' and was roundly cheered which broadened the smile on his face. And standing not far away was the inventor of the smoke screen (which was to save lives) Wing Commander Brock RNAS of Brock's Fireworks. Afterwards we were given stations to go to by platoons (about 40 men) and at each place there was a clay model about 3 feet by 3 feet of the Mole and harbour entrance. The narrator gave detailed news of the latest intelligence reports of a few hours earlier with regard to movements of ships, etc., alongside the Mole, etc.

Then the hottest news of all : the defences comprised one thousand troops on the Mole, and in armament sixty-two guns of 4 inch to 11 inch (including 7 on the Mole) spread six miles each side of Zeebrugge.

So, where our early training was presumably as a single unit against a target in France, we are now *'part of a force'* where each part will have something to do to ensure the blockships are able to reach the canal entrance.

Vice-Admiral Keyes came aboard the next day and confirmed what we had been told, gave us the dates, and wished everybody the very best. He was given a prolonged cheer and without a doubt he was very happy.

Our first attempt was on 11th April and in the evening we embarked on *Iris* and made the rendezvous with the whole force; what a thrilling sight it was, nearly 150 craft. The motor launches and coastal motor boats, about one hundred, were manoeuvring about like ants to get into their position and believe me it gave one an intense lift up with the feeling that everything possible was being done to ensure success from every angle. And over on the right side of the force, in the lead was Vice-Admiral Keyes on HMS *Warwick* and atop the small mast of the destroyer was the Admiral's flag which looked the size of a blanket! It was of battleship size and being on the tiny mast of a destroyer looked out of proportion, but again this item gave one a feeling of pride.

We nearly made the target on the 11th; with only one hour to go we had to turn back, and everybody felt very disappointed, but our disappointment was brushed aside with the Admiral telling everybody he could have let the force go ahead into possible disaster and nothing achieved, and far better to wait to achieve success. The Admiral was roundly cheered on the *Hindustan*, and we could hear the cheers he got on the blockships.

On the 13th, a very short trip, and with this cancellation it meant being caged up on the *Hindustan* for nearly two weeks which seems a long time when a force is primed to go. However certain things were organised and some things were relaxed to keep men's minds active and to prevent monotony. Gambling is a very serious offence in the Royal Navy, but here the brakes were taken off, and after all, nobody had much money and we may not be around much longer to enjoy it!

The game Crown and Anchor (Robbery if you like!) was run by 'Snowy' Wadd (very fair hair) of Leicester, and a partner. They both had body belts well loaded with their takings. One day an officer rolled up his shirt and put it on the board, 'You've busted me,' he said. Snowy put a value on it of 3d or a tanner, and the investor lost, only to have someone whose luck was in (temporarily!) buy it back for him. At the end of the day the Crown and Anchor kings gave back many small things to the loser, and maybe back again next day. Snowy and his partner vowed that on stepping on the Mole they'd put down the canvas Crown and Anchor board and shout, 'Come on, you lucky fellows!' They did it, and maybe had that board been autographed and around today it could be worth a bit at Christie's!

Time passed away smoothly during that period and we were thrilled when we had the standby in the forenoon of the 22nd. A final muster at stations for the clay models, and with the latest intelligence reports of only three or four hours earlier, we all knew the Mole as though we'd lived there. The period of delay certainly brought out that good point.

And away we went in *Iris* in the evening of 22nd April with everybody chatting to each other, getting the job done with willingness and determination. And Major Eagles and his officers moved around here and there for a cheery talk to all.

Everything was going according to plan, and about 11 p.m. we had a tot of rum which had to be drunk in the presence of the Platoon Commander, and during the coughing and swallowing of the tot our Lieutenant Inskip gave as he'd always done his very best wishes to be followed by the Platoon Sergeant 'Cock' Philips (a cockney) giving good luck and handshake.

The tot of rum had just about settled down, when shortly before midnight (zero time), dark and raining, the MLs alerted the guards on the Mole and, it's hardly believable, but, in a flash, the darkness of the night was converted into day by scores and scores of the brightest star shells. Thanks to Wing Commander Brock, we were safe and it was good to see the smoke screen drifting towards the Mole and further in like a sea fog. High explosive shells began to fall, and just over to the right of us no more than 100-200 feet away a whopper dropped into the water; the water spout looked to be something like 12 feet across and probably 20-40 feet high. Sergeant Philips shouted, 'Check lifeboats'. Had it been a bit closer it could have been liferafts or gone forever.

Again, everybody is in tip-top form knowing we are being on target, and with the words from Lieutenant Inskip minute by minute – nearly there, just about the length of two football pitches to go, 4 minutes to go – and then, would you believe it, everything gone so well and very nearly there, and fate steps in with the wind turning completely around (now from shore) and blowing the smoke to behind us and there we are, *Vindictive*, *Iris* and *Daffodil*, only 300 yards from the Mole and in broad daylight so to say (from star shells and searchlights) and we were fully exposed for a minute before the guns at the end of the Mole opened fire while the ships had boosted speed to the shelter of the Mole.

There were casualties but, this is the point to be stressed, had those gunners opened fire immediately it would have been disaster. What caused them to remain quiet for one minute is anyone's guess. Maybe seeing a ship the size of the *Vindictive* practically on top of them, staggered them, or maybe they had to switch from star shell to high explosive, or something else. Whatever it was, the ships were able to get alongside.

It had been urged on us to maintain silence as much as possible, but, when that submarine loaded with HE blew up and shattered the viaduct, there was one mighty cheer such as one hears at Wembley !

Time and events passed quickly, and it was surprising how quickly we received the word : the blockships have gone in. With that the main task was accomplished and the 'Go Home' signal was made.

Our troubles were not over by any means. Just after we pulled away from the *Vindictive* efforts were made to activate the smoke screen apparatus at the stern to conceal us; it wouldn't function, and very quickly we were spotted by the guns and, bang, bang, bang, we received hits and casualties, and would have undoubtedly been sunk but for the immediate action of an ML rushing in to shield us with smoke. Commander Gibbs RN on the bridge lost both of his legs, and while tourniquets were being applied he died, with devotion to duty on his lips with these words, 'Leave me alone, leave me alone, I want to get these men back.'

And here's another, on the deck below and on the port side was 'Chitty' (Pte) Chittenden (cockney) who had lost both legs and tourniquets applied, singing his old canteen song : 'I like pickled onions, I like piccalilli, pickled cabbage is all right with a bit of cold tripe on Sunday night, etc., etc.' and anybody who went to him, 'H'you going on Chitty,' got the reply : 'Don't worry about me, look after the others.' And undoubtedly there were many more cases like these on other ships of the force. Our Lieutenant Inskip went instantly, and Major Eagles; no chance for them to issue comforting and cheery words which was their daily way of life.

Everybody who was able, had tasks towards saving life, by the first aid training we had at Deal, or of providing fuel to feed the boilers.

The bridge of the *Iris* was in bad shape for navigating and the youngster who was now captain of the ship, a lieutenant, had little left by way of instruments. I think he was left with a hand compass. However around 3 a.m. a ML after a search carefully approached the *Iris* and shouted to us : 'Oi, you're in the middle of a bloody minefield, get out quick, the tide is running out, follow me.' (A welcome visitor !)

Not long after that another challenge 'What ship ?' by loudspeaker, and repeated, while the dark shadow was creeping towards us. It was thought to be German – and we had to throw everything weaponny overboard and make believe we were a hospital ship, with the challenger still creeping towards us; it came again 'What ship?', and the young lieutenant who'd tried to use a flashlight (torch) and his own voice called to us on the *Iris*: 'When I say three, everybody shout *Iris*.' That we did, and the challenger called out, 'This is the flagship, HMS *Warwick*.' Ugh, what a relief that was!

Shortly afterwards the voice of the Admiral asked how things were, and told us *Vindictive* and *Daffodil* were OK, and he would send us help. He was roundly cheered. About 4 a.m. HMS *Phoebe* (destroyer) came to us and secured lines to tow us back to Dover, but with something like a 6 foot to 8 foot swell the towline snapped and *Phoebe* tried twice more, and same thing. The motion of the sea was one thing to break a line, and one must also remember a destroyer does not carry very heavy lines.

So eventually *Iris* arrived at Dover a little before 3 p.m., and on the dockside an unexpected welcome from 'Sir' Roger Keyes. In his hand was a telegram and he shouted to us, 'This is the telegram I received from HM King George V giving me a knighthood. You all did the job and I will never forget you.' He never did.

Before leaving *Iris* we paid our last respects to those who'd gone, and left by train for RM Depot at Deal, to be checked in various ways. Arriving Deal, we had the grimmest of all parades, 'The Roll Call'. The order of the day was read to us by which HM the King had decreed there will never again be another 4th Battalion in the Corps.

On return to Chatham we were a depleted unit with something like 40% casualties, and the march down Military Road from the station was not all that cheerful with somebody now and then getting into the ranks seeking information, where is so and so? What happened to him? and so on. The 40% mentioned above must not confuse casualties of the whole operating force, which were less than 10%, extremely good when one looks back at the newspapers of the day with large type $\frac{1}{2}$ inch to 1 inch across the front page – 'Yesterday's casualties in France 20,000, 30,000, 40,000 and more.'

Earlier I mentioned the rendezvous off Dover with the MLs moving about like ants: unknown to me at the time, in one of those small boats was a native of this city, Victoria, British Columbia, Canada – a Lieutenant (then) Bourke who I met on coming here in 1948. Before joining the RN (with eyesight below normal!) he was just a fruit farmer and such a quiet and unassuming man that one would not have thought he could electrify himself to the absolute limit which gained him the Victoria Cross at Ostend. Well, there is an example of the team spirit which existed in the whole force. And he, like many more, has passed on, and those of us still around stick together with the team spirit and constantly keep in mind 'The Tribute' with the last line 'We will remember them.'

Lieutenant Inskip was killed and *Captain del Strother* dangerously wounded. *Private Wadd* was wounded, and *Bugler Hefferman* was killed: he was mentioned in despatches.

Lieutenant Bourke was awarded the DSO and specially promoted for 23rd April, for showing the greatest coolness and skill in handling his motor launch. He repeatedly went alongside *Brilliant* under very heavy fire and took off 38 officers and men. He took in tow and brought back to harbour another motor launch which was damaged. At the Ostend operation of 9th/10th May he was awarded the VC (see page 210).

4

Submarine C3

The aim of the two submarines, was to prevent German reinforcements passing on to the Mole across the viaduct during the action. The submarines employed were old C Class, $C1$ and $C3$, built in 1906 and 1907, and displacing 316 tons. It was calculated that the boats driven at a speed of 6 knots against the viaduct would penetrate the light bracing of the piers up to their conning towers. Each submarine carried two motor skiffs and a light scaling ladder. A picket boat commanded by Lieutenant Commander Francis H. Sandford was in attendance to rescue the crews. $C1$ did not arrive as its tow-line parted. $C3$ under Lieutenant Richard Sandford rammed the viaduct, and exploded its charges, destroying a considerable section. Sandford was awarded the VC; he was rescued by his brother in the picket boat.

*

From O. McNab: J. Howell-Price

My father, Lieutenant John Howell-Price, RNR, (who died in 1937) was of the crew of six in submarine $C3$ which breached the Mole at Zeebrugge at the beginning of the attack.

Lieutenant John Howell Price DSC, was awarded the DSO at Zeebrugge for his invaluable assistance in placing C3 between the piles of the viaduct before the fuse was lighted and she was abandoned. 'His behaviour in a position of extreme danger was exemplary.'

*

From K. Taylor: In the engine room

My brother-in-law, Allan George Roxburgh, was in the engine room of the submarine $C3$ that rammed the Mole at Zeebrugge. They were all volunteers; they knew it was a dangerous job in which they might lose their lives but they were not told what it was. They practised for the job, and made trial raids until the final day.

Their means of escape from the submarine after ramming the Mole

145

was to run along the Mole (which would mean capture) or by motor boat. The propeller of the boat was damaged in being lowered into the water and they had to row. They were being shot at all the time and Allan Roxburgh and one other were the only two not wounded. He was awarded the CGM and Croix de Guerre with palms. He died December 1960.

The citations for *ERA Roxburgh, Stoker Bindall, PO Harmer,* and *Leading Seaman Cleaver* read: 'The ratings above mentioned were members of the crew of Submarine *C3*, which was skilfully placed between the piles of the Zeebrugge mole viaduct and there blown up, the fuse being lighted before the submarine was abandoned. They volunteered for and under the command of an officer eagerly undertook this hazardous enterprise, although they were well aware that if the means of rescue failed and that if any of them were in the water at the time of the explosion they would be killed outright.'

*

From J. R. Pitt:

Captain Francis Sandford DSO, RN, a torpedo and explosives specialist, was prominent in staff work in preparation of the demolition arrangements for Zeebrugge and for fitting out submarines in general. He carried out the rescue of his own brother and the crew of submarine *C3* of which his brother was in command and who was subsequently awarded the VC. Both of course were taking part in the raid on Zeebrugge on St George's Day 1918.

The two brothers were members of a very remarkable family of 5 sons of a notable 19th century 'worthy' of Devon, the Venerable Archdeacon E. G. Sandford of Exeter. Another brother was an England Rugby International in 1906, and all five excelled in their chosen careers.

Captain Sandford was specially promoted for Zeebrugge for his preparation of the demolition arrangements and the fitting out of the submarines. He carried out the rescue of *C3*'s crew by means of a service picket boat, in which he covered 170 miles during the voyage to and from the Belgian coast.

*

5

The Blockships

The difficulties of the blockships, *Thetis*, *Iphigenia* and *Intrepid*, were not restricted to entering the canal – although that problem would seem enough. In addition they had to sink themselves in a manner which would ensure (a) they could not easily be moved, (b) they would prevent the passage of enemy craft, and (c) their presence would cause the channel to silt up. The tide at Zeebrugge rises 15 feet; the blockships therefore needed to be where the upper structures would be within 6 feet of high tide level, to obstruct the path of shipping effectively. For the maximum value to be obtained from the silting up process the blockships needed to be as squarely across the channel as their length permitted and then the bottoms could be blown out, releasing tons of cement which would rapidly be covered with silt and take months, if not years, to move.

*

From G. Cory-Wright: a hot seat

My late father was in command of the blockship *Intrepid* at Zeebrugge.

He got onto a Carley float after the *Intrepid* was scuttled. Unfortunately the flares had not been removed and ignited on contact with the water. He spent a very unpleasant half hour floating in the harbour making a perfect illuminated target for the Germans. He was awarded the DSC.

Lieutenant Alan Cory-Wright's citation read : 'Showed great coolness during the action, and by his bravery and cheerfulness throughout set a fine example to his men.'

*

From R. H. Thorp: Percy Dean commanded 'ML 282' and showed outstanding courage in rescuing men from the blockships. The reference to 'Iris' and 'Daffodil' is mistaken.

Perhaps the following information might prove of interest to you.

I refer, in particular, to the exploits of Percy Dean who commanded, either the *Daffodil* or the *Iris*, (two ferry boats formerly employed in the Liverpool service between the port and nearby suburbs). These two boats were commissioned by the Admiralty to block the harbour at Zeebrugge in order to restrict the activities of the German submarines (then known as U-boats) which were then taking an immense toll on our shipping facilities. The exploit proved to be an outstanding success and for his courage and gallantry Commander Percy Dean was awarded the Victoria Cross.

Fortunately, he survived the affair, and after the War he returned to continue his business as a State Merchant. His business was conducted from Canal House, Eanam Wharf, Blackburn, Lancs. The business ceased to function about 1950. He died comparatively young, but I believe he left a son of whom I have no further knowledge. Beyond his activities in the War he took little or no interest in public affairs. So far as I remember he was a very modest man and little was known of him beyond his own domestic circle. He was a member of the Royal Volunteer Naval Reserve and it was in that capacity he was chosen to lead the Zeebrugge Raid.

May I say, in passing, that an oil painting of Percy Dean VC, hung on the staircase to the local Museum and Library in Library Street, Blackburn.

I hope this letter, although lacking the detailed information you may require, might lead you into other channels which will prove more fruitful. My sole object in writing you is to ensure that the name and exploits of Percy Dean receives a prominent place in the proposed publication. He was a man of outstanding courage and, in my generation, a local idol.

From T. Harrild: the blockships at Ostend

My daughter living in Woking brought me a cutting from a newspaper re : Zeebrugge. Well I was not in that part of the raid, but I was in HMS *Brilliant* with the *Sirius* on the raid to get between the piers at Ostend, but owing to the shifting of the Stroom Bank buoy we ran aground, and being stuck there was very unhealthy with the searchlights and shore batteries firing at a sitting target just off shore.

After the war I was in *P21* and we used to take the 'King's Messenger' to Ostend and on one occasion I went ashore and looking in a shop window I saw two postcard photos of the *Brilliant* and *Sirius*, which must have been taken the next morning with the *Brilliant* on fire. Well I have these photos and also the Matrix of the Raid printed by *Daily Mail*, the first to let the public know of the event.

At the time I was an Ordinary Signaller aged 18. If I remember rightly our COs were Commander Godsal and Lieutenant Crutchley, whom I think took the *Vindictive* to Ostend and were killed.

One thing I'm rather annoyed about is that there is no mention on my Naval history sheet of the *Brilliant* or the Raid.

Lieutenant Victor Crutchley was awarded the DSC for 23rd April for showing great coolness under heavy fire, and setting a fine example to his men. He immediately volunteered for the second operation, where he was awarded the VC (see page 209).

*

From E. Vaux: account by Lieutenant Vaux
HMS *Iphigenia*, c/o GPO 8th April

I am shortly off in this good ship on rather an interesting job – in fact, this is the ship and the job that I have been employed in preparing since 6th February (the day I paid off the *Marvel*). Of course it is most frightfully secret, hence my camouflage to you in saying that I was going (a) to recommission the *Marvel*, (b) on experimental work, (c) going to *Dwarf* as first lieutenant, etc., etc., sorry, but it was absolutely necessary. I was extraordinarily lucky in getting it, as it is a volunteer job and there are only a few officers in it. By the time you get this epistle it will be all over and I shall be either home or a prisoner of war or no longer, hence the letter explaining.

I am nominally navigator here, in addition there is the captain, the first lieutenant and engineer, all of which are first-rate fellows and we are a very cheery mess. We hope to be off tomorrow with any luck, but the weather may not be suitable, in which case, we shall have to wait a bit longer. By the way, when I went up to Liverpool the other day, I was sent up by Admiral Keyes to bring the *Iris* and *Daffodil* (the two that are going alongside the Mole at Zeebrugge) down. They were both Liverpool ferry steamers running from Woodside across, but unfortunately they weren't ready when the two pukka captains had turned up, so down I came to Chatham.

I was very lucky in being the second officer of the five blocking ships to arrive at Chatham (the rest didn't come till about a month later) as I was pretty busy helping to look after them, as they were in their initial stages then; also I took one or two trips down to the Admiral at Dover with despatches, etc. Just after I had joined this stunt about 8th February I went up to the Admiralty and saw a lot of Brass Hats. One of them took me into a room and asked me if I wanted to go, then if I was married and if I was engaged, etc., etc. It was most thrilling, quite a musical comedy sort of business; in fact, I used to sleep with my notes, etc., buttoned to my chest, so to speak! It was rather amusing at Chatham too. Lots of fellows used to ask me what I was doing, so I had to invent all sorts of stories to put them off the track.

I don't think it's much use my telling you exactly what we are going to do as(a) we've got to do it first (b) it will be out in the papers before you get this. Anyway the whole aim of the operation is for three ships of which this is one, to steam into Zeebrugge and sink, thereby blocking the entrance and exit of the port, which, if successfully done, will stop somewhere about 50 per cent. of the sinking of merchant vessels – also for two ships to do the same at Ostend. All the rest of the party in the operation are merely to help us to get in, though, of course, they have got just as tough a job if not tougher. If the Hun is not expecting us I think we ought to do it O.K., but if he is all ready it's going to be a pretty tough proposition, as we have to steam past their guns at practically point blank range. Getting away is also a bit of a problem. If the cutter is seaworthy, I pull away in her like blazes, after the ship is blown up and sunk, out to sea and hope to get picked up by a destroyer or something. If I can't manage that, I shall row to Holland – only 7 miles – walk ashore, demand 24 hours to repair my ship (this is quite O.K. as by international law, a warship may put into a neutral port for 24 hours to repair damages – my cutter will certainly be a man-of-war, as it will have pistols aboard! and probably a broken oar as damages!), then pay a visit to the British Attaché or what not and get him to cable for a destroyer or motor boat to take me back – voila, quite simple. Of course that is assuming we are lucky enough to get in and lucky enough to get out again.

By the way, we are lying in the Swin now, not far from Chatham. I got a whole lot of food from Fortnum.

Lieutenant Philip Vaux was awarded the DSC for valuable services as navigating officer of *Iphigenia* in a position of considerable danger at times under heavy fire.

*

From E. Elliot: the Cement

At the time of the Raid, my late husband was the Chief Engineer at the Earle's Cement Works at Ellesmere Port in Cheshire. I was not married to him there, but in later years he told me that at that time there was a rushed job at the Works. All hands were roped in to help load the obsolete battleships with cement before they were taken to be blockships to stop German submarines leaving and entering the Brugge Canal.

I have been extremely interested in both great wars, because of course they have taken place in my lifetime. Their venues and geographical situations have had a great influence during the last few years. I have travelled a great deal and whenever and wherever possible I have visited places concerned, not perhaps historical as yet, but which in time will become so.

I have seen the bridge on the river Kwai, Kranji (Singapore), the Burma railway, entered Changi Jail, been to Corregidor and recently spent some time visiting the British Cemetery at El Alamein.

To continue the first part of this letter (I know I have digressed). Two years ago I left Amsterdam by Dutch Cargo Ship for a voyage out East. The first morning, thinking to be at sea I was most surprised on looking out of my cabin window to find us passing close to a lighthouse at the end of a long mole or breakwater. I could hardly believe my eyes, for the passengers had not been told of this event. We had called at Zeebrugge to take on a quantity of dynamite – kept as a secret for some time. This was discharged later in the voyage at Carite – in Manila Bay; of course, knowing our ship to be at Zeebrugge for only a very short time, I climbed down the ladder and went ashore.

I took a very thoughtful walk along the Mole to the lighthouse. My thoughts turned back to over 50 years ago and the events of that brilliantly thought out piece of strategy and tactics. The bitter wind blew in from the North Sea (it was winter) but I will always remember having seen one more place where brave deeds had been performed during my lifetime.

*

Account sent in by Mrs O. Partridge – Kent newspaper account

The bottling up of Zeebrugge will always count one of the most glorious feats of a service which has built up a tradition of accomplishing the impossible and while it has been recorded in official documents, where it may serve to stir future generations of England's Jack Tars to emulation, it is good to have the story of it as it presented itself to the lower deck man who participated in that night's great doings. Such a narrative as we heard the other day from Leading Seaman Edwards, of Plumstead, in the Seamen's Hospital, Greenwich, where he lies making a good recovery from honourable wounds, stirs the blood and helps us to realise in some degree our debt to our gallant boys of the Senior Service.

Edwards, who has four shrapnel wounds in the right leg and two in the right arm, was helmsman of *Iphigenia*, one of the two crafts which made a magnificent end at the entrance to the harbour of Zeebrugge. 'I doubt,' (he said) 'whether you could have found anywhere a company more fitted to the enterprise than that which was chosen – and I am not saying so because I was one of them. We all knew exactly what we were to do, and if everybody save myself had been killed on my old craft I could have taken her to the appointed place, so thoroughly had we been instructed. Only one spirit prevailed – to get there and do the job successfully! At supper, at ten o'clock on that wonderful night there was a good deal of conversation, and while all realised the risk that we must run and few expected to come out alive, I heard only one opinion. "We don't mind the sacrifice so long as it's a success and helps things along!" It is one of the most marvellous things I have seen in eleven years of seafaring life that so many of us came out unhurt.

'As we went in *Vindictive* led, with *Iris* and *Daffodil*, then *Thetis*, *Intrepid* and *Iphigenia*. We got within about two miles of the Mole before the Germans commenced their barrage, and from what we had been told we knew that once we were inside we were comparatively safe. Under cover of bombs dropped by our airmen and of fire from our monitors we went through the barrage, and as we approached the Mole we came under the light of the star shells which the enemy sent up. Gun and pom-pom firing told us that the *Vindictive* had reached her objective, and in we went. Right, left, and ahead of us there were batteries, but everything went lovely; we got round the Mole, and were ordered to take stations. Just then we saw *Thetis* in difficulties, and we went astern and manoeuvred so as to get past her. As we went by *Thetis* a shell caught our foremost funnel and made a big gash. All that I heard from our commander, who was on the bridge, was a remark that our artificial fog apparatus was put out of action. We got the order to shift to the aft wheel; the next was "Hard a-port". Illuminated by the star shells and the searchlights, we could see the jetty, on which there were several machine-guns. But before we reached the point for which we were making we hit a barge, on which there were four machine-guns, clean amidships, and carried it from its moorings.

'A moment later we got jammed right across the entrance and received the order to abandon ship. My chum, whose duty it was, nipped down to the engine-room to connect up the mines and blow the bottom out of her. While this was being done *Intrepid* drew up alongside of us. My job was done, so I took up a rifle, pointed it at some figures which I took to be machine-gunners on the jetty, and I believe I managed to get two of them. Then we took to the boats, and it was not until just before she reached the water that it was found the cutter I was in was damaged. I tore off my coat, and with my sea-boots and a few odd things made a bundle with which I tried to bung up the hole, but it was no use. The tide was running, and when we came in the water that was being churned up by the screw of *Iphigenia* the cutter was sinking. With shrapnel flying overhead I swam to the other boat, and just as I reached it I felt something in the right arm. They pulled me aboard her, and I found the coxswain, wounded in both legs, at the tiller. There were several dead in the boat. I remember remarking, "They have caught me at last," and then moved my arm, relieved to find it was not broken. Before this I must have been hit in the leg, but I did not know it, and when a motor-launch came up I mustered sufficient strength to clamber aboard, although I had been within an ace of becoming unconscious. The next thing I remember is being hauled aboard *Warwick*, which carried me to Dover and from there I came on here.'

*

From E. Oldaker, niece of Captain S. G. West

Captain Sidney Greville West DSC, OBE, RN
The part he played in the attack on Zeebrugge on 23rd April 1918
for which he was awarded the Distinguished Service Cross

In 1918 he was sent from HMS *Benbow* as an Engineer Officer with the rank of sub-lieutenant, for the Zeebrugge raid. His assignment was to set the time bomb that blew up one of the blockships (the *Iphigenia*) and bottled up the U-boats in their headquarters behind the Mole or breakwater. Two other blockships were also sunk *Thetis* and *Intrepid*.

After the event all key people were interviewed by Admiral 'Evans of the Broke'. Captain West had formed a mental picture of the Admiral – an idealised compound of Nelson, Beatty and King George – but was dismayed at being ushered into the presence of a short, balding old gentleman with practically no chin. Within five minutes his hero worship was completely restored by the vigour directness and acumen of the Admiral whom Captain West later described as a 'Tiger in sheep's clothing'.

Captain West, together with all the key people, was invited to add a touch of paint to the famous oil painting of the Zeebrugge raid which now hangs in the Royal Exchange. Those who did so were later presented with a miniature print of the painting.

Mate Sidney Greville West's citation for the DSC read : 'Throughout the preparations and the operation this officer worked his department in an admirable manner. After the alarm bell for blowing the charges had been rung he returned to the engine room in order to start the engines ahead and did not finally leave until he received an order from the commanding officer to do so. He was thus of the greatest assistance in the accurate placing of the blockship.'

*

6

Destroyers and Monitors

Those who took part in the Zeebrugge operation in destroyers or monitors are liable to discount their value or the risks they took. However, as the *North Star* was sunk and *Warwick* nearly so, this undue modesty should be seen only in relation to the inner core of the conflict on the Mole and in the harbour. Life on the support boats was no bed of roses on 23rd April 1918.

*

From C. J. Winter – In the engine room

I took part in both the Zeebrugge and Ostend raids 1918, serving as a stoker in HMS *Warwick*, the flagship of Admiral Keyes on both occasions.

*

From H. G. Undey – HMS Phoebe

I was at Zeebrugge April 1918 and was on destroyer HMS *Phoebe*. The *Phoebe* and *North Star* went in to guard *Vindictive* against German destroyer attack. We got right inside the harbour making artificial fog, the wind was blowing on to the shore. Then all of a sudden it changed and blew out to sea and left us at point blank range of the German guns. It was like daylight with the German star shells lighting the place up. *North Star* got hit and was sinking; we went alongside, got a wire rope aboard but the wire rope snapped so we went alongside again. The Captain shouted to everyone to jump aboard that could, then we had to leave otherwise we would get it ourselves. The funnels were partly shot away and we lost two killed.

*

From H. G. Hawkes: HMS Mentor

My late father served in the Dover Patrol as a W/O in HMS *Mentor* and took part in the raid on Zeebrugge 1918.

*

From Commander H. Evans

I was a midshipman RNVR in the destroyer *Trident*. We towed submarine *C3* to Zeebrugge, and towed *Daffodil* home to Dover; during the action we patrolled off the end of the Mole to deal with any German TB's that might escape. I was in charge of the two guns and had a front view 'from the stalls'.

During the earlier action attempt when we all turned each off Zeebrugge someone turned the wrong way and we rammed the destroyer *Sceptre*, cut her bows open and exposed her mess deck lights. Luckily on the seaward side. A few feet the other way would have exposed our lights to the shore. We could not go astern with *C3* on a string behind us. A few minutes later we were nearly rammed by the blockships which luckily dodged ahead of us.

Trident was also in the Ostend party on 9th/10th May 1918. We found an abandoned ML in the fog and I was sent away in the whaler to board her, but she blew up when we were being lowered. We escorted *Warwick* and *Velox*, which were lashed together back to Dover.

As far as I know I am the only officer left from *Trident*, and I know of only one seaman. We used to have a Zeebrugge Officers Dinner, but gave up about ten years ago when Bishop Broadmore died and our members shrank to ten.

There will be a 'Vindictive Day' Service at Ostend on Sunday 15th May.

*

From P. Ellison: HMS Erebus

An uncle of my late husband, Vice-Admiral Charles Samuel Wills CMG, DSO, was commander of HMS *Erebus* at Zeebrugge. The following is taken from an obituary notice in my possession, but the date of Admiral Wills' death or name of the newspaper is not given:

Admiral Wills (then Captain) commanded the monitor *Erebus* in the bombardment of Zeebrugge during the operations at Ostend and Zeebrugge in April 1918, and special reference was made to the work of his vessel in despatches of the Vice-Admiral of the Dover Patrol.

It will be recalled that the *Erebus* with her sister ship the *Terror* (Captain C. N. Burton) at 11.20 p.m. on the night of the historic attack on the Mole opened the long range bombardment which proved so effective in making the larger part of the Garrison take cover, a fact which greatly facilitated subsequent operations, and which dealt so great a blow to the morale of the German forces. It was undoubtedly the effects of this exacting operation which undermined Admiral Wills' health and which, together with a wound in the head received in the action, eventually gave rise to the grave breakdown, causing his death. The *Erebus* was afterwards blown up, etc.

Another short (un-named and un-dated) cutting states :

After two years in command of the armed merchant cruiser *Laconia* he was appointed to the command of the new monitor *Erebus* and saw much service on the Dover Patrol, being frequently in action off the Belgium coast. He was wounded when the *Erebus* was torpedoed and for his work in that ship was Mentioned in Despatches and awarded the DSO and also the Legion of Honour, etc., etc.

*

Account by Captain J. S. Cowie CBE, RN from Bermuda:
HMS *Warwick*

Herewith, at long last, my piece about Zeebrugge – I hope it reaches you in time.

You will, I am sure, appreciate that it relates only to Zeebrugge, and not to the subsequent attack on Ostend on 10th May. In that affair *Warwick* was mined, and only just succeeded in getting back to Dover (held together by her mine-rails).

THE ASSAULT ON ZEEBRUGGE

At the time of the assault I was the sub-lieutenant of HMS *Warwick* (Commander Victor Campbell) in the Dover Patrol.

A fleet destroyer of the W class, *Warwick* (who was also equipped to lay mines) had to some extent been made capable of carrying out the functions of a flotilla half leader. For example, she carried a qualified navigating officer and an RNVR doctor, and her W/T installation had been enlarged.

On the occasions when the Vice-Admiral Dover proceeded to sea, it was the practice for him to wear his flag in *Warwick*, and to have with him various members of his staff, and this arrangement was followed for the Zeebrugge operation. By this I mean the actual assault on 23rd April, not the earlier attempt made on the night of the 11th/12th, which had to be abandoned due to a change in the direction of the wind.

However, as the official account noted 'some useful lessons were learnt'. Also, in so far as I was concerned, some new cuss-words.

As in all destroyers, my duties as the sub were many, but primarily I was the Torpedo Control Officer. Normally, my action station was on the bridge, but as it was expected that there would be an exceptional amount of noise, it had been decided that the whole ship's armament should be in 'local control'. This put me at the torpedo tubes, situated just abaft the engine-room hatch, with full authority to fire torpedoes at my own discretion.

Together with *Warwick*, the destroyers *North Star* and *Phoebe* formed the Inshore Division, and in the final paragraph of our orders all three ships were cheerfully forecast as being certain losses.

The first thing that I recall was the bursting of an enormous enemy parachute flare overhead. For a few moments night was turned into day, and I could see *Vindictive* coming in. From then on *Warwick* and various other craft proceeded to make artificial chemical smoke screens and duck into them, and it became difficult to judge distances.

At some time during these early doings, the engine-room hatch opened, and the Engineer Commander (Rampling) stuck his head out. Down on the foot-plate I could see our small black kitten drinking from a saucer of milk. 'I've never known this ship let off such regular salvos,' shouted the Chief. When I replied that we had not fired a single gun, and that he had only heard shells from enemy coast-defence batteries bursting, he thanked me very much and descended, closing the hatch behind him and (presumably) went on feeding milk to the kitten.

My next recollection is of the planned blowing up of the ancient submarine *C3* with five tons of explosives in her bow compartment, under the viaduct in the Mole. At the time, *Warwick* was near the viaduct. I *saw* the explosion, but did not *hear* it, an indication of the intensity of the general background noise.

Then *Vindictive* hauled off, with flames pouring from her shot-perforated funnels. *Warwick*, who again was rather close in, had to take drastic action to avoid being run down by her.

I have no precise idea of our next movements, but we presumably got round to the eastern or inner side of the seaward end of the Mole, and I sighted what appeared to me to be a German destroyer, and brought the torpedo-tubes to the 'ready'.

I was just about to pull the firing lever when I realised that the vessel I was aiming at was not an enemy destroyer some little distance away, but one of our own motor-launches (MLs) very close to us. I ordered the tubes to be trained fore and aft, and she came alongside.

She was low in the water, and seemed to have a vast number of people on board, but somehow we hauled them all up. The badly wounded ones were made as comfortable as possible and slowly fleeted forward along the mine-rails to an improvised operating theatre in one of the seamen's messes.

A demolition charge was placed in the already badly damaged ML and the time-fuse lit. As we were about to move clear of her our 1st lieutenant, Trumble, was killed by the accidental firing of one of her Lewis guns he was attempting to salve. He was *Warwick*'s only fatal casualty.

Our next encounter was with the two other ships of our division, *Phoebe* and *North Star*. The latter had run too close in, been hit by enemy shore batteries, and was sinking. Her survivors were transferred to *Phoebe*, and *Warwick*, after a final look round, headed for Dover at full speed.

I was ordered down to the Captain's day cabin to dispense hospitality, the Admiral's lady having arranged for two hampers from Fortnum and Mason's to be placed onboard just before we sailed from Dover, a remarkable feat of clairvoyance on her part.

Of the various characters assembled in the Captain's cabin, two will remain forever in my memory – Stuart Bonham-Carter, commanding *Intrepid*, and his Engineer Officer, Lt Bury.

One would have thought that having been miraculously snatched from a watery grave, so to speak, they would have had something to say about the fact, but not so. They were solely concerned with the rights and wrongs of Bonham-Carter's action in blowing Bury and his skeleton staff up through the deck of *Intrepid* with the machinery wrapped round their necks, without giving the pre-arranged warning to evacuate the engine and boiler rooms.

At midnight I reluctantly parted from them, and went up to the bridge to keep the middle watch.

Never a dull moment in the life of a sub-lieutenant.

Lieutenant Stuart Sumner Bonham-Carter was awarded the DSO and promoted for handling *Intrepid* with great skill and coolness in a position of considerable danger under heavy fire. 'Great credit is due to him for his success in sinking *Intrepid* in the Bruges Canal.'

Commander Victor Campbell, Engineer Commander Rampling, Lieutenant Trumble and *Lieutenant Bury* were mentioned in despatches.

*

7

Motor Launches and Coastal Motor Boats

Captain Carpenter said of the small craft, 'We felt they could be relied upon to tackle any situation, however difficult or unexpected.' He went on to quote the case of one of the CMBs which had its bows damaged in a collision. One of the sailors promptly put his backside in the hole and kept it there while the boat gathered sufficient speed for the bows to ride clear of the water. The CMB was then proceeding at 27 knots and had to continue at this speed circling the convoy which was only making 10 knots. Another CMB had engine trouble just after setting out, was towed back into Dover by a trawler, repaired the engines and set off again – five hours late. They then crossed the Channel – 60 miles in two hours – and arrived so fast they nearly ran ashore at Blankenberghe. This was on the earlier expedition; a similar incident occurred on the 22nd April.

An ML normally could carry 40-50 passengers. At Zeebrugge and Ostend, when they were picking up survivors, some carried over 100.

*

From C. Saunders: a liking for danger
My uncle, Lieutenant-Commander Raphael Saunders, commanding *ML 128*, was ordered to approach the Mole and send up flares. However, his engine failed as he was going through the smoke screen, and his ship drifted out of the smoke to within range of the defences. He himself seemed to bear a charmed life; the crew member beside him was killed, the ship was riddled with bullets, and a fragment broke the glass of the binnacle (compass housing) under his hand, without even scratching him.

He was a member of the RNVR before the war, and joined up as an Able Seaman. He received special promotion for the Zeebrugge raid, and the DSO for Ostend.

When the Second World War broke out he badgered the Admiralty for a ship. As he was then 64 years old they would only offer him a desk job; getting bored with that he joined the bomb disposal squad, until he was retired!

I am sorry I cannot tell you any more, but he was essentially a reticent man, except for telling us of incidents which did not reflect glory on himself. But he had a dry wit, and although he died in 1959 aged 83 he is still often missed.

Lieutenant Raphael Saunders received special promotion at Zeebrugge. He volunteered for rescue work but owing to a breakdown in his engines did not arrive in time. He however went in and took off the crew of *Motor Launch 424*, when that vessel was sinking under heavy fire. At Ostend he was awarded the DSO. Together with *ML 283* he went in after *Vindictive* to look for survivors. When near the shore he came under heavy fire – his signalman was killed, and Lieutenant Brayfield and one of the crew wounded. He showed great coolness, setting a fine example to his men throughout, and was of the greatest assistance in organizing the smoke screen.

*

From R. Cunningham: missing at sea

My cousin has sent me a slip from the *Daily Telegraph* of 7.3.77 about Zeebrugge. My brother Andrew C. Cunningham, a midshipman in the RNR, was reported missing on 12th April 1918, during a preliminary attack, to test out the defences of Zeebrugge, prior to the big attack on the entrance to Zeebrugge Harbour when a blockship was sunk to seal off the harbour to German Submarines both in and outside the harbour. My brother's body was never recovered, but a Lieutenant Lawson, I think, and a few other members of the coastal motor boat crews' bodies were washed ashore at Ostend. These CMBs were used as submarine chasers at that time in the Channel or stationed at Dover and Ostend, i.e. the Dover Patrol. During the preliminary raid in Zeebrugge their job was to go in close to the Mole at Zeebrugge and throw up flares, while the Naval battleships lying far from land bombarded Zeebrugge harbour, to test the German defences for the big attack on the 23.4.18. The British Official Report stated that one of their coastal motor boats had been sunk and the Official German Report said that they had sunk a British torpedo boat. I contacted the German Red Cross at that time for any news of my brother, but their reply was negative; no prisoners had been taken, and no bodies had been recovered by the Germans.

I read a book cany years ago, giving an account of war in the air, and the author mentioned being shot down in the sea by attack fire, and picked up by a CMB off Zeebrugge, but this story gave the date of 10.4.18 and not 12th April, when the Admiralty informed my father that my brother Andrew was posted missing, so there is some confusion by the book's date and the Admiralty's date. My brother Andrew was first a cadet on HMS training ship the *Conway* on the Mersey. Then he joined the RNR, and was posted as midshipman on HMS *Changunola* and for three years patrolled on that ship between Glasgow and Iceland and was waiting for his promotion to sub-lieutenant, when he was with the Dover Patrol and killed at Zeebrugge.

He would have been 19 years old if he had lived to his birthday, 24th June 1918. I understand that there is a monument to the Dover Patrol standing on the cliffs of Dover and when I left London to come to South Africa on 25th January 1924, was passed through the Straits of Dover about 3 p.m. and saw what looked like a monument or war memorial on the cliffs and thought that is where Andrew's name is on the monument to the Dover Patrol. His name is also on the War Memorial at my old home town Moffat in Scotland and in the book of Scottish dead at Edinburgh Castle and at my old school at Beith in Ayrshire.

I understand that the CMBs at that time were the fastest boats in the Navy doing over 45 knots and that they carried depth charges, and if a German periscope was sighted, the CMB went for same at full speed, and threw two depth charges, one to either side, then came back to see if any oil surfaced. Without this preliminary attack to test out the German defences, the main attack on 23rd April may not have been so successful.

*

From E. E. Noyes: Harry Tate's Navy

I don't think we can be of much help for, although my father was full of reminiscences about Gallipoli, Zeebrugge, Jutland, etc., we ourselves have forgotten much that he told us.

He was at both Zeebrugge 23/4/18 and Ostend 10/5/18 and the only minor things we can call to mind are as follows :

The MLs bought from the USA and manned by the RNVR were scornfully referred to as Harry Tate's Navy by the regular RN chaps but never the less the regulars had a hearty respect for their courage and tenacity in the face of dreadful odds.

The contingent of Australians from the flagship *Australia* and who sailed in the *Vindictive* and the blockships were the subject of much admiration for their gallantry and good humour despite their heavy losses.

The old ferry boat *Daffodil* came in for much barracking but I can't remember the circumstances.

When the radio controlled ML with 500 tons of TNT hit the *Erebus* there were some crude comments but a great relief that somebody had thought of the idea of the side blisters.

I remember my father saying that one of his messmates who was somewhat of an artist – we still have some of his work in the form of an oil painting of HMS *Erebus* and some decorated German 2 inch HE shells – was swearing like hell that his so and so artistic work would be ruined and why the hell Jerry couldn't have gone the other side and up the ward room.

Concerning the raid itself everyone seemed to have a terrific admiration for Keyes and the concept but considered that it was almost certain death for those on the *Vindictive*, the blockships and the relief vessels. There was great disappointment that the plan for the blockships was not 100% successful.

My father came in contact with several survivors from the *Vindictive* (or from the *Iris*) – some of them badly wounded – but they all gave credit to the fighting qualties of the Hun but also admiration for the tenacity and bravery of those involved in the landing with special reference to the Australian contingent.

Concerning the bombardment of the Belgian coast my father was what was then known as 'Captain of the Gun' – a title now extinct – in the 15 inch turret and he remarked that the rate of fire had exceeded by far anything previously attained in battle or practice and the chaps in the ammunition hoists were passing out with fatigue while the temperature in the turrets was higher than my father had experienced in the tropics.

The above is about all – it isn't much but it is now difficult to recall the very many anecdotes of such a long career in the navy.

*

From C. W. Keel: after the battle

My elder brother George Ernest Keel was a Chief Engineer aboard what was then known as a CMB (coastal motor boat) whose duty it was (I believe) to lead in the old battleships to be sunk in a position to block the U-boats entrance.

The late Sir Roger Keyes was the Admiral in charge and I again believe was one of the plan originators. At the same time Ostend was to be attacked. Zeebrugge was a success but Ostend only partially so.

My brother survived Zeebrugge but I believe from my late mother, that volunteers from the survivors of both attempts were called for to attack Ostend for the second time. My brother wrote a letter to my mother (which I was not allowed to read) but which stated the heavy odds against returning. He was killed in action at Ostend on 10th May 1918. After the war was over I travelled by a coal boat to Le Havre France and from there made my way to Ostend and located my brother's grave along with others in the British part of a French Cemetery. In this was a poorly kept plot with a kind of register of names in the little Church. I was then about 18 years of age with little money in a strange land but found great kindness at a British Mission to Seamen (I think) at Ostend which was in charge of, I think, a Reverend Grant and his wife.

They did everything to comfort me at the time with personal supervision to see that good food and bedroom, bath, etc., be provided. My late mother received a printed message from the late Sir Roger Keyes but he added his personal addition in his writing stating that my brother had died while gallantly doing his duty.

Being 16 at the time my mother felt that I should not be allowed to know all, but the above is what I recollect of Zeebrugge and Ostend 1918.

Before entering the Navy my brother was always connected with petrol engines and motor cycles and took one of the first twin-stretchered motor cycles to France bringing out the wounded. He became attracted to the petrol engined CMBs of the navy and was Chief Engineer in the attack on the submarine bases. His service medals I retain, being the only surviving male member of the family.

*

From M. Watts:

My late husband, Lieutenant Commander Arthur Watts DSO and Bar, RNVR took part in both the Zeebrugge and Ostend raids in April 1918. My husband was in command of *ML 239*, leader of a smoke screen unit. He was awarded the DSO for Zeebrugge and Ostend (see page 208 of *Zeebrugge and Ostend Despatches* of Sir Roger Keyes. Published by Oxford University Press 1919).

I have quite a clear memory of some things he told me – I was a lot younger than he was – but I have a good memory still! Of course, it is a long time ago – he left nothing written – so my memories may be of no interest to you.

My husband, who was an artist who contributed to *Punch*, the *Radio*

Times and many periodicals of the time in the 20's, was killed in a civil flying crash in 1935.

Acting Lieutenant Commander Arthur Watts won special promotion at Zeebrugge; together with Lieutenant Commander Mieville, Lieutenant Dixon and Lieutenant Drummond, he was a leader of the smoke unit and by his skill and judgement contributed to the great success of the smoke screen in his section. His citation for the DSO at Ostend read: 'This officer was in command of *ML 239* and the leader of a smoke screen unit. He led his unit with skill and judgement in a very exposed position, and it was largely due to him that the screen was so extremely successful in his section.'

*

From H. E. Hampson: Smokescreens. Sir Roger Keyes' thoroughness

I was, at the time engaged in the manufacture of smoke screen apparatus for that exploit; these were made on the premises of the firm for whom I worked as an oxy-acetylene welder and assembled in the submarine basin of the naval dockyard, they were then bolted on to lighters and towed across the Channel in order to cover the movements of the concrete filled *Vindictive*. Although somewhat Heath Robinson in design, they did by all accounts a very useful job and contributed in no small measure to the success of the operation.

The C in C Dover Patrol, Admiral Roger Keyes was often to be seen in the dockyard taking a keen interest in the assembly of these crude but effective pieces of equipment which also screened his flagship (HMS *Warwick*) on the crossing.

*

From J. F. Morris: his brother's account

D. R. Morris, Midshipman RNR (HMS Conway *– 15/1/1916 to Feb. 1918). Letter of 28th April 1918. HMS* Arrogant, *C/O G.P.O. London.*

'I am glad to say that I am quite safe, except for a wound in my left arm. However, it is not serious. We had a terrible fight but quite enjoyed it, and, of course, we won. No doubt you will see an account in the papers. I got a Lewis Gun bullet put into me, just as we got to Zeebrugge Mole, but managed to keep on firing until all was over. Of course, there were quite a lot wounded, but not many seriously. One of our middies had 14 wounds and is very bad. He is in hospital in Dunkirk. I never thought I should see Ostend and Zeebrugge so soon.'

In the local paper the above letter is repeated and also 'When we arrived outside Zeebrugge 15 inch shells were flying about, and we got it pretty hot. We sighted the *Vindictive* and as she was getting badly hit, and no smoke screen to shield her, we decided to get our screens going. We then went between her and the Mole, which is 160 yards away. The result was that the enemy could not see the *Vindictive* and she was able to put her men ashore. In a few minutes we were all hit. We had 36 hours without sleep, and had hardly any food, so you can guess we were pretty exhausted.'*

He was gazetted on 8th March 1918 at the age of 16. He served in a ML at Zeebrugge. Later he was in Egypt and Palestine mainly on a converted yacht HMY *Managem* and operated off the Syrian Coast. This seems to have finished in 1919 and he went on the *Konigin Luise* to take troops back to Australia in June 1919. This went on until February 1921.

Up to the time of the depression he served with the various Ellerman Lines and died at sea, in the Persian Gulf in June 1944.

*

From A. Stobbs: the mystery of the MLs

I write to say that I recall hearing, as a very small child, my father recounting one or two particular strange tales of his Dover Patrol days.

He was Lieutenant F. Garnet Stobbs, RNVR, based in Felixstowe Dock and, during his service commanded four motor launches, as they were known; three of them on the Dover Patrol. Those were, HMMLs *14, 59, 3* and *2* in that order I believe.

He was posted in *ML 59* to the Zeebrugge project but, at the last moment was medically down-graded to his annoyance, so was switched from *ML 59* to *3* therefore.

I still have the group photograph of his intake at the RN College, Greenwich, their tutor – for whom he had a high regard – Montenarro was the name I believe.

One thing I recall is his saying it was a mystery how those craft held together in high seas. Apparently on top of a wave, the deck planks would open; he would put a half crown coin in an aperture and, at the bottom of the trough it was immovable!

I can also recall an early memory of attending a Sunday morning service on the deck of the old *Ganges* and to this day the scene

* See Hilton Young's account, page 79.

flashes back whenever I hear this hymn 'O God our help in ages past. . . .'

*

From Wing Commander Mackie: the boom defence

My father was Anthony Charles Mackie DSC, Lt RNVR (Dover Patrol). Like a good sailor he was quite good at exaggeration, but I was brought up on yarns about this operation (I was born 7.7.14). I understood he assisted in the start of the operation by dismantling their huge boom defence warning bell at the end of the Mole. His ship was damaged but he picked up survivors and returned home.

Admiral Keyes was more than a hero.

He sailed his open day boat on the East Coast, near Maldon in Essex until he died some years ago.

Lieutenant Anthony Mackie received the DSC for his services at Ostend on 9th/10th May. He was mentioned in despatches for specially distinguished service, in his command of *ML 279*. He 'pluckily carried on his smoke screen work under fire for one and a half hours after breaking the starboard shaft, retiring with the rest of the flotilla when operations were completed under one engine.'

*

From W. Marlow – 'Shiner' Wright

One of my great friends in life was J. C. Wright (Shiner) whom I believe was 2 i/c in *Daffodil* under Lieutenant Campbell DSO.

My first encounter with 'Shiner' Wright was when I joined London Division RNVR No 9 Coy in 1910. He was then C.P.O. His great love was training a field gun crew for competing with the terms of the Royal Navy. This he did most successfully in so much as our team ran in the final at Olympia against HMS *Excellent*.

After Zeebrugge the story amongst his contemporaries at the time (certainly not coming from him) was that a VC and a DSO were allotted' for this exploit and that Campbell and Wright tossed a coin to decide which should receive which.

Lieutenant James Courtenay Wright was awarded the DSC at Zeebrugge; in fact he was second in command of HM *Motor Launch 282* under Percy Dean, VC. He showed great courage and coolness in embarking the crews of *Intrepid* and *Iphigenia*. It was largely due to the magnificent manner in which he and others carried out their duties that so many officers and men were rescued from the blockships in the canal at Zeebrugge. He was dangerously wounded.

*

Account by Lieutenant S. D. Gowing, sent in by B. Muir (daughter): Synopsis for a book which was never written

Plan for heavy bombardment of Zeebrugge and Ostend by monitors, with smoke-screen made by MLs; impossible for unscreened ships to approach shore batteries. Captain McLean from Grand Fleet arrives to train MLs in concerted manoeuvring and smoke-screen work. Night passage to Belgian coast with thirty MLs and four monitors. Bombardment at dawn, three hours. Heavy fire. Smoke-screen successful. Destroyer action . . . Ostend and Zeebrugge docks destroyed . . . home over Goodwins.

MLs transferred to Dunkirk for smoke-screen and bombardment work. Daily actions. Intensive raids on Dunkirk nightly and bombardment by heavy German guns. Ostend railway depot destroyed by monitor fires. German destroyer raid on Dunkirk . . . Germans shoot up the town, pass through at full speed, torpedoing the monitor. Beached and sent home. The *Erebus* takes her place.

Decision to mine the Straits from shore to shore . . . 12,000 deep-laid mines . . . hush-hush job. Commander Metcalfe (Jackson) in charge. *ML 21* (S. D. Gowing's ship) detailed to accompany him. Ten week's work in winter gales.

Metcalfe on last voyage shot himself with a rifle from the cabin rack *Daffodil* (armed trawler) brings him home.

Training and preparation . . . worked out to time-tables. Fine staff work. The fleet sails.

The two submarines part at midnight for their separate objectives. MLs ahead. S. D. Gowing in command of *ML 551*) take positions off harbour. . . Point blank range. . . German star shells. . . Hell let loose. . . *Vindictive* arrives with half her crew killed . . . storms the Mole but unable to silence the guns. . . Destroyer action. . . Pier work of Mole blown up by submarine charged with explosives that has rammed herself under the piles. German cyclist corps racing in to reinforce plunged into gap and is drowned wholesale. Blockships force the harbour, one knocked out, the two others sink themselves in canal mouth according to plan. MLs rescue the crews . . . all that remain alive. Complete success of operation. *Vindictive* sounds recall signal and retires, shot to pieces and all funnels blazing.

At Ostend the wind changes at the critical moment . . . smoke-screen blown off shore. The blockships sunk close under shore guns. Crews rescued by MLs . . . *551* runs ashore and screens the Hindenburg battery during retirement of the Flotilla. Return to Dunkirk.

Decision to go back to Ostend immediately with *Vindictive*. The second attack. The Germans ready for us. More mines and yet more guns. The run in-shore. MLs shot up. The screen succeeds. *Vindictive* makes the piers before the guns get her. Sinks herself across the harbour. Raked by machine guns and heavies. Survivors of crews taken off by MLs. Transferred to Commodore's flagship outside, which is mined during the retirement but reaches port. Zeebrugge and Ostend bases destroyed. No U-boats able to enter. 17 corked up inside.

[The account of 'my father's war' ends as follows :]

The last push. . . . Squadrons of heavy-gun monitors with MLs drive along Belgian coast engaging the shore batteries . . . the Army advances. German army fighting rearguard action in retirement from Belgium.

Night falls . . . last of German troops retreating from Ostend. *MLs 281* and *551* reach the harbour and land the King and Queen of Belgium. Their reception by a liberated people.

(My father received the Croix de Guerre and was also mentioned in despatches.)

*

From A. A. Croft: presence of mind (!)

My late brother-in-law, Dudley Babb, took part in the Zeebrugge Raid on 23rd April 1918 as a sub-lieutenant.

He distinguished himself by his presence of mind – or backside – by sitting on a flare which German machine-gun bullets, splashing up around the Carley float on which he was, had ignited. He was subsequently offered a decoration or promotion; he chose the latter – more money in it – and became, I believe, the youngest two-ringer in the Service.

Sub-Lieutenant Babb received special promotion. He was navigating officer of *Intrepid* and by his bravery and cheerfulness throughout the action he set a fine example to his men.

*

From H. E. Thompson: diagram of the smoke screen

I have delved back through the mist of time and managed to recall the shape and approximate measurements of the apparatus used to make smoke during the attack on Zeebrugge long, long ago. In this matter I

DIAGRAM OF SMOKE APPARATUS
Supplied by H. E. Thompson

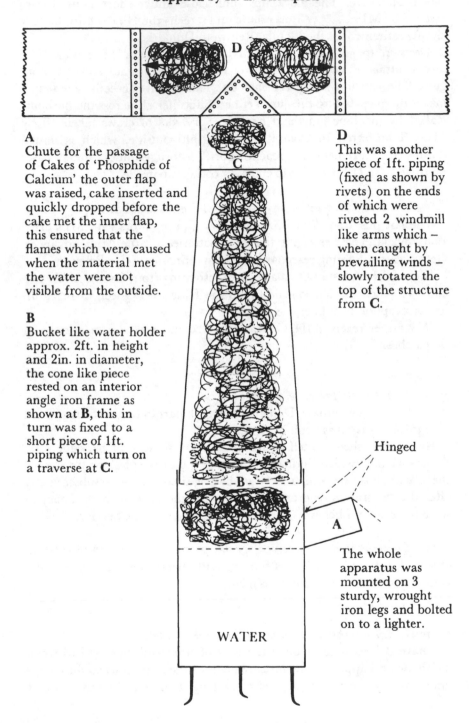

A
Chute for the passage
of Cakes of 'Phosphide of
Calcium' the outer flap
was raised, cake inserted and
quickly dropped before the
cake met the inner flap,
this ensured that the
flames which were caused
when the material met
the water were not
visible from the outside.

B
Bucket like water holder
approx. 2ft. in height
and 2in. in diameter,
the cone like piece
rested on an interior
angle iron frame as
shown at **B**, this in
turn was fixed to a
short piece of 1ft.
piping which turn on
a traverse at **C**.

D
This was another
piece of 1ft. piping
(fixed as shown by
rivets) on the ends
of which were
riveted 2 windmill
like arms which –
when caught by
prevailing winds –
slowly rotated the
top of the structure
from **C**.

Hinged

The whole
apparatus was
mounted on 3
sturdy, wrought
iron legs and bolted
on to a lighter.

WATER

have been assisted by my wife who worked at the same establishment as myself and who also did her bit in the making of the same; between us we have managed to agree the design.

*

Account by Sir Ion Hamilton Benn: the Ostend operations
(Sent in by J. Cumin-Scott)

None of the books that I have seen about Zeebrugge and Ostend operations gives an account of what happened at Ostend on the night of the 11th April 1918, which resulted in the buoys being shifted by the Germans before St George's Day, causing the failure of the blocking operations on that night.

> Orders for operation Z.O. – April, 1918.
> Ships coming from Thames, Dover and
> Dunkirk to rendezvous 5 miles off
> Zeebrugge Mole and 5 miles off Ostend –
> Stroombank Buoy No 7 respectively.

The 20 MLs to make the smoke screen came up from Dunkirk, leaving there at 9.30 p.m., arriving at the rendezvous five miles from Ostend in good time. In *ML 532* I took station close to Commodore Lyne's destroyer. The plan was that *ML 532* should go into Ostend with the blockships and rescue the crew of the *Brilliant* after she had been sunk between the piers, and that Lieutenant Commander Robin Hoare in *ML 283* should do the same for the crew of the *Sirius*. Lieutenant Roland Bourke in *ML 276* was to follow us in case *ML 532* or *ML 283* was knocked out. The other MLs were to take station on the best line for the smoke screen according to the wind, anchoring about 250 yards from the harbour entrance.

At zero hour the Commodore hailed me saying, 'Zero hour, no word from the Admiral, proceed in execution of orders, wind if any NNE.' I thereupon instructed Eric Welman, RN, to go ahead; he commanded the CMBs which were to light the entrance to the harbour with flares, a very dangerous mission. These 'skimming dishes' had a speed of over 30 knots, but the smoke they made was rather poor. The MLs followed at a speed of 15 knots, our instructions being to make a smoke screen between the Stroombank Buoy No 7 and the Bell Buoy at the Harbour entrance to cover the two blockships *Brilliant* and *Sirius* from the shore batteries, and especially from a battery with big guns, a little to the east of Ostend.

After running 14 minutes I saw the Stroombank buoy No 7 right ahead. The MLs were placed as arranged, but there was practically no wind. Meantime, the Germans having heard our approach put up every kind of star shell, flaming onions, rockets, etc., and fired a lot of two-pound tracer shells in strings of 13, like coveys of partridges, but the biggest guns did not fire. Our smoke went straight up in pillars, expanding as it went up like inverted pyramids. I was reminded of the scene I once saw in the caves of Staffa lit up by torches of the guides, great stalactites coming down from the roof. This was no good for the block-ships so I at once ordered all MLs to get under way and move slowly round from Buoy No 7 to the Bell Buoy; this spread the smoke and made good cover, except for the last couple of hundred yards.

Alas, the blockships did not show up. After two hours, when the tide had fallen too low to admit of entering Ostend, I gave instructions to withdraw.

At Dunkirk I learned that ten minutes after zero hour the Commodore received a message from the Admiral to say the operations were abandoned for lack of wind, but there was no means of letting me know; being miles away followed by a string of noisy launches no signals could be seen or heard.

Several of the MLs were damaged by gun fire, but none was sunk; on the other hand, two of the CMBs were lost and it was reported that one at least had been salved by the Germans.

Consequently, when it was decided that a further attempt was to be made on the night of 22nd/23rd April I asked the Commodore whether the buoys (especially Stroombank Buoy No 7) were in the charted position, and learned that Lieutenant Welman had on the 18th/19th fixed the position of No 7 and found it correct. The Commodore also sent an aeroplane over on 21st April and was told that No 7 was in its correct position. However, on the night of 22nd/23rd, having got the zero signal from the Commodore, we ran 14 minutes on the same course as before and saw no No 7 where we expected it to be, but saw a twinkle about 1,500 yards away to the norrard, and proceeding there found it marked Stroombank Buoy No 7. I therefore concluded that the Commodore's destroyer had not been in exactly the same position as on the 11th. On both occasions the position had been fixed by dead reckoning, and the speed of the tides and currents varies from day to day owing to the direction of the winds in the North Sea, etc. Subsequent events proved that the position was right and that No 7 had been moved by the Germans.

That night there was a moderate on shore breeze, and a nice smoke screen was laid, until later the wind shifted and spoilt it.

As the blockships did not show up at the time expected, I went out a short distance looking for them; then a few minutes later I saw through the smoke two large vessels which appeared to be coming out from Ostend. My first thought was that they were German destroyers and that we were in for a very bad time, but getting another glimpse realised they were the blockships (they had first gone to the right position for Buoy No 7 and had subsequently found it where we had).

They turned on the buoy in the direction believed to be the harbour entrance. *ML 532* then went ahead making as much smoke as possible. By this time the shore batteries and big guns had opened up hot fire. *ML 532* carried on until we saw dunes right ahead and knew that we were to the eastward of the harbour. Turning at full speed we went back to warn the *Brilliant* but as we came alongside she struck a sandbank and sheered across the channel. At the same time a shell struck *ML 532* carrying away the bows from the keel to the deck with anchor, winch and chain. We were all knocked down – I fell against the binnacle and was somewhat damaged. When we picked ourselves up we saw the *Sirius* was on fire and also aground close to the *Brilliant*. Seeing *ML 532* was out of action Lieutenant Commander Robin Hoare in *ML 283* went alongside the *Brilliant* and took off Captain Godsal and the crew. It was fortunate that Lieutenant Bourke in *ML 276* was following us as he took off Lieutenant Commander Hardy and the crew of the *Sirius*; then both the MLs made for Dunkirk very heavily laden with the crews of these two ships. Meantime, *ML 532* had drifted away in the smoke, both engines had been shifted on their beds by the shock, breaking the exhaust pipes, consequently both engineers were badly gassed. Getting no response to my signals to stop engines, Lieutenant Kirkwood, a young New Zealander, jumped down and stopped them, returning on deck in a rather dazed state he told me both engineers were on the floor, whereupon our Cook, F. Bowles, went down and carried them both on deck, where they recovered after an hour or two.

Before the operation on the 10th I had given orders that each ML should have a small red bulb fixed to the top of her mast so that they might be easily distinguishable at night. As it turned out this saved us in the *ML 532* from a German prison. We were about 600 yards from Ostend completely broken down, kept afloat by a bulkhead of less than an eighth of an inch thick. I had just said to the helmsman, 'It looks like breakfast on Sauerkraut' when I caught sight of a tiny red light far away to seaward and I turned on the searchlight and signalled 'SOS, SOS, SOS,' fortunately some of the rescued crew of the *Sirius* were sitting in the stern of *ML 276* facing aft. They saw the signal and passed word to

Lieutenant Bourke who immediately came back to us. There was some difficulty in getting in tow, as one rope after another broke, but this was accomplished and we were towed slowly about halfway back to Dunkirk. By this time the engineers had managed to patch up an exhaust pipe and had got one engine going so I told *ML 276* to cast off and take the rescued men, some of whom were wounded, to Dunkirk as quickly as possible. *ML 532* carried on slowly and arrived there about mid-day on the 23rd.

Robin Hoare had already got a DSC, he was awarded a DSO at the first Ostend operation; a Bar to the DSO for the second Ostend operation, and also in July 1918, the Albert Medal for another Special Act of Gallantry.

Roland Bourke was awarded the DSO. He and Lieutenant Drummond both got VC's on 10th May, when HMS *Vindictive* was put into Ostend Harbour, but that is another story.

W. Wigg – Leading Seaman in *ML 532* and F. Bowles, the Cook, were both awarded the DCM.

Wigg had been with me for 16 years in various yachts and held a Master's ticket. Bowles, part owner of a Tollesbury fishing smack, was cook in the Kaiser's Schooner *Meteor*. When the war broke out he was given a pass home, but no wages, £60 due – he joined me in HMY *Greta* in September 1914.

THE 9th MAY, 1918

The Zeebrugge Bruges Canal was the depot for German submarines and destroyers operating in the Channel, and Bruges was also connected with Ostend by canal.

As we had failed to block Ostend on 23rd April, Admiral Keyes decided to have another try using the *Vindictive* under Captain Godsal and the old depot ship *Sappho* under Captain Hardy, the two officers who had commanded the *Brilliant* and the *Sirius*.

He sent me back to Dunkirk to discuss plans with Commodore Lynes and make arrangements for the smoke screen and rescue MLs.

When I told the Commodore that I intended to lead the MLs he looked at me and said, 'Do you think it is quite the thing for an elderly man and an MP to be going to Ostend three times inside a month?'

I replied, 'I am a member of the Ostend Yacht Club and on my last visit I left two of my front teeth behind!'

The failure of 23rd April was due to the Germans moving the Stroombank Buoy to another and smaller channel to the NE, and also to the wind shifting at the turn of the tide from an on shore to off shore breeze which blew back our smoke screen and exposed the *Brilliant* and *Sirius* to the full blast of the big guns of the shore batteries. It was decided that this time the blockships should ignore all buoys and go in at the top of high water from a point fixed about ten miles from the harbour; that MLs should station in a straight line about half a mile off shore, and as it was uncertain where the blockships would pass through this line the two nearest MLs would follow to rescue the crews.

The *Sappho* broke down on her way up from Dunkirk and the *Vindictive* went on alone; a thick sea fog developed which made it difficult to find the entrance between the piers. She eventually succeeded with the help of a million candle power buoy which was lighted at the entrance by one of Captain Welman's gallant little CMBs, but this, of course, exposed the *Vindictive* to the fire of all the harbour batteries.

After passing the entrance between the piers Captain Godsal went outside the conning tower to get a better view and gave the order 'Hard a starboard' to bring the *Vindictive* square across the channel. At that moment a bit shell hit the conning tower and Godsal was never seen again. The second-in-command, Lieutenant Sir John Alleyne, was knocked out by the concussion, but Lieutenant Crutchley, though badly shaken, gave the order 'full speed astern' on the port engine to help the vessel swing, but it was too late and she took the ground at an angle of about 25 degrees.

My *ML 532* was in dockyard hands so I went with Lieutenant Commander Watson in *ML 105*. We took up the position in the centre of the line believing it was the place where the *Vindictive* would pass, but we did not see her at all until the CMB lighted up the entrance. *ML 254* was the nearest to her and *ML 276* was not far away. Lieutenant Drummond in *ML 254* followed her inside the piers. While doing so he was badly wounded in two places and his second-in-command Lieutenant Gordon Ross was killed. The seaman at the wheel was also wounded but they managed to get the ML alongside the *Vindictive* and take off two officers and 37 men. *ML 254* then backed out. Half an hour later she was picked up in a sinking condition by the destroyer *Warwick* with Admiral Keyes on board.

Meantime Lieutenant Bourke in *ML 276*, after raking the piers with the Lewis gun, went into the harbour to see if anyone was left alive in the *Vindictive*. Finding no one he backed out; on passing the stern he thought he heard a cry and so went alongside again without result. As he backed out for the second time he was sure he heard a shout and therefore went in again, this time on the other side of the ship, where he found two men in the water being held up by a petty officer in a half sunken rowing boat. Sub-Lieutenant Petrie managed somehow to get these men on board; one of them proved to be Sir John Alleyne.

ML 276 was subsequently picked up outside by one of our monitors and towed into Dunkirk. I examined her next morning and found the mast had been shot away about 7 foot from the deck and there were 55 holes in her between wind and water. Before these operations on the Belgian Coast I had given strict instructions that no petrol tank should be more than half full, so that the petrol would be below the water line. But for this precaution both these MLs would have certainly been lost with all on board.

The holes in *ML 276* were plugged up temporarily and I escorted her to Dover and from there she was escorted to Chatham Dockyard for repairs, she went under her own power in both passages. A month later she came back to Dover all spick and span. On arrival I told Lieutenant Bourke that as we were very short of MLs he should fill up the petrol, be on hand, and be ready to go to sea if necessary. An hour later he came to me and said, 'It is no use, Sir, the petrol tanks are leaking badly.' I sent for the Dockyard Superintendent. He confirmed that the main tank was leaking badly and part of the deck would have to be taken off in order to get the tank out. This was done and I found that on one side there was a hole inwards about 2 inch in diameter and on the other side there were 13 small holes going outwards shewing that a shell had entered and broken into pieces inside; one would suppose that there must have been an explosion, but the tank was not distorted in shape. The tank was put on a lorry with instructions to the driver to stop in front of the Admiral's office, and I went and told the Admiral. He, as I expected, looked at me and said, 'Why, that is quite impossible'. I replied that I fully expected he would say that, the tank was outside the front door for him to see for himself. It is said that there cannot be an explosion if there is no air, so I think it likely that the missile was one of the 2 inch tracer shells, a great number of them were fired by the Germans that night and that having pierced the tank it flew into pieces.

It transpired subsequently that there was no need to block Ostend as the Canal from Bruges was too shallow for the large German U-boats and destroyers which were confined there until the end of the war by the blocking of Zeebrugge.

Both Drummond and Bourke were awarded the Victoria Cross.

Commander Ion Hamilton Benn DSO MP received special promotion for 23rd April. By his energy and fine spirit he inspired the officers and men of the motor launches with devotion to duty and readiness to self sacrifice. During the engagement he was in *ML 582*, in one of the most inshore berths, and went alongside *Brilliant* under very heavy fire, after she had ground. He was awarded the Croix de Guerre. For his services on 9th/10th May, he was made a CB. His mention in despatches for specially distinguished service read : 'This officer led the motor launches in *ML 105* with conspicuous ability and success. This is the third occasion Captain Benn has led the inshore motor launch division off Ostend under a very heavy fire. Captain Benn has set a very fine example of bravery and devotion to duty to the officers and men of the motor launches of the Dover patrol, which he has commanded for nearly three years and has thus contributed greatly to the success which has attended the gallant efforts of these small raft in carrying out the dangerous duties assigned to them during these operations off the Belgian coast.'

Lieutenant Robin Hoare was awarded the DSO at the first Ostend operation for taking off 50 of the crew of the sinking *Sirius*; he then proceeded to *Brilliant* and took off 16, then back to *Sirius* for the remainder of the officers and crew. He received a bar to the DSO at the second Ostend operation. He was ordered to follow astern and assist two other motor launches detailed for rescue work. He remained at the Stroom Bank Buoy position until *Vindictive* had passed, and then followed her, patrolling east and west within a quarter of a mile of the shore under heavy fire, searching for survivors until 3.20 a.m. when all hope of finding anyone still alive had passed.

Lieutenant Eric Welman DSC, was specially promoted and awarded the DSO at the first Ostend operation for handling the units of the coastal motor boat flotilla under his command in a masterly manner, rendering the great service in screening and rescue work. He was always in the most exposed positions across the harbour entrance covering *Vindictive*, *Iris II* and *Daffodil* by smoke screen. He received a Bar to the DSO at Ostend for organising and leading the coastal motor boats in a most spirited manner. He encountered an enemy torpedo boat near the entrance to Ostend, which switched on searchlights and opened fire. He at once closed with her, and engaged her with Lewis guns to such good effect that she withdrew and left the channel clear for the approach of the blockships. He also received the Croix de Guerre.

Lieutenant Malcolm Kirkwood received the DSC for his work at the first Ostend operation. After his ship was damaged alongside *Brilliant* and the engineers gassed, he went down to the engine room which was full of fumes, and started the starboard engines, thereby saving the ship from either being sunk or captured. Shortly afterwards he lost consciousness and was only rescued with difficulty.

Commander William Watson was mentioned in despatches and promoted for the first operation. He was mentioned for specially distinguished service at the second operation; he was in command of *ML 105*, and was of great assistance to Captain Benn in arranging and supervising the smoke screen. This involved going from end to end of the line and taking his vessel close inshore several times, when he came under heavy fire. He showed great courage and coolness throughout the operation.

Captain Lynes had been appointed by Keyes to direct the early attempt to block Ostend, and Keyes entrusted the second operation to him also. He directed it in a most able manner, proceeding himself in HMS *Faulknor,* and supporting the *Vindictive* from an inshore position. He was made a Commander of the Legion of Honour.

Lieutenant Sir John Alleyne DSC was awarded the DSO for the second Ostend operation. He had volunteered from a monitor of the Dover patrol for service in the *Vindictive*. He refitted the navionational arrangements destroyed in *Vindictive* on 23rd April and on 9th/10th May was invaluable because of his local knowledge. He showed great coolness under fire, and skilfully navigated the *Vindictive* to the entrance in Ostend Harbour. He was severely wounded when his captain was killed.

*

Account by N. Rogers

Rear Admiral Roger Keyes was in charge of the Dover Base. The Zeebrugge raid was despatched from the dockyard at the Eastern Harbour at Dover where the Coastal Motor Base was situated. I was one of the crew on *CMB 28A* under the command of Lieutenant Hill, RN. The crew consisted of five with Sub-Lieutenant Fogg Elliott, two ERA's and a wireless telegraphist of which I was the latter. The W/T operator was also signaller with semaphore flags and hoists.

The boat was 55 feet long built by Messrs J. I. Thornycroft Ltd. at Hampton, Middlesex, and had two 12 cylinder engines (FIAT). The armament was two 18 inch torpedoes fired from the stern above propellers, two Lewis Machine Guns, and two depth charges. The maximum speed was 40 knots. A wireless cabin was situated at the rear of the cockpit with an aircraft with a range of about twenty miles.

As the hull of the boat was of wood to prevent barnacles forming on the hull the CMB's were lifted out of the water by slings and chains and placed on chocks on trucks. It was not considered wise to go to sea in rough weather. The task was two months at Dover patrolling the Straits of Dover and one month at Dunkirk submarine hunting in the Belgian coast.

The wireless operators were not permitted to actually take part in the operation to minimize casualties.

HMS *Vindictive* and the flotilla of motor launches and CMB's left Dover on the eve of St George's Day 1918 to meet up with other vessels from Harwich and other ports. The CMB's were under the command of. Lieutenant Eric C. Welman, *CMB 28A* took its position in the line, but unfortunately developed engine trouble and had to return to base. The ERAs discovered the defect, repaired it, and the boat was able to follow the flotilla and take its place as originally planned. One of the skippers of another CMB was Lieutenant Reed, DSO and bar, who took part in both Zeebrugge and Ostend raids. He later was in the Russian raids against the Bolsheviks, but unfortunately was shot in the head whilst raiding.

The Mole was breached by using an old submarine filled with explosives and rammed into the Mole, and was a counter attack to attack German defensive action whilst channel was blocked. This was effected by Lieutenant R. D. Sandford, RN, who was picked up by a Motor Launch after the explosion. On his death some time later, he was buried in Eston Cemetery, near Middlesbrough, Cleveland, where a monument was erected.

The return of *Vindictive* to Dover after the operation was a most inspiring sight, and miraculous that she was able to make port. The official photographs published in the press could not possibly shew the damage which she had received.

I visited the scene at Zeebrugge in the summer of 1920, and the *Thetis*, *Iphigenia* and *Invincible* were still in the position in which they were sunk, and it was possible to go aboard at low tide.

Lieutenant Hill was mentioned in despatches.

Lieutenant Dayrell-Reed DSO received a bar to his DSO at the second Ostend operation; in command of a coastal motor boat he carried out a successful attack on the pier ends, afterwards laying and maintaining good smoke screens close inshore throughout the remainder of the operation under heavy fire.

*

8

The Raid from Various Standpoints including the Air

From Mr S. C. Brown, Secretary of the Zeebrugge Association

Our leader the late Admiral Sir Roger Keyes (as he then was) was President of this Association and a founder member. He frequently expressed the wish that the annual Memorial Services at Zeebrugge should be carried on until the last man! This we shall endeavour to do. Of the original 997 members only 130 are now left, with an average age of 84!

Strangely enough the Belgian people make much more fuss of the action than do our own people; mainly because they regard Zeebrugge as the spark which lit the flame of freedom for Belgium.

*

From Mr F. J. Rickson: the effect on morale in France

... I was at the time of the Zeebrugge operation serving with the 1st Battalion Royal Inniskilling Fusiliers, 36 Ulster Division as a machine gunner. We had been heavily involved in the German offensive of 21st March 1918, and were desperately holding on in the Ypres Salient. We knew nothing about the raid on Zeebrugge which took place on 23rd April 1918, but I came to learn of this splendid operation sometime afterwards when I became a casualty, and found myself in a military hospital in France. The Zeebrugge raid was hailed as a great naval feat, and one that could shorten the war, but above all, more or less put a stop to the sinking of our supply ships, carrying food, and vital war supplies. The effect of the raid, 'bottled' up the U-boats already in the harbour, and prevented the U-boats which were out at sea from getting in, this action virtually put an end to the U-boat peril operating against this country.

*

From Colonel J. G. M. Stamp: training after the war

... I was *not* there, but between the wars this episode was a standard work used in tuition at the Coast Artillery School formerly at Shoeburyness, Essex. I attended an Instructors' course there in 1934, and the name of the famous Captain Carpenter, VC, RN, is indelibly imprinted in my mind, as are the names of the two Mersey paddle steamers *Iris* and *Daffodil*, which with bows head on to the side of the *Vindictive* went full-steam ahead to keep her alongside the Mole, while troops threw up grappling irons to hold ladders with which they scaled up on to the Mole.

Meanwhile a small submarine was wedged between the piles supporting a small bridge which connected the Mole to the shore 'stub', and there blown up, and some German troops hurriedly sent up on bicycles rode into the water, not seeing the gap in the dark.

*

From Mrs Winifred Miller: the ultimate cost

I'm nearly eighty now but one of the most poignant memories of my youth concerns a boy who was at Zeebrugge. He was not a special friend and I didn't know his family but he was a member of our youth club. His name was Percy Biden.

We were dancing one Saturday evening and I wished him Many Happy Returns of his birthday. He was to be twenty-one on the following Thursday.

'Wait until I get there,' he said. And he didn't. He died, of wounds received at the battle, during the next few days. He knew he might.

Half the young boys from that youth club never returned from the War. And they were very young.

*

From Mrs D. Garrod

I cannot lay claim to being very closely associated with the Zeebrugge raid, but in about 1908, while on a visit to my uncle, who was at that time a fleet surgeon in charge of the Royal Naval Hospital at Great Yarmouth, I became friendly with a very charming and high-spirited boy called Dallas Brooks, who was the son of the Naval chaplain at the hospital. We spent many hours cavorting at the local skating-rink – where Dallas was a constant source of danger to the other skaters by his antics! A few years later the same fearless daring and courage was in evidence at Zeebrugge – when he was awarded the DSO.

Lieutenant Reginald Dallas Brooks' citation (*Vindictive*) for the DSO read: 'He imbued his men with the highest degree of devotion to duty. The manner in which the howitzer in its exposed position on the quarter deck was used under his personal direction was very fine.' He was specially promoted to Acting Captain.

*

From Mrs J. H. Barnes: Security

Mine is a very humble memory, but I think you might be interested – even if it is not material worth recording in your book.

When leaving the Royal Naval School my one ambition was to join the WRNS. This was possible, and at the time of the Zeebrugge attack I was attached to the Seamen's Regulations office at Chatham Barracks.

In a huge ledger I was entering the names of men with the ships to which they were being drafted. On collecting a new batch of names from the Chief Petty Officer the letters SSV instead of HMS appeared. I remember saying 'Chief, *SSV* – are they passenger ships?' He just said, 'Never mind m'dear – enter 'em up.'

It was a few days later that I knew I had entered the names of those splendid men bound for Zeebrugge, and that SSV stood for Secret Service Vessels.

*

From Mrs J. Gardiner: an air observer in 202 Squadron RAF, in a DH4

My cousin, Leonard Timmins, DFC, who died about fifteen months ago, took part as an observer in the raid on Zeebrugge. He was shot down into the sea and subsequently taken prisoner. I believe he spent some months in a camp in Russia and remained in that country to take part in what he referred to as 'The Churchill War' after the end of the Great War.

I recall him saying that the worst part of being brought down into the sea was when he broke his front teeth, pulling off his gloves.

He was awarded the Flying Cross, but I do not know for what action.

*

From Dr W. Timmins about the same incident

My father served as an observer in 202 Squadron RAF and did reconnaissance in the Zeebrugge area before and after the raid, being shot down into the sea and captured two days after the raid and remaining a POW until the end of the War.

The aircraft in which he was an observer was a DH4 – he was awarded the DFC in 1918, I think about the time of the raid. I remember seeing some old aerial photos he had of the sunken blockships but when he remarried and moved house these pictures disappeared.

*

From Mr A. H. Savage – in a DH9

The Royal Naval Air Service had a few squadrons of land-based aeroplanes lent to co-operate with the Army – and known as the Naval wing. I was flying DH9s (daylight bombers) with No 11 Naval Squadron (renumbered 211 after the Royal Air Force came into being on 1st April 1918) operating from an aerodrome near Dunkirk.

In the very early hours of 23rd April we were hauled out of bed and took off for destination unknown led by Flight Commander Ireland (a Canadian). We flew in V formation, each machine carrying twelve 16 lb bombs. I had only eight bombs and a camera and flew behind and 200 feet above the other five. We flew out to sea – half way to Dover, climbing trying to gain height – we normally tried to get to 14,000-15,000 before crossing the lines but on this occasion the leader's engine was ropey and we turned inland at only 12,000 feet – towards Zeebrugge.

When he fired his Very pistol we all dropped our bombs together – on the Mole – apparently to harass repairs. The formation split up and we beetled out to sea to get out of the anti-aircraft fire – which was very heavy – and every machine in the formation was a bit peppered. But we all got back safely.

It is quite possible that some of the photos which I later saw published in newspapers – showing the damage the Navy had done – were taken by my machine.

*

From Mr L. Brett: No 6 Squadron RNAS

In April 1918 I was a 1st class air mechanic in No 6 Squadron RNAS stationed at Dunkirk for the particular purpose of bombing the port of Zeebrugge. We were equipped with the long distance bombers DH 9, the aim being to distract the enemy while HMS *Vindictive* was shelling the harbour as part of the combined services operation.

You may be interested to know that the battle-scarred White Ensign from HMS *Vindictive* hangs in Rye Church. I visited the church last year and touched the flag. The church itself is most interesting, and well worth a visit.

*

From Mr A. C. Kilburn

In the First World War I was in the RNAS and I was stationed on the Western Front near Nancy. We carried out long distance night bombing raids into Germany in our Handley Pages. Towards the end of the war, I and several other pilots were sent back to England to Bircham

Newton in Norfolk. A few huge four engined super HPs had just been made – the V 1500 – and with these it was intended to bomb Berlin. The Armistice came and it never was bombed.

In th spring of 1919 I was the junior pilot in one of these machines with which we tried to do a non-stop record flight London (Manston) – Madrid. The weather prevented it from being a non-stop flight. After several weeks in Spain we tried to do it Madrid–London non-stop; however over the Bay of Biscay the machine started to disintegrate at 5,000 feet (probably owing to the heat in Spain). Mercifully we got down safely and were rescued by fishing boats. My senior pilot on this trip was C. H. Darley DSC, DFC – a brilliant HP pilot – we were also at Bircham Newton together. He was at the northern end of the Western Front and I *think* his squadron there was 214 but I am not sure. For the Zeebrugge raid he blew up the lock gates and got the DSC. Our HPs were not very speedy – about 70-20 m.p.h. – and I know from personal experience that the fire from the defences could be very unpleasant, as I am sure it must have been for Darley on this raid.

Very sadly Darley was burned to death when he crashed in a Vickers-Vimy which he was piloting. It happened at Bracciano near Rome on 29th September 1919.

*

From Captain A. J. Coulthard: preliminary reconnaissance

I am no doubt a trifle biased but it seems to me that insufficient justice has been done to my kinsman the late Lieutenant Robert Coulthard (and Lieutenant J. D. Fysh) in every account I have seen of the Zeebrugge raid except possibly the Air Ministry publication *A Short History of the Royal Air Force* (1929) which for a number of reasons dealt very briefly with this epic of the Royal Naval Air Service.

I have been informed that had it not been for the almost synchronised phasing out of the RNAS and the removal of its personnel from the Royal Navy almost from that very day, an award for gallantry would almost certainly have been made and the event have received more subsequent publicity in that so much hinged upon the report these two men obtained. I think I am correct in saying that much of the beneficial effect of the raid was the result of this report.

On a personal note Robert Coulthard was later in 1918 forced down at sea whilst flying a Special Mission and was reported dead and a Memorial Service was held for him at his parish church. He was in fact picked up by the Germans and eventually repatriated on 13th December 1918. He used to carry a report of the Memorial Service in his pocket. He later became a pioneer of African Game Preserves and died in 1961 in Nigeria.

*

From Miss J. Watts: Admiral Keyes' personal reconnaissance

In case it is of interest, you may like to know that the late Captain Alick V. Bowater, RNAS, was the pilot who took Admiral Sir Roger Keyes on his reconnaissance flight before the Zeebrugge operation.

The Admiral insisted on seeing the whole area in spite of heavy anti-aircraft fire which made the flight extremely hazardous even to the final landing in adverse weather conditions at (I believe) Dover.

I do know that for many years Captain Bowater attended the Reunion Dinner on St George's Day and, I understood, was the only airman to have that privilege.

*

Extracts from the diary and notes of Sub-Lieutenant G. McCoul, later Surgeon Captain McCoul. The diary is informative on the preparations and atmosphere beforehand. HMS Swift, a destroyer, was involved in the first Ostend operation.

I was very young, eighteen and two months when I joined HMS *Swift* from the Grand Fleet, and I find it very difficult to concentrate on Zeebrugge-Ostend especially as the night in question was not of as much interest to me as the abortive night of 17th April was, and in view of the fact that we were mined on 7th May and excessively damaged, just before we were to be Admiral's flagship for the second attack on Ostend.

Furthermore to anyone in the Dover Patrol for any length of time, Zeebrugge and Ostend were just another bit of excitement in a long period of more or less constant excitement in our forays against the Hun.

I should explain some of the terms used. Dark-night patrol was usually worked by *Swift* out of Dover and extended from just on dark to, say, eight o'clock. The Daylight Patrol or Coast Patrol was worked from Dunkerque and might be either by day (usually) or by night. Seatime was enormous. 'The Roads' was where we lay when we were at Dunkerque. (I have spelt the town this way throughout. It seems to have become anglicised.) About half-a-mile from shore. Very rarely in harbour.

We did more sea-time than perhaps was conducive to good health, and lack of sleep was almost as big an enemy as the Germans. I note that I did 137 days censoring and censored 11,088 letters and 601 parcels in that time. This was the only job I disliked.

The piece on the Zeebrugge and Ostend operation was written while on leave after the mining.

(Although only eighteen he had already passed *2nd* MB.)
(Comments in italics are notes later added by Surgeon McCoul.)

Joined *Swift*. Then on Dark Night Patrol. 11.11.17.

6th December: Just finished boiler cleaning, suppose to have night off when Action Stations, 'Weigh Anchor', (*an unusual event : submarine passing down Channel.*) Full ahead, out of harbour – out all night – saw nothing, In again – straight out to Dunkerque to pick up Duke of Westminster (Armoured Cars) and Churchill.

12th December: Up the coast on Patrol. Sank 7 loose mines. German aircraft which fussed about overhead. Didn't drop anything so we didn't bother them.

Apparently our only 6 pdr anti-aircraft gun jams at the sixth shot and we don't like to start anything with it.

11.50 a.m. Six German destroyers were sighted and closing to 10,000 yards we engaged. Both their and our first were wide and then they suddenly got the range. (*Miranda, Afridi* and French destroyer had left us to lay a buoy.) We got a salvo of three about 30 yards off our starboard beam to start with, then as the other ships were getting it just as hot as we were, the *Minos* altered course and the Hun concentrated on the point of turn. The first salvo there was just over the *Minos*, the second barely short of *North Star* and as our Captain turned late we got a salvo of 5 instead of 3 which got us about 10 yards astern and shook us up somewhat. Then the German shore batteries started with heavy stuff and we cleared off after shipping a few pieces. No casualties. They had 7 seaplanes observing which gave us some anxiety. Back to Dunkerque and lay in 'Roads' just in time to see a pretty good German air-raid after Dinner. Ring side seats with the odd one falling round us and a number of Duds.

13th December: Day-Light Patrol. Up the coast and ran right into the Huns only a few hundred yards away coming out of a fog-bank. They used shrapnel which was unpleasant. They made good shooting and loosed up two torpedoes which missed. For some reason the Commodore broke off the engagement although we had twice their number.

Later I learned the reason was that we were fighting over a minefield and they were not.

Up tonight with the mine layers *Ariel, Telemachus, Meteor, Ferret* and *Legion*. We apparently don't want any trouble with the Hun with all these mines, at any rate before they are laid.

14th December: Huge stunt. *Afridi* got lost and while lost dropped 3 depth charges and claimed a submarine.

'Huge Stunt': I seem to remember referred to the opinion on board us that a ship had no business claiming a victim when they didn't know where they were. They were well out of line. Visibility very bad.

10th January 1918: No entry since 14.12 but the following is noted under this date:

Our 6 inch gun went out of action and we were supposed to be going to Chatham for a new one but in the event we laid off for a few days and had a nice new one put in.

On 18th December we did gunnery and torpedo firing with the Broke off Folkestone and then went on Dark Night Patrol for a few nights and then back to Dunkerque and on patrol up the coast. We had a scrap with German torpedo boats and got it in the neck, a hit on the starboard propeller which meant a visit to Chatham.

14th February: German destroyer raid on Dover. Some shells in the town. On patrol just then and quite near. Saw the *Kosmos*, a trawler blown up but we could not partake as it was out of our patrol area.

A ship on Patrol could not leave its area to enter another area. Otherwise would be confusion.

15th February: Dover bombarded by a submarine. This was in our area and we rushed in. Saw nothing.

18th February: Belgian coast Daylight Patrol. Bombarded Ostend and were bombarded in return.

19th February: Up the coast to intercept reported destroyer reinforcements from Zeebrugge at midnight. Nothing seen.

21st February: Night patrol. Firing near Dunkerque. Air-Raid ashore.

5th March: Patrols out of Dover since 25.2.18. Nothing much to note. Then back to Dunkerque, for Coast patrol.

On 28/2 in running action with TBDs in the morning and later in the day with aircraft who bombed us. No hits. Aiming very bad from 6,000 feet.

Again later to look for a missing airman, one of ours. Found his lifebelt and a floating petrol tank.

5th March: Return to Dover after a long and weary spell of exceptionally bad weather for the last month.

15th March: Nothing much doing. 6 days boiler cleaning and laid off on account of thick fog.

27th March: Not much time to write anything lately. Most of the time at Dunkerque. A few nights ago we were on Eastern Barrage and when we came back we found there had been a raid down the coast by 18 Hun destroyers.

Botha and *Morris* were lying at anchor in the roads with three Frenchmen. At the alarm slipped anchor and pursued up West Deep and then to Middlekirk Bank and came across 7 Germans returning to Ostend. *Botha* rammed one and claimed to have torpedoed another. The *Morris* lost *Botha* and came across another German TBD and torpedoed her. She then encountered an abandoned German TBD. This was sunk by gunfire by *Morris* and the French. The Frenchman *Meyl* arriving late out of harbour then arrived and 'all *Gloire* and Garlic' torpedoed the first ship she saw. This was the *Botha*.

It was said at the time that 'Botha' officers on the Bridge fought the action in their pyjamas.

I believe the 'Meyl' towed 'Botha' back to harbour.

In the afternoon we were up the coast with *Terror* who put 39 x 15 inch into Ostend. As a retaliation the Germans bombarded Dunkerque for three days in succession with 'Moaning Minnie'. A very long range weapon. There have also been six Dunkerque air raids in as many nights.

We have also been helping in sweeping a minefield which appears to have been one of ours which seems queer unless its getting ready for something else.

Just back from last night's effort which was a sweep into the Bight with the Harwich Striking Force to intercept reinforcements for Zeebrugge and Ostend. Two of our destroyers mined. The *Exe* and the *Ariel*.

One of better memories: dawn – an ocean full of destroyers at speed in a calm sea.

16th April: Not much time to write. We have had three days boiler cleaning and returned to Dunkerque.

On 17th we went up the coast as usual. This time with four monitors and bombarded Ostend for thirty minutes. Fire was returned but no one was hit.

Later German TBDs bombarded Adenkerke.

20th April: Captured the wreckage of a German seaplane and a caged dead pigeon. Weather rotten. Air raid on us while in the Roads.

Comedy: Some miles away two German seaplanes were observing. One had engine failure and the other came down beside him and our 6 inch gun opened up. As we got nearer and our firing must have been getting some near misses we could see that the second pilot was taking the first on board. Our shooting then became worse the nearer we got to them. Finally the two of them taxied off out of sight leaving the wreckage behind. Our RNR midshipman later upbraiding the gun layer for his bad shooting, was told: 'Gentlemen of the Royal Navy do not shoot sitting ducks . . . Sir!'

21st April: Sea gone down. Wind changed to SE Barometer steady.

At this point I did a separate entry for the Zeebrugge and Ostend operations. Volunteers manned the blockships, the 'Vindictive', the submarine 'C3', the 'Iris' and 'Daffodil', etc., etc., but at no time as far as I am aware was the Dover Patrol (or the ship's company of the 'Swift') asked to volunteer. I think Commander Amedroz's opinion the correct one (he was Captain of the 'Swift') which was more or less that while others could volunteer for anything they chose our job was simply to carry on our simple duty as we were doing every day and night and to attempt to ensure satisfactory conditions for a successful conclusion.

Zeebrugge and Ostend Operation

On my return to Chatham in February after repairs, there were one or two obsolete cruisers being filled with concrete and old iron, which filled me with curiosity. On enquiry the Captain told me that it was for 'some horrible stunt up the coast'. The next day he went to Dover and on return said that we were to be the Admiral's flagship. *Decision not carried out as we had too deep a draught and were too big a target. The 'Warwick' was the finally chosen ship.* That was all the information he could give us at the time. We then returned to Dover and went on to Dunkerque and bombarded the coast and did other things presumably already mentioned. He also informed us that he had been told that everyone had 'volunteered' but that he had said that as this was part of our normal duty we had no need to 'volunteer' and that he considered his ship's company to be well tried professionals.

I felt very proud at that moment to know that I really 'belonged'. *As I have done ever since.*

The first Ostend operation was a dark calm night with a slight breeze from the NE. As we had been kicked out of being flagship we had been given the job of taking care of the smoke making launches and patrolling 2½-3 miles from the beach to stop any of their TBDs making trouble. We were over their minefield most of the time.

The bombardment began just as we reached our patrol line. It was terrific and seemed to be all up and down the coast, but then as far as we were concerned there was a lull. It was a fine sight. Although the smoke hid detail from us, the whole area seemed lit up. Everything banging away and star shells at each end of our patrol line, which was Zeebrugge at one end (or near) and Ostend at the other.

We could see the motor launches inshore putting up their smoke and apparently doing all right.

One of them suddenly put up a couple of red Very lights and we went in to help. There was no sign of them when we got there, *three bodies fetched up on Malo beach two days later*. So we put up some smoke and came away, while a few machine guns opened up and their bullets winged around but no one was hit. *At this point before we made our smoke I could see with the naked eye some barbed wire on the beach.*

It was beginning to get day-light and as we had not received any withdrawal signal we swept down to Ostend at full speed to see what was happening there. We were suddenly into smoke again and almost as quickly out possibly only about 2,000 yards from the end of the piers at Ostend. *We had to do a 180° turn at speed. I remember seeing the gun crews ashore running to the guns and the Captain on the bridge yelling, 'Inch by bloody inch by heck'. All their shots were 'overs'.*

They gave us it pretty hot but we got out again all right. We returned to Dunkerque and found that owing to the wind blowing the smoke back the whole show had been a failure.

Ostend was a failure and a second raid was planned and we were to be flagship. But we were mined somewhere off Griz-Nez on Eastern Patrol with two dead and 11 wounded.

7th May: 2.33 a.m. we struck a mine with our port propeller guard. The explosion blew in the port side of the wardroom and the subs cabin aft (*one continuous hole*). The Sub (Nicholson) was off duty, in his cabin and asleep. Ditto self and Mr Coughlan (Commissioned Mechanician), The Gunner (Mr Turner) was on duty as after watch. A. B. Robson was with the ammunition party whose action stations was the ward-room. Nicholson and Robson killed outright and instantaneously. Coming back on one propeller we were all over the place and finally bumped Dover Pier which concertinaed 15 feet of our bows.

I don't remember being blown up. Nicholson and Mr Coughlan, Mr Turner and self inhabited the same cabin flat. When I came to (*I was out for seconds only I think*), I was sitting amongst a lot of broken glass and the debris and conscious only of a tinkling sound still being heard.

It is interesting to note that in the 2nd World War I was immediately above the point of impact of the torpedo which sank the 'Ark Royal' and I was deluged with yellow water which missed me going up but even filled my jacket pockets coming down. I was conscious all the time and heard the same sound 'tinkling' like broken glass being poured out of a bucket. I was on the flight deck a considerable height above the explosion (say 20 yards). Before the 'Ark' I was in HQ Air Raid Shelter when what was said to be a 500 lb. bomb hit us so near that a tongue of flame came round two right angles into the shelter. Apart from a 'whoosh' and heavy pressure I heard no bang and I have come to the conclusion that if you are near enough to an explosion you hear no bang.

The first thing I saw was Mr Coughlan who had been blown out of his bunk (like myself) into the Cabin Flat. We both 'came to' together, grinned rather idiotically and asked each other simultaneously what had happened. Neither of us being able to answer we went very shakily up on deck. No one was there immediately and we just hung on to each other, breathing fresh air which seemed very good. Then the gunner came and called out our names (it was pitch dark) to see if we were O.K. On the sub's name being called we let out a yell and went down the hatch with a rush, only to find the cabin blown in and Nicholson dead and badly mutilated about the head.

I could not get at my medical supplies as my cabin was smashed up and the medical chest was jammed against other things. The gunner however got me a reserve supply up forward and we lifted the sub into the cabin flat and I started to cover his head up as it was such a horrible sight and I thought it better to get it done straight away before the hands should see it.

Brains and bits of flesh were blown across the cabin flat all over the wreckage of my own cabin.

About half way through this someone yelled out that I was wanted. I rushed down to where the Bosun had collected the wounded (all 5 members other than A. B. Robson). I did them up as best I could. Mr Coughlan then came down and told me that Robson was missing, so we went down into the Ward-Room to have a look around.

We found the port-side of the ward-room blown in and the place full of water. Everything was smashed to atoms and there was no sign of Robson. While I was still searching Coughlan started a pump and we then flooded the magazine and shell room. Still not finding Robson I concluded he was in bits and reported to the bridge to the Captain.

Comedy: this is not in my Diary but I remember it well. At this point I got on to the upper deck still wondering what had happened. Still dark and I had lost my torch. I was aware of what seemed to me to be another ship with a sailor swinging a stable lantern. I shouted up to him, 'What ship are you?' only to get the reply, 'The 17th West Kents.' I am not sure about the 17th. It may have been some other number but he was a soldier on duty on Dover Breakwater.

This done I went down aft and finished cleaning up the sub and had him put on a stretcher and put him on deck. I then, having obtained a torch went back to the Ward Room and began another search for Robson. I found a leg cut off at the knee still in its seaboot and that was all.

During all this we had been making home on one propeller. I don't know for how long. Suddenly water came rushing through the hole in the ward-room about knee high, I thought we were sinking and dropped the leg and rushed for the upper deck. When I was about half way up the ladder there was a terrific crash and I came down again with a hell of a bump and I began to wonder where I was, what I was doing and whether I was going to drown as water was swilling about all over. I heard Bill, the Navigator's bull-terrier, whining and realised he was shut in the Navigator's cabin which was only a yard or two away. I was tempted to leave him – he was no friend of mine – but in the event I went back for him. I found him even more frightened than I was. I had no trouble with him. As soon as I opened the cabin door he dived past me and was first up the ladder which was askew and hanging by only one nut. At this moment I thought we had been either mined or torpedoed or in collision. Actually steering badly we had been carried by the tide bang in to the breakwater and stove in our bows to a considerable extent. While we were fiddling about shoring up forward and trying to hit the harbour entrance I discovered we had more injured. Chiefly men from the Dynamo Room whose faces had hit the dials, etc., as we hit the breakwater.

I bound them up while we were getting to our buoy and got a pumping vessel alongside and I took my wounded ashore.

More comedy: While we were doing this the Chief Engineer (Eng. Comm. Hughes RN) came running along the upper deck calling, 'Close all water-tight doors.' Again we were in the CPO's Mess and the Hatch Cover was slammed down on us. Nobody liked this at all. The Bo'sun was helping me and he suddenly whispered to me, 'Where's yer 'at Sir.'

I said I didn't know, he then said 'I'd find it if I was you, yer 'airs fair standing up on end.'

It is a curious fact that our Midshipman whose cabin was forrard under the Bridge slept through the Mine episode and only woke up when we hit the breakwater.

Repairs took 11 weeks and I got a very long leave.

26th August: Still at Dunkerque. Up the coast with Commodore, a few other destroyers and small monitors in attendance on *Terror* and *General Wolfe* to try out *Wolfe*'s new 18 inch gun on Ostend. Weather too bad. Two depth charges. Saw nothing.

31st August: Up the coast 04.30. Off Ostend we were observed from the beach and were bombarded for a short while. Their first four were near misses on the *Wolfe*. *Termagant* division had to put up smoke and hide everything. Weather prevents shoot.

8th September: In Roads at Dunkerque. Signal came to 'Weigh' but Captain and No 1 ashore. Great excitement. I thought the Huns must have been sighted but the signal was cancelled and a CMB was sent to pick up an airman who had come down in the sea. Left for Dover with Mails.

11th September: Suddenly demobilised to continue medical studies. Last words of Commander Amedroz, my much admired Captain, 'So you are going off to exams. Remember knowledge and wisdom are not the same things and when you face your examiners it might help if you remember that any bloody fool can ask questions and you'll need both to outwit them.'

*

From Mr W. E. Gray: 213 Squadron, After the Raid

In daylight, following the Zeebrugge attack, I was one of five pilots in Sopwith Camels from 213 Squadron, sent to low-bomb large sheds on the landward end of the Mole. Each carried a 112 lb. bomb, to be released without bomb-sights in a low dive – and each having had a practice run at free-hand bombing on our airfield.

Approaching from seaward, we swung in from the landward end and dived, in line ahead, to release our bombs at a few hundred feet above the Mole; nearly all were direct hits on the sheds, and we made our way out to sea again without getting damaged.

Our squadron was attached to the Royal Navy, Dunkirk, throughout 1918, commanded by Squadron Commander Major Ronald Graham DSO, DSC.

*

From E. A. Steel – After the battle

I am afraid that I am unable to contribute anything directly connected with that heroic attack on the Mole at Zeebrugge, as I was but a thirteen-year old schoolboy living in Rochester at that time, but I have every reason to remember that historic occasion.

As in the case of many other boys, I had a relative serving in the Navy and it so happened he was temporarily based at Chatham at that time. He was serving on a minelayer then being fitted out. On a visit to my home he invited me alone to visit his ship and have tea with him on board! Needless to say I did not hesitate to accept the invitation and so, one Sunday afternoon, I proudly accompanied him through the Dock-yard gates – and being saluted too by the sentry on duty – to visit the minelayer. I now come to the point: on the way I saw many ships in dock, but at one point I saw two, or perhaps three, ships in the most dreadful condition that one could imagine. Funnels peppered, a bridge torn completely away and gaping holes in the hull. One part of a hull was almost torn away from the other and it was amazing to me that the vessels could have survived to find their way back to Chatham. The scene is still impressed on my memory. It was then that I was told the ships had seen action at a place called Zeebrugge.

My next exciting experience was to go on board one of HM's mine-layers. It was all the more exciting to see the mines already in position, so it would not be long before the ship would receive orders to patrol the North Sea.

It was a jolly good tea!

*

9

The Second Ostend Raid

Contrary to popular belief the second Ostend Raid –on 9th/10th May – achieved a fair measure of success, although the cost was high. However the planning was not nearly as precise as it had been for Zeebrugge. An example of this was the fact that there was initially no experienced navigator on the *Vindictive*. Lieutenant Sir John Alleyne, then serving on the monitor the *Lord Clive*, realised the deficiency and as he himself had an excellent knowledge of the area, volunteered for the post. As a navigator on a monitor which was accustomed to station itself off the Belgian coast while it bombarded the interior, Lieutenant Alleyne had become well-versed in the ways of the tides, the shoals and the Germans. He was allowed to volunteer but then Rear-Admiral Boyle, who was Admiral Keyes' Chief of Staff, ordered that Alleyne should be dropped off at Dunkirk. Alleyne, who contrived not to receive the order (knowing it was pending) kept out of the way until *Vindictive* set off.

He was astonished to find that *Vindictive*'s gyro compass was out-of-date, there was no up-to-date sounding apparatus on board either, and that no one else had adequate experience in navigation. Lacking the proper apparatus, he had to time his progress up the coast by his own watch. He still owns it – but it stopped when he fell into the sea after he had been wounded. However, timing progress in this way alerted him to the fact that the Germans had altered the buoys. Apparently it was a common practice by both sides during the naval war and he fully expected it. Unfortunately no one had expected it on the first Ostend raid.

However, in spite of all these problems Alleyne brought the *Vindictive* right into the harbour. As they were within a few feet of the harbour wall, on which the Germans had heavy machine-guns, the decks of the *Vindictive* were swept by constant streams of bullets. It was also subject to heavier bombardment. Alleyne was wounded and pulled back into the conning tower by Godsal and Crutchley. (A ship may be steered from bridge, conning tower, or aft.) The bridge was no longer useable and

Godsal stepped outside the conning tower to take a look at the scene and was instantly killed. *Vindictive* had reached the vital part of the channel and was blocking as much as one ship could. Unfortunately her sister ship *Sappho* was not there to block the other side as she had fallen out through engine trouble. Nevertheless, as mentioned earlier, *Vindictive* was left in a position where she would cause the maximum inconvenience to the Germans.

As soon as Crutchley and Bury had blown the charges on *Vindictive* and she had settled down into her place, abandon ship was ordered and a most difficult evacuation then took place. CPO Reed carried the wounded Alleyne and put him into a skiff were there were already two other wounded men. *ML 254* then came alongside *Vindictive*. She was commanded by Lieutenant G. H. Drummond whose thigh was promptly broken by the German fire which was still landing on *Vindictive*. Drummond stayed at his post, even after being wounded twice more while *Vindictive* was searched for survivors. None were found. With her cargo of dead and wounded picked up before she limped out through the fog. There she was picked up by Admiral Keyes' flagship, the destroyer *Warwick*. Hardly were the complement of the battered ML transferred to *Warwick* than the latter hit a mine. Fortunately she was not badly holed enough to make her sink and lashed to *Velox* and towed by *Whirlwind* she too limped back to Dover.

Meanwhile two other MLs were still searching the area for possible survivors. One was *ML 276* under Lieutenant Bourke. It came in close to *Vindictive* and there found the skiff, which had now capsized in the swell, but still had Alleyne and the other two wounded men grimly clinging to it. *ML 276* was hit by yet another shell as she crawled out, full of bullet holes, and with many wounded on board. She was eventually taken in tow by the monitor *Prince Eugene*. Bourke, together with Drummond and Crutchley, received the VC.

*

From Captain R. D. King-Harman DSO, DSC: The 'Vindictive' at Ostend

I missed your letter in the *Telegraph*, but am glad to hear from your letter to me received today you are undertaking the writing of a book on Zeebrugge. There is plenty of room for an account such as you propose of what I still regard as among the greatest feats of arms of the Royal Navy.

I am sorry to disappoint you in adding anything to your book. My ship was one of the destroyer escorts and as such we really played only an onlooker's role. I do not feel I can tell you anything of much interest or value. I do not know if your book will include anything about the second and successful attack on Ostend, the first blocking attempt at the same time as the Zeebrugge one having failed. The Zeebrugge affair has always had the limelight and rather obscured the second Ostend operation when the harbour there was successfully blocked by the *Vindictive*. Most people at the time thought it was suicide to try and repeat the blocking only three weeks later. If your account does happen to include Ostend, I think you could get something of interest out of a friend of mine, then Lieutenant Sir John Alleyne, now Captain Sir John Alleyne DSO. He volunteered for the job of navigator and got the ship right into the desired spot between the piers before he was badly wounded and unable to move. The captain, whose name I forget, was killed and the only other surviving officer, Lieutenant Crutchley, got the surviving men together with Alleyne, into the motor launch detailed for the job. Crutchley, now Admiral Sir Victor Crutchley VC, was given the VC.

If the operation is being dealt with by you, Jack Alleyne could give you some very interesting details of it, if he could be induced to talk, which I rather doubt.

I saw him last year, when he was active and hearty at the age of 87, when he told me that he had been obliged to give up hunting at 86 because he had become too blind to see the fences. Crutchley is still going, but I do not know his address. He is a nice chap and if you wanted any information from him I am sure he would give it to you.

米

From Lieutenant Commander J. H. McGivering: Drummond VC

I was very interested in your letter in the *Daily Telegraph* today, as my late father John McGivering (1884-1971) was in the RNVR in the 1914 war and at one time commanded HM *ML 339*.

He and my mother knew Lieutenant Commander G. H. Drummond VC, and all that I can recall of their activities is the story that he (Drummond) had beautiful manners and played the piano like an angel : the more he drank, the better his manners became, until he would say to father, 'I say. Mac. old man, I wonder if you would be so kind as to give me a hand to my cabin – I fear I cannot walk !'

When Drummond went to get his VC, from King George V the King asked what he did in civilian life. Drummond said, 'I was a professional invalid, Sir !' which caused the King to roar with laughter, much to the horror of the courtiers. That is the essence of father's stories, and he used to say that Drummond had fallen out of his pram as a child and broken or dislocated his neck, with the result that he was unable to turn it, and was obliged to turn his whole body to see left or right.

I served under Captain Sir John Alleyne, Bart. at Freetown in about 1943 and occasionally met him on business but did not discover that he went aboard *Vindictive* to swing compasses (he was navigator of a ship that now escapes me,* but it is in the Despatches) and stowed away (if I remember rightly) and went on the raid.

Gordon S. Maxwell was a poet when he was not dropping smoke-floats from *ML 314* and gave father a copy of his *The Rhymes of A Motor Launch* in 1927, published by Dent in 1919. It is on the table beside me now and contains many items sung or recited at a concert in HMS *Arrogant* at Dover the night before they sailed for the raid.

My mother, 90 last October, used to say that she and my late sister went aboard either *Iris* or *Daffodil* at Portsmouth after they returned from the raid, and they saw sand on the decks to soak up the blood but I fear she does not now remember the incident.

Father was at Wick at the time of the raid, but knew most of the officers in MLs. We still have the coloured print of Wilkinson's *ML 193* over the fireplace in the sitting-room and a (dirty) white Ensign that flew in *339*.

Lieutenant-Commander Drummond was specially promoted at Zeebrugge for his work as leader of a smoke unit, and won the VC at Ostend. *Lieutenant Gordon Maxwell* was mentioned in despatches.

*

From F. M. Macfarlane: the fate of 'ML 254'

The Distinguished Service Medal was awarded to my father for service on the *MB 549* but my father was also on the *ML 254*. After the crew of the *Vindictive* were taken off, the *ML 254* had to be sunk as she was in a bad state and would have fallen into enemy hands. She was charged with explosives but before leaving her my father nipped down to the engine room to rescue his pipe and tobacco and also snatched a family photograph on his way up.

He carried a wounded officer to safety and was three times mentioned in despatches. All he received from the raid was a splinter in his thumb.

Chief Motor Mechanic A. M. Macfarlane was awarded the DSM at Ostend on 9th/10th May. He was mentioned in despatches for specially distinguished service; he had volunteered for dangerous rescue work. It

* The monitor, *The Lord Clive*.

was largely due to the magnificent manner in which he and his fellow shipmates carried out their duties that so many of the officers and men of the *Vindictive* were rescued.

*

From E. M. Selway: 'left for dead' (Ostend)

My father, Thomas Henry Knowles, was a member of the Royal Marine party which sank the *Vindictive* across the harbour. He is now dead, but I remember his account of the action.

He told me that he was one of a party of Marine volunteers which took part. After the ship was sunk he and the others were stranded on a mole, being shelled by gun emplacements on the other moles. He was very badly wounded, and was put in the hold of the rescue ship with the bodies of those who had been killed, as he also was thought to be dead. On his return the King and Queen visited him in hospital.

The commander of the operation demanded the VC for all those taking part, but King George V would not accede to this, and so my father and his comrades took part in a ballot for one VC and he did not get it.

*

From J. Lambert: an interesting point about the change in the wind

My father Rawsthorne Procter took part in the raid as a lieutenant in command of a ML (No 556).

Unfortunately I can give you very little information – my father died in 1946 – and my father never told us a great deal about it – apart from the fact that he made the smoke screen. He used to wax indignant about others occupied in the same task, they failed to notice the change in direction of the wind or to correct their position for laying the smoke screen accordingly.

He was awarded the DSC for his efforts – he never missed the annual St George's day dinner.

Lieutenant Proctor's citation read : 'This officer was in charge of a section of motor launches screening monitors during the bombardment of the Ostend shore batteries. He exhibited conspicuous ability and initiative under heavy fire and materially contributed to the success of the operation.'

Glossary

VADP	Vice Admiral Dover Patrol
RNAS	Royal Naval Air Service
PMO	Principal Medical Officer
How	Howitzer
Focsle	Forecastle
F-top	Foretop
TBD	Torpedo Boat Destroyer
RMA	Royal Marine Artillery
RMLI	Royal Marine Light Infantry
ML	Motor Launch
CMB	Coastal Motor Boat

VESSELS AND CRAFT TAKING PART IN THE SIMULTANEOUS BLOCKING OPERATIONS AT ZEEBRUGGE AND OSTENDE

The Zeebrugge Enterprise
(a) *Special services during the oversea voyage*
Aerial Escort:
  61st Wing of Royal Air Force.
Other services:
  Special service vessel *Lingfield*. Motor Launches Nos 555, 557.

(b) *Offshore Forces*
Outer Patrol:
  Scout : *Attentive*
  Destroyers : *Scott, Ullswater, Teazer, Stork.*

Long-range Bombardment:
  Monitors : *Erebus, Terror.*
  Destroyers : *Termagant, Truculent, Manly.*

(c) *Inshore Forces*
Flagship:
  Destroyers : *Warwick* (Flag of Vice-Admiral R. J. B. Keyes).
Blockships:
  Light Cruisers : *Thetis, Intrepid, Iphigenia.*
Storming Vessels:
  Light Cruiser : *Vindictive.*
  Special vessels : *Iris, Daffodil.*
Attack on Viaduct:
  Submarines: *C1, C3,* and one picket boat.
Aerial Attack:
  Aircraft : 65th Wing, Royal Air Force.
Other Operations:
  Destroyers : *Phoebe, North Star, Trident, Mansfield, Whirlwind, Myngs, Velox, Morris, Moorsom, Melpomene.*

Motor Launches: Nos 79, 110, 121, 128, 223, 241, 252, 258, 262, 272, 280, 282, 308, 314, 345, 397, 416, 420, 422, 424, 513, 525, 526, 533, 549, 552, 558, 560, 561, 562.

Coastal Motor Boats: Nos 5, 7, 15, 16A, 17A, 21B, 23B, 24A, 25BD, 26B, 27A, 28A, 30B, 32A, 35A.

The Ostende Enterprise

(a) *Bombarding Forces*

Monitors: Marshal Soult, Lord Clive, Prince Eugene, General Craufurd, M.24, M.26, M.21.

Destroyers : *Mentor, Lightfoot, Zubian.*

Motor Launches : Nos 249, 448, 538, and three others.

French Destroyers and Torpedo Boats : *Lestin, Roux, Bouclier,* and Torpedo Boats Nos 1, 2, 3 and 34.

French Motor Launches : Nos 1, 2, 33, 34.

British Siege Guns in Flanders.

(b) *Inshore Forces:*

Blockships:

Light Cruisers : *Sirius, Brilliant.*

Destroyers:

Swift, Faulknor, Matchless, Mastiff, Afridi, Tempest, Tetrarch.

Motor Launches:

Nos 11, 16, 17, 22, 23, 30, 60, 105, 254, 274, 276, 279, 283, 429, 512, 532, 551, 556.

Coastal Motor Boats:

Nos 2, 4, 10, 12, 19, 20, 29A, 34A.

Covering Squadron for both Enterprises

Forces from Harwich:

Light Cruisers, seven.

Leaders, two.

Destroyers, fourteen.

CITATIONS FOR THE VICTORIA CROSS AWARD
23rd APRIL and 9th/10th MAY, 1918

Commander (Acting Captain) Alfred Francis Blakeney Carpenter, RN
For most conspicuous gallantry.

This officer was in command of *Vindictive*. He set a magnificent example to all those under his command by his calm composure when navigating mined waters, bringing his ship alongside the mole in darkness. When *Vindictive* was within a few yards of the mole the enemy started and maintained a heavy fire from batteries, machine guns and rifles on to the bridge. He showed most conspicuous bravery, and did much to encourage similar behaviour on the part of the crew, supervising the landing from the *Vindictive* on to the mole, and walking round the decks directing operations and encouraging the men in the most dangerous and exposed positions. By his encouragement to those under him, his power of command and personal bearing, he undoubtedly contributed greatly to the success of the operation.

Captain Carpenter was selected by the officers of the *Vindictive, Iris II* and *Daffodil,* and of the naval assaulting force to receive the Victoria Cross under Rule 13 of the Royal Warrant, dated the 29th January, 1856.

*

Lieutenant Richard Douglas Sandford, RN
For most conspicuous gallantry.

This officer was in command of Submarine C3, and most skilfully placed that vessel in between the piles of the viaduct before lighting his fuse and abandoning her. He eagerly undertook this hazardous enterprise, although well aware (as were all his crew) that if the means of rescue failed and he or any of his crew were in the water at the moment of the explosion, they would be killed outright by the force of such explosion. Yet Lieutenant Sandford disdained to use the gyro steering, which would have enabled him and his crew to abandon the submarine at a safe distance, and preferred to make sure, as far as was humanly possible, of the accomplishment of his duty.

Lieutenant Percy Thompson Dean, RNVR (Motor Launch 282)

For most conspicuous gallantry.

Lieutenant Dean handled his boat in a most magnificent and heroic manner when embarking the officers and men from the blockships at Zeebrugge. He followed the blockships in and closed *Intrepid* and *Iphigenia* under a constant and deadly fire from machine and heavy guns at point blank range, embarking over 100 officers and men. This completed, he was proceeding out of the canal, when he heard that an officer was in the water. He returned, rescued him, and then proceeded, handling his boat throughout as calmly as if engaged in a practice manoeuvre. Three men were shot down at his side whilst he conned his ship. On clearing the entrance to the canal the steering gear broke down. He manoeuvred his boat by the engines, and avoided complete destruction by steering so close in under the mole that the guns in the batteries could not depress sufficiently to fire on the boat. The whole of this operation was carried out under a constant machinegun fire at a few yards range. It was solely due to this officer's courage and daring that *ML 282* succeeded in saving so many valuable lives.

*

Captain Edward Bamford, DSO, RMLI

For most conspicuous gallantry.

This officer landed on the mole from *Vindictive* with numbers 5, 7 and 8 platoons of the marine storming force, in the face of great difficulties. When on the mole and under heavy fire, he displayed the greatest initiative in the command of his company and by his total disregard of danger showed a magnificent example to his men. He first established a strong point on the right of the disembarkation, and, when satisfied that that was safe, led an assault on a battery to the left with the utmost coolness and valour.

Captain Bamford was selected by the officers of the RMA and RMLI detachments to receive the Victoria Cross under Rule 13 of the Royal Warrant, dated the 29th January, 1856.

*

Sergeant Norman Augustus Finch, RMA

For most conspicuous gallantry.

Sergeant Finch was second in command of the pompoms and Lewis guns in the foretop of *Vindictive*, under Lieutenant Charles N. B. Rigby, RMA. At one period the *Vindictive* was being hit every few seconds, chiefly in the upper works, from which splinters caused many casualties.

It was difficult to locate the guns which were doing the most damage, but Lieutenant Rigby, Sergeant Finch and the Marines in the foretop, kept up a continuous fire with pompoms and Lewis guns, changing rapidly from one target to another, and thus keeping the enemy's fire down to some considerable extent.

Unfortunately two heavy shells made direct hits on the foretop, which was completely exposed to enemy concentration of fire. All in the top were killed or disabled except Sergeant Finch, who was, however, severely wounded; nevertheless he showed consummate bravery, remaining in his battered and exposed position. He once more got a Lewis gun into action, and kept up a continuous fire, harassing the enemy on the Mole, until the foretop received another direct hit, the remainder of the armament being then completely put out of action. Before the top was destroyed Sergeant Finch had done invaluable work, and by his bravery undoubtedly saved many lives.

This very gallant sergeant of the Royal Marine Artillery was selected by the 4th Battalion of Royal Marines, who were mostly Royal Marine Light Infantry, to receive the Victoria Cross under Rule 13 of the Royal Warrant dated 29th January, 1856.

*

Able Seaman Albert Edward McKenzie

For most conspicuous gallantry.

This rating belonged to B Company of seaman storming party. On the night of the operation he landed on the Mole with his machine-gun in the face of great difficulties and did very good work, using his gun to the utmost advantage. He advanced down the Mole with Lieutenant-Commander Harrison, who with most of his party was killed, and accounted for several of the enemy running from a shelter to a destroyer alongside the Mole. This very gallant seaman was severely wounded whilst working his gun in an exposed position.

Able Seaman McKenzie was selected by the men of the *Vindictive, Iris II* and *Daffodil* and of the naval assaulting force to receive the Victoria Cross under Rule 13 of the Royal Warrant dated the 29th January, 1856.

*

Lieutenant-Commander George Nicholson Bradford, RN

For most conspicuous gallantry at Zeebrugge on the night of 22nd-23rd April, 1918.

This officer was in command of the Naval storming parties embarked in *Iris II,* When *Iris II* proceeded alongside the Mole great difficulty was experienced in placing the parapet-anchors owing to the motion of the ship. An attempt was made to land by the scaling ladders before the ship was secured. Lieutenant Claude E. K. Hawkings managed to get one ladder in position and actually reached the parapet, the ladder being crushed to pieces just as he stepped off it. This very gallant young officer was last seen defending himself with his revolver. He was killed on the parapet.

Although securing the ship was not a part of his duties, Lieutenant-Commander Bradford climbed up the derrick which carried a large parapet-anchor and was rigged out over the port side. During the climb the ship was surging up and down and the derrick crashing on the Mole. Awaiting his opportunity he jumped with the parapet-anchor on to the Mole and placed it in position. Immediately after hooking on the parapet-anchor, Lieutenant-Commander Bradford was riddled with bullets from machine-guns and fell into the sea between the Mole and the ship. Attempts to recover his body failed.

Lieutenant-Commander Bradford's action was one of absolute self-sacrifice; without a moment's hesitation he went to certain death, recognising that in such an action lay the only possible chance of securing *Iris II* and enabling her storming parties to land.

*

Lieutenant-Commander Arthur Leyland Harrison, RN

For conspicuous gallantry at Zeebrugge on the night of 22nd-23rd April, 1918.

This officer was in immediate command of the Naval storming parties embarked in *Vindictive.* Immediately before coming alongside the Mole, Lieutenant-Commander Harrison was struck on the head by a fragment of shell which broke his jaw and knocked him senseless. Recovering consciousness, he proceeded on to the Mole and took over command of his party who were attacking the seaward end of the Mole. The silencing of the guns on the Mole head was of first importance and although in a position fully exposed to the enemy machine-gun fire, Lieutenant-Commander Harrison gathered his men together and led them to the attack.

He was killed at the head of his men, all of whom were either killed or wounded.

Lieutenant-Commander Harrison, although already severely wounded and undoubtedly in great pain, displayed indomitable resolution and courage of the highest order in pressing his attack, knowing as he did that any delay in silencing the guns might jeopardise the main object of the expedition, i.e. the blocking of the Zeebrugge-Bruges canal.

*

Lieutenant Victor Alexander Charles Crutchley, DSC, RN

This officer was in *Brilliant* in the unsuccessful attempt to block Ostend on the night of 22nd-23rd April, and at once volunteered for further effort.

He acted as First Lieutenant of *Vindictive* and worked with untiring energy fitting out that ship for further service. On the night of 9th-10th May, after his Commanding Officer had been killed and the second-in-command severely wounded, Lieutenant Crutchley took command of the *Vindictive* and did his utmost by manoeuvring the engines to place the ship in an effective position.

He displayed great bravery both in *Vindictive* and in *ML 254* which rescued the crew after the charges had been blown out and the former vessel sunk between the piers of Ostend harbour, and did not himself leave the *Vindictive* until he had made a thorough search with an electric torch for survivors under heavy fire.

Lieutenant Crutchley took command of *ML 254* when the Commanding officer sank exhausted from his wounds, the second in command having been killed. The vessel was full of wounded and very seriously damaged by shell-fire the forepart being flooded. With indomitable energy and by dint of baling with buckets, and shifting weight aft, Lieutenant Crutchley and the unwounded kept her afloat, but the leaks could not be kept under and she was in a sinking condition with her forecastle nearly awash, when picked up by HMS *Warwick*.

The bearing of this very gallant officer and fine seaman throughout these operations off the Belgian Coast was altogether and an inspiring example to all thrown in contact with him.

*

Lieutenant-Commander Geoffrey Heneage Drummond, RNVR

Volunteered for rescue work in command of *ML 254*.

Followed *Vindictive* to Ostend : when off the piers a shell burst on board killing Lieutenant Gordon Ross and Deckhand J. Thomas, wounding the coxswain and also severely wounding Lieutenant Drummond in three places. Notwithstanding his wounds, he remained on the bridge, navigated his vessel – which was already seriously damaged by shellfire – into Ostend harbour, placed her alongside *Vindictive* and took off two officers and thirty-eight men some of whom were killed and many wounded whilst embarking.

When informed that there was no one left alive on board, he backed his vessel out clear of the piers before sinking exhausted from his wounds. When HMS *Warwick* fell in with *ML 254* off Ostend half an hour later the latter was in a sinking condition.

It was due to the indomitable courage of this gallant officer that the majority of the crew of the *Vindictive* were rescued.

*

Lieutenant-Commander Roland Bourke, RNVR

Volunteered for rescue work in command of *ML 276* and followed *Vindictive* into Ostend, engaging the enemy machine-guns on both piers with Lewis-guns.

After *ML 254* had backed out, Lieutenant Bourke laid his vessel alongside *Vindictive* to make further search. Finding no one, he withdrew but hearing cries from the water he again entered the harbour and after a prolonged search eventually found Lieutenant Sir John Alleyne and two ratings, all badly wounded in the water, clinging to an upended skiff, and rescued them.

During all this time the motor launch was under very heavy fire at close range, being hit in 55 places, once by a 6 inch shell – two of her crew being killed and others wounded. The vessel was seriously damaged and speed greatly reduced.

Lieutenant Bourke however managed to bring her out and carry on until he fell in with a monitor which took him in tow. This episode displayed daring and skill of a very high order, and Lieutenant Bourke's bravery and perseverance undoubtedly saved the lives of Lieutenant Alleyne and two of the *Vindictive*'s crew.

AWARDS AND DECORATIONS FOR ZEEBRUGGE AND OSTEND, 23rd APRIL

Victoria Cross
Capt Alfred Carpenter, RN
Lt Richard Sandford, RN
Lt Percy Dean, RNVR
Capt Edward Bamford, DSO, RMLI
Sgt Norman Finch, RMA
AB Albert McKenzie
Lt-Cdr George Bradford, RN (posthumous)
Lt-Cdr Arthur Harrison, RN (posthumous)

Companions of the Order of the Bath
Capt Hubert Lynes, CMG, RN
Capt Wilfred Tomkinson, RN
Capt Ralph Collins, RN
Maj Bernard Weller, DSC, RMLI

Companions of the Order of St Michael and St George
Capt the Hon Algernon Boyle, CB, MVO, RN
Capt Henry Douglas, RN

Companions of the Distinguished Service Order
Cdr Edward Osborne, RN
Cdr Alfred Godsal, RN
Lt-Cdr Kenneth Helyar, RN (*North Star*)
Eng Lt-Cdr Ronald Boddie, RN (*Thetis*)
Lt Keith Robin Hoare, DSC, RNVR
Lt Harold Campbell, RN (*Daffodil*)
Lt Stuart Bonham-Carter, RN (*Intrepid*)
Lt Cecil Dickinson, RN (in command of demolition party)
Lt Oscar Henderson, RN (*Iris II*)
Lt Eric Welman, DSC, RN
Lt John Annesley, RN (in command of a CMB)
Lt Edward Billyard-Leake, RN (*Iphigenia*)
Surg Frank Pocock, MC, RN (*Iris II*)
Lt John Howell-Price, DSC, RNR (*C3*)
Lt Roland Bourke, RNVR

Lt Hugh Littleton, RNVR (in command of MB)
Capt Arthur Chater, RMLI
Lt Reginald Dallas Brooks, RMA (*Vindictive*)
Chaplain Charles Peshall, BA, RN (*Vindictive*)
Lt Theodore Cooke, RMLI

Bar to the DSO
Lt Francis Harrison, DSO, RN

Distinguished Service Cross
Lt Francis Lambert, RN (*Thetis*)
Lt Victor Crutchley, RN (*Brilliant*)
Lt Alan Cory-Wright, RN (*Intrepid*)
Lt Cuthbert Bowlby, RN (in command of CMB)
Lt Philip Vaux, RN (*Iphigenia*)
Lt George Belben, RN (*Thetis*)
Eng Lt Wilfrid Long, RN (*Brilliant*)
Eng Lt William McLaren, RN (*Sirius*)
Surg William Clegg, MB, RN (*Vindictive*)
Lt Leonard Lee, RNVR
Lt James Wright, RNVR
Lt John Robinson, RNVR (in command *ML 424*)
Lt Arthur Bagot, RNVR (in command *ML 283*)
Lt George Bowen, RNVR (in command *ML 110*)
Lt Malcolm Kirkwood, RNVR
Lt Harold Rogers, RNR (*Daffodil*)
Sub-Lt Cedric Outhwaite, RNVR (in command CMB)
Mate Sidney West, RN (*Iphigenia*)
Lt Charles Lamplough, RMLI (Marine storming party)
Lt George Underhill, RMLI (Marine storming party)
Sub-Lt Peter Clarke, RNR (in command CMB)
Sub-Lt Leslie Blake, RNR (in command CMB)
Sub-Lt Alfred Knight, RNR (*Sirius*)
Gnr Thomas Galletly, RN (*North Star*)
Art Eng William Sutton, RN (*Daffodil*)
Art Eng William Edgar, RAN (*Iris II*)
Serg Maj Charles Thatcher, RMLI
Serg E. E. Kelly

Bar to the DSC
Lt Edward Berthon, DSC, RN (*Sirius*)
Sub-Lt Maurice Lloyd, DSC, RN (*Iphigenia*)

Conspicuous Gallantry Medal
Ch Motor Mech James Attwood, RNVR
Ch Motor Mech Sydney Fox, RNVR

Ldg Deckhand William Weeks, RNR
Sig Thomas Bryant (*Iris II*)
Sto Henry Bindall (*C3*)
PO Walter Harmer (*C3*)
Ldg Sea William Cleaver (*C3*)
ERA Allan Roxburgh (*C3*)
Ldg Sea Albert Davis (*Iphigenia*)
Ch ERA Frank Gale (*Thetis*)
Pte William Hopewell, RMLI
Serg Frank Knill, RMA (*Vindictive*)
AB Ferdinand Lake (*Iris II*)
Pte John Press, RMLI
PO David Smith (*Iris II*)
PO Edwin Youlton (*Vindictive*)

Distinguished Service Medal

HMS *Vindictive*
Ch Air Mech Clifford Armitage,
   RNAS
ERA Norman Carroll
ERA Herbert Cavanagh
Sto William Crawford
MAA Charles Dunkason
Arm Arthur Evans
Ldg Sig Albert Gamby
AB Arthur Geddes
ERA Herbert Harris
Sto PO Thomas Haw
Sto James Hayman
PO Herbert Jackson
AB Richard Makey
SBS Arthur Page
Ch Sto Alfred Sago
Sto Joseph Smith
ERA Alan Thomas
PO Thomas Wood

HMS *Iphigenia*
Plumber Charles Batho
ERA Arthur Burton
Sto Victor Bush
Arm Edwin Gibson
CPO Henry Jeffries
CERA Ernest Johnson
Sto Walter Joy
AB Leonard King
AB Frederick Woodroofe

HMS *Intrepid*
AB Herbert Bambridge
CERA Thomas Farrell
ERA John Ferguson
AB Frederick Hide
PO Percy Inge
Sto John Palmer
Sto PO Albert Smith
ERA Herbert Smith

HMS *Thetis*
Sig Harold Clinch
Ldg Sto Frederick Freestone
PO Alfred Messer
AB Edgar Radley
Sto George Summers
PO Ernest Tanner
Ldg Sea Charles Winfield
Sto PO James Wynn

HMS *Brilliant*
Sto William Furze
AB Walter Giles
ERA Bertie Heath
PO Joseph Reed
Sto PO John Wardropper Turner

HMS *Sirius*
CERA Harry Cramp

AB Handel Lawe
Sto Leonard Packman
Sto PO Thomas Scales
PO William Vincent
AB Edward Ware

HMS Iris II
Ldg Sea William Bassett
Sto PO Henry Mabb
Pte Charles Martyn, RMLI
ERA Stanley Odam

HMS Daffodil
ERA Harry Baker
PO James Cownie
Sto Frederick Easter
Ldg Mech George Pemberton

Seaman Storming Party
('A' Company)
PO George Antell
Ldg Sea George Bush
AB Harold Eves
AB Frederick Larby
AB William Lodwick
AB Horace Nash
AB John Reynolds
Ldg Sea Dalmorton Rudd
AB George Staples

('B' Company)
Ldg Sea William Childs
PO Frederick Joyce
AB Thomas Ripley
AB Benjamin Charlestone
AB Frederick Summerhayes
AB Albert West
AB Frank White

('C' Company)
AB William Bishop
AB Walter Butler
Ldg Sea Veines Hawkins
Ldg Sea Edward Thompson
PO John Webb

('D' Company')
AB Andrew Carnochan
AB Francis Kelland
Ldg Sea George Shiner
AB Thomas Tusler
PO Henry Wenman

4th Battalion, Royal Marines
Pte John Adam
Serg Crispin Budd
Serg Reginald Burt
Pte Albert Clark
Serg George Hewitt
Corpl William Kingshott
Pte Leonard Lane
Pte Albert Lee
Lce Serg Frank Radford
Pte Walter Wakefield
Corpl Bert Wells

RMA Detachment
Gnr Edward Hearn
Gnr Norman McPhee

HMS Phoebe
AB Robert Catchpole
CPO Frederick Forster
Sto PO Henry Rainbow

HMS North Star
CERA George Carter
PO Robert Cockburn
CPO Robert Hall

HMS Warwick
Yeo Sigs Alfred Elliot

Picket Boats, Motor Launches and
Motor Boats
Ch Motor Mech Roy Alexander,
   RNVR
Dkhnd Frank Bowles, RNR
Dkhnd Albert Brooks, RNR
Dkhnd Charles Cowling, RNR
PO Thomas Crust
Ldg Dkhnd Percy Dalman, RNR

Dkhnd William Francis, RNR
Dkhnd William Golding, RNR
Ldg Dkhnd Arthur Grain, RNR
Ldg Teleg William Halsey
Ldg Dkhnd James Heaver, RNR
Ch Motor Mech Stanley Hill, RNVR
Ch Motor Mech Frederick Holmes, RNVR
Dkhnd Frank Johnson, RNR
Dkhnd Charles Lawrence, RNR
Ldg Dkhnd Donald McAllister, RNR
Sig Clement Page, RNVR
Ch Motor Mech Howard Pank, RNVR
Motor Mech Robert Pratten, RNVR
Ch Mootor Mech Charles Pulsford, RNVR
Air Mech John Shrewsbury, RNAS
Dkhnd Cyril Slough, RNR
Ch Motor Mech Leslie Spillman, RNVR
Ldg Sto Edwin Starks
Sig John Stewart
Ch Motor Mech Harold Thornton, RNVR
Dkhnd William George Warnes, RNR
Ch Motor Mech Edward Whitmarsh, RNVR
Ch Motor Mech Arthur Wilkins RNVR
Ch Motor Mech Edward Windley, RNVR
Ch Motor Mech Howard Wolfe, RNVR

Announced later :
Pte H. Proctor, RMLI
Bugler L. Guttridge, RMLI
Sgt W. Thomson, RMLI
Pte W. Gilkes, RMLI

To receive a Bar to the
Distinguished Service Medal
PO Charles Biss, DSM (Dev), Seaman storming party, 'C' Company
CPO Aubrey Tagg, DSM, HMS *Intrepid*
Ldg Dkhnd William Wigg, DSM, RNR, *Motor Launch 532*

Mentions
The following Officers and Men were mentioned in dispatches by Vice-Admiral Sir Roger J. B. Keyes, KCB, CMG, CVO, DSO, Commanding the Dover Patrol, for distinguished services on the night of the 22nd-23rd April, 1918 :

Capt Charles Wills, CMG, DSO, RN
Capt Charles Bruton, RN
Capt Ernest Wigram, DSO, RN
Capt George Blount, DSO, RN
Capt William Howard, DSO, RN
Cdr Henry Halahan, DSO, RN (Killed in action)
Lt Col Pryce Peacock, RMA
Maj Frank Brock, OBE, RAF (Killed in action)
Maj John Cull, DSO, RAF
Maj Bertram Elliot, DSO, RMLI (Killed in action)
Cdr Reginald Watson, DSO, RN
Cdr Frederick Strong, DSO, RN
Cdr Edward Altham, RN
Cdr Reginald Parry, RN
Cdr Henry Oliphant, MVO, DSO, RN
Cdr Arthur Bedford, RN
Cdr Valentine Gibbs, RN (Died of wounds)
Cdr Fischer Watson, DSO, RN
Cdr Reginald Amedroz, RN
Cdr Victor Campbell, DSO, RN

Cdr Patrick Harrington Edwards, RNVR
Lt Cdr Sebald Green, RN
Lt Cdr (Act Cdr) Claude de Crespigny, RN
Lt Cdr Robert Hammond-Chambers, DSO, RN
Lt Cdr Frank Bramble, RN
Lt Cdr Francis Haselfoot, RN
Lt Cdr W. F. Sandford, RN
Lt Cdr Charles Knox-Little, RN
Lt Cdr Arthur Harrison, RN
(Killed in action)
Lt Cdr George Bradford, RN
(Killed in action)
Maj Alexander Cordner, RMLI
(Killed in action)
Maj Charles Eagles, DSO, RMLI
(Killed in action)
Lieut Arthur Chamberlain, RN
(Killed in action)
Lt Harold Coulthard Walker, RN
Lt Llewellyn Morgan, DSC, RN
Lt Aubrey Newbold, RN
Lt Ronald Dunbar, RN
Lt Claude Bury, RN
Lt William Bremner, RN
Lt Edward Hill, RN
Lt the Hon Cecil Edward Spencer, RN
Lt Claude Hawkings, RN
(Killed in action)
Lt Charles Paynter, RN
Lt Kenneth Kirkpatrick, RN
Eng Lt Arthur Lougher, RN
Lt George Spencer, DSC, RNR
(Died of wounds)
Lt Archibald Dayrell-Reed, DSO, RNR
Lt James Andrew, RNVR
Lt Harold Wellesley Adams, RNVR
Lt Herbert Tracey, RNVR
Lt Gordon Maxwell, RNVR
Lt Wilfred Kelly, RNVR
Lt Rawsthorne Procter, RNVR

Lt Albert Webb, RNVR
Lt Sidney Gowing, RNVR
Lt Max Downing, RNVR
Lt Allan Geddes, RNVR
Lt Collamer Calvin, RNVR
Lt Graham Hewett, RNVR
Lt David Macvean, RNVR
Lt William Wilson, RNVR
Lt John Senior, RNVR
Surg Sidney Grimwade, MB, RN
Surg Arthur Green, RN
Surg Frederick Payne, RN
Capt John Palmer, DSC, RMLI
(Prisoner of War)
Act Lt Guy Cockburn, RN
Act Lt Wilfred Stanfield, RNR
Act Lt Leopold Hegarty, RNR
Act Payr Herbert Woolley, RN
Sub-Lt Frank Ramsay, RN
Sub-Lt Henry Hancox, RN
Sub-Lt Humphrey Low, RN
Sub-Lt Alexander Young, RNVR
Surg Prob Philip du Toit, RNVR
Surg Prob George Abercrombie, RNVR
Mate Victor Price, RN
Lt Daniel Broadwood, RMLI
Lt A. L. Eastlake, RE
Act Lt Hubert Phayre de Berry, RMLI
Act Sub-Lt Thomas Heap, RNR
2nd Lt Arthur Norris, RM
Gnr Arthur Powell, RN
Gnr Christopher Bysouth, RN
Warrt Eng Dugald Campbell, RNR
Mid Norman Herbert, RNR
Mid Felix Mossop, RNR
Mid Allan Robertson, RNR
Tempy Lt Joseph Watts, RMLI
Tempy Lt Edward Taylor, RMLI
Co Sergt-Maj Ernest Kilby, RMLI
AB Ambrose Adams
Sto William Adams
Gnr John Akrill
PO Charles Arnold

Senior RA Geoffrey Arthur
Sgt John Bailey, RMLI
Sgt William Baker, RMLI
Dkhnd Herbert Barlow, RNR
Elect Art Leonard Beer, (Since died)
Dkhnd Albert Bell, RNR
AB Frederick Berry
Senior RA Harry Bevington
AB Arthur Bishop
AB William Bone
PO Ernest Borrott
Sto Benjamin Boxall
ERA Henry Bradfield
Dkhnd Edward Brennan, RNR
Sto PO Frederick Bridge
PO Herbert Britton
Yeo Sigs John Buckley (Killed in action)
AB Reginald Bult (Died of wounds)
PO Arthur Burberry
Ldg Sea Frederick Burke
PO John Callaghan
Ldg Dkhnd Jack Cannon, RNR
AB James Carter
Off Std Percy Carter
AB Arthur Cassell (Missing)
AB Joseph Causton
AB Charles Clark
AB John Cochrane
Sto James Cole
Off Std Frederick Collyer
Dkhnd James Connolly, RNR
Sto William Connor
AB Arthur Constable
PO David Cook
Sto John Coxhedge
Corpl William Craig, RMLI
Sto PO William Crockett
ERA William Cross
AB Jesse Culmer (Died of wounds)
Ch Motor Mech W. George Culverwell, DSM, RNVR
Gnr William Dance, RMA
Yeo Sigs William Daymon
AB Cecil Duncan

PO John Edwards
ERA Norman Edwards
Sto Philip Edwards
CPO George Ellen
Air Mech Roland Entwistle, RNAS
AB David Evans
Ldg Sea Frank Evans
Pte John Evans, RMLI
Motor Mech Robert Everett, RNVR
Sto Edwin Fisher
Ch Motor Mech Atholstone Foster, RNVR
AB Albert Franklin
AB Edward Friday
Ldg Sea Cecil Fullwood
AB Daniel Gilbey
Pte William Gilkes, RMLI
AB Henry J. Gillard
Air Mech William Gough, RNAS
Gnr James Grady, RMA
Dkhnd Arthur Gurr, RNR
Bugler Leonard Guttridge, RMLI
Pte George Hall, RMLI
Sto 1st Cl Robert Hall
PO Michael Hallihan (Killed in action)
AB George Hanson
PO George Harlow
Off Std Alfred Harris
Dkhnd Albert Hartung, RNR
Pte James Hawksworth, RMLI
PO Arthur Heard
Ch Motor Mech Gerald Hebblethwaite, RNVR
Bugler Charles Hefferman, RMLI (Killed in action)
AB Arthur Hilling
Pte Frederick Hoath, RMLI
Ch Motor Mech Walter Hocking, RNVR
CPO Albert Hurrel
Yeo Sigs Albert James, DSM
AB Charles Jarrett
AB Charles Jeffries

Pte Nelson Jermy, RMLI
Arm Albert Jobson
Ch Ship's Cook Harry Jones
Vict Assist Percy Kenworthy
Vict CPO Samuel Kimpton
CPO George Lancaster
AB Richard Lawrence
Ldg Sea William Arthur Lee
Ldg Sto William Stephen Lee
Ldg Dkhnd Fred Lissenden, RNR
AB Frederick Lorriman
PO Samuel Lowe
Dkhnd Donald MacAlister, RNR
ERA Robert McCorquodale
Dkhnd John McCrackan, RNR
Sto Herbert McCrory
Dkhnd Angus McIntyre, RNR
 (Died of wounds)
Ch Motor Mech Friend Mackie,
 RNVR
Dkhnd George McKruly, RNR
 (Killed in action)
AB Leonard Maidment
CPO William Main
Pte Percy Mann, RMLI
AB Richard Mantle
AB Albert Matthews (Killed in
 action)
CERA William May
Ldg Sea William Mereweather
Dkhnd Sidney Meridith, RNR
Ch Motor Mech Roland Meyer,
 RNVR
PO William Miller
AB John Milroy
Dkhnd John Morrison, RNR
Pte Frederick Mundy, RMLI
AB Jeremiah Murphy
AB Leo T. Newlands
Sig Herbert Nickerson, RNVR
PO Edwin Noble
AB Albert Olive
Sto PO David Palmer
Sgt Henry Parker, RMLI
Ch Motor Mech Meredith Parker,
 RNVR

Shipwt Frederick Partis
AB Francis Patton
PO Charles Pearson
Sto George Philp
PO Charles Pitt
Ldg Sea William Potter
Sto William Potter
Ldg Dkhnd David Pottinger, RNR
Senior RA Edwin Poynter
Pte Herbert Proctor, RMLI
Gnr William Ranson, RMA
AB Frederick Richards (Missing)
Ch Motor Mech Henry Rist,
 RNVR
SBA Albert Robinson
Motor Mech James Robinson,
 RNVR
Dkhnd Alec Rowland, RNR
Ch Air Mech William Ryan,
 RNAS
AB Frederick Salter
Ldg Sig William Sansome, DSM
PO George Schoon
Ldg Sto Valentine Selth
Corpl Noel Sharrock, RMLI
Sto Arthur Smith
Ch Motor Mech Ernest Smith,
 RNVR
Dkhnd James Smith, RNR
Ch Motor Mech Laurence Smith
PO William Smith
AB Archer Southgate
PO John Spencer
PO Walter Stevens
Ord Sea Robert Symons
CPO Edgar Terry
Sgt William Thomson, RMLI
Air Mech Keith Thow, RNAS
AB Stanley Trumper
Dkhnd Richard Turner, RNR
AB Sidney Vincent
Air Mech George Warrington,
 RNAS
AB Alfred Watkins
Ch Sto Alfred Watts
AB Thomas Wescott

Ldg Sea Thomas Westwood
ERA Robert White
PO Thomas White
Ch Motor Mech Garnet Wolseley
    Wickson, RNVR
Sto PO Arthur Wiggins
Ch Sto Albert Wilson (Killed in
    action)
Sig Arthur Wilson, RNVR
AB William Woodhead
Ldg Sea Albert Woodley
AB George Worth
Dkhnd Philip Wright, RNR

The following officers were mentioned by Vice-Admiral Sir Roger Keyes for services in connection with the preparatory work of the operations :

Rear-Adml Cecil Dampier
Col Charles Lambe, CMG, DSO,
    RAF
Capt Alexander Davidson, DSO,
    RN
Capt Herbert Grant, RN
Lt-Col Frederick Halahan, MVO,
    DSO, RAF
Maj Peregrine Fellowes, DSO,
    RAF
Eng Lieut-Cdr Macleod Edwards,
    RN
Staff Payr Walter Northcott, RNR
Payr Alec Haine, RN
Lt Ivan Franks, RN
Lt Frank Archer, RNVR

Special Promotions for Service in Action:
Cdr (act Capt) Alfred Carpenter, RN to be Capt
Cdr Ralph Sneyd, DSO, RN (commanded *Thetis*)
Lt Cdr Robert Rosoman, RN
Lt Cdr Hubert Gore-Langton (in command of *Phoebe*)
Lt Cdr Henry Hardy, DSO, RN (in command of *Sirius*)
Lt Cdr Francis Sandford, DSO, RN
Lt Cdr Bryan Adams, RN
Sub-Lt Felix Chevallier, RN (in command of Nos 1 and 3 demolition
    parties in *Daffodil*)
Sub-Lt Dudley Babb, RN (*Intrepid*)
Sub-Lt Angus Maclachlan, RN (*Brilliant*)
Gnr John Cobby, RN (*Vindictive*)
Eng Lt Cdr William Bury, RN (*Vindictive*)
Ch Art Engr Frederick Steed, RN (*Phoebe*)
Eng Sub-Lt Edgar Meikle, RN (*Intrepid*)
Art Eng Percy Brooker, RN (*North Star*)
Staff-Eurg James McCutcheon, MB, BA, RN (*Vindictive*)
Major Bernard Weller, DSC, RMLI
Capt Edward Bamford, DSO, RMLI
Capt Arthur Chater, RMLI
Sub-Lt George Nicolle, RNR (in command of CMB at Ostend)
Sub-Lt Peter Clarke, RNR
Mid Henry Clifford, RNR

Mid John Wheeler, RNR
Asst Par Edward Young, RNR
Cdr Ion H. Benn, DSO, MP
Act Lt Cdr William Watson, RNVR (*ML 105*)
Act Lt Cdr Lionel S. Chappell, DSC, RNVR (*ML 558*)
Act Lt Cdr Robin Hoare, RNVR
Act Lt Cdr Jean Mieville, NVR (*ML 280*)
Act Lt Cdr Arthur G. Watts, RNVR (*ML 239*)
Lt Alex Dixon, RNVR (*ML 258*)
Lt Geoffrey Drummond, RNVR (*ML 254*)
Lt Edward Hilton Young, MP, RNVR
Lt Raphael Saunders, RNVR (*ML 128*)
Lt Roland Bourke, RNVR
Lt Percy T. Dean, RNVR
Sub-Lt Thomas Turnbull, RNVR
Sub-Lt Williams Scott, RNVR
Lt Theodore Cooke, RMLI
Act Capt Dallas Brooks, RMA
Cdr Edward Osborne, RN
Cdr Alfred Godsal, RN
Lt Cdr Frank Bramble, RN
Lt Cdr Francis Haselfoot, RN
Lt Harold Campbell, RN
Lt Stuart Bonham Carter, RN
Lt Richard Sandford, RN
Lt Eric Welman, RN
Lt Edward Billyard Leake, RN
Eng Lt Cdr Ronald Boddie, RN
Eng Lt Wilfred Long, RN
Mate Sydney West, RN
Surg Frank Pocock, MC, RN
Lt Archibald Dayrell-Reed, DSO, RNR
Mid Felix Mossop, RNR
Nineteen Croix de Guerre were conferred by the French President and Rear-Admiral Keyes was made a Grand Officer of the Order of Leopold by the King of the Belgians.

AWARDS GRANTED FOR OSTEND
9th/10th MAY

Victoria Crosses
Lt Cdr Geoffrey Drummond, RNVR
Lt Cdr Roland Bourke, DSO, RNVR
Lt Victor Crutchley, DSC, RN

Companion of the Order of the Bath
Cdr Ion Hamilton Benn, DSO, MP, RNVR

Companion of the Order of St Michael and St George
Capt Ernest Wigram, DSO, RN
Distinguished Service Order
Cdr R. Parry, RN
Cdr W. W. Watson, RNVR
Engr Cdr W. A. Bury, RN
Lt Cdr J. L. Mieville, RNVR
Lt Cdr A. G. Watts, RNVR
Lt Cdr R. Saunders, RNVR
Lt Sir J. M. Alleyne, DSO, RN

Bar to the DSO
Lt Cdr R. Hoare, DSO, DSC, AM, RNVR
Lt A. E. Welman, DSO, DSC, RN
Lt A. Dayrell-Reed, DSO, RNR

Distinguished Service Cross
Lt R. McBean, RN
Lt W. Bremner, RN
Lt A. L. Poland, RN
Lt R. Procter, RNVR
Lt A. Mackie, RNVR
Lt F. F. Brayfield, RNVR
Lt A. Geddes, RNVR
Sub-Lt G. Shaw, RNR
Sub-Lt J. Petrie, RNVR

Bar to the DSC
Lt the Hon C. Spencer, RN
Lt C. F. Bowlby, DSC, RN

Conspicuous Gallantry Medal
P. O. J. Reed, DSM
Ldg Dkhnd D. G. Rees, RNR

Distinguished Service Medal
Ldg Sto J. Akid
Sto R. Bailey
AB F. Bore
Sto W. Carter
AB J. Chambers
Ch Motor Mech F. Chivers
Ldg Sto T. Chitty
Sto Cross
Motor Mech A. Davis, RNVR
Sto G. Elliott

Ldg Dkhnd W. Farthing
Shipwt G. Frater
Sto PO G. Fryer
Sto F. Gilroy
Sig D. Heale
Sto M. Henry
PO R. Jeffreys
Sto W. Johnson
Ch Motor Mech G. Jones, RNVR
Sto PO S. Jordan
Sto W. Joslin
Ch Motor Mech G. Kerr
Sto E. Largey
Ldg Sea A. Ling
Ldg Sto B. Lowe
Ch Motor Mech E. McCracken
Sto S. McCracken
Ldg Dkhnd G. McGee
Ch Motor Mech L. McGinley
Ldg Dkhnd J. Maclean
Ch Motor Mech H. McMillan
Ch Motor Mech L. McMillan
Ch Motor Mech L. McQueen
Ch Motor Mech E. S. Mountain
Ch Motor Mech A. Macfarlane
Sto F. Neville
Sto PO J. Newington
Sto J. Norris
Sto P. O'Reilly
Sto H. Park
Ldg Sto S. Pearce
Mechn J. Pelham
ERA F. Pickerell
Yeo Sigs T. Pinches
PO C. Potter
Mc Motor Mech R. Rae
Sto J. Relf
Ldg Sea E. Robertson
Sto F. C. Russell
Ldg Stoker A. Saunders
Air Mech D. Smith
Sto J. Statton
AB V. Surridge
Dkhnd C. Surtees
Dkhnd Sutherland
Ch Motor Mech J. Talbot

Stoker J. Taylor
Ldgh Dkhnd G. Turner
AB H. Wilson
Stoker W. T. Wood

Bar to the DSM
ERA N. Carroll
ERA H. Cavanagh
Ch Yeo Signs D. Foley

Mentioned in Despatches: in addition to the foregoing:
Capt Wilfred Tomkinson, CB, RN (in command of the destroyers)
Cdr Frederick Strong, DSO, RN (in command of a destroyer)
Cdr Victor Campbell, DSO, RN (in command of *Warwick*)
Cdr Patrick Parker, RN (engaged Ostend batteries with *Prince Eugene*)
Cdr James Clark, DSO, RN (Staff of Commodore, Dunkirk)
Cdr Francis Sandford, DSO, RN

In command of off-shore destroyers :
Cdr H. Oliphant, MVO, DSO, RN (senior officer offshore force flying
    pennant of Cdre Lynes)
Cdr B. Ramsay, RN
Lt Cdr A. Cooper-Key, DSO, RN
Lt Cdr H. Braddyll, RN
Lt Cdr W. H. Sandford, RN
Lt Cdr G. L. Warren, RN
Lt J. R. Johnston, RN
Lt C. Ringrose

Lt R. H. Caldwell, RN
Lt F. H. G. Trumble (killed in action)
Eng Lt Cdr R. Rampling, RN

Lt Cdr W. L. Jackson, RN

Lt M. MacCallum, RNVR (*ML 292*)
Lt J. Gordon, RNVR (*ML 397*)
Lt A. Bagot, DSC, AM, RNVR (*ML 283*)
Sub-Lt C. W. Scott, RNVR (*ML 562*)
Mid H. L. Proctor, RNVR (*ML 283*)

Mto PO C. McDonald (missing)
PO H. Martin (missing)
Ldg Sto Kemp (missing)
AB W. Mobling (killed in action)
AB R. Garbutt (missing)

Sig G. Linegar (missing)
Sto P. Smithers (POW)
Stoker C. Fisher (missing)
Dkhnd C. Gillett (killed in action)
Ldg Dkhnd Hamshaw (killed in action)
Dkhnd W. Clark
Dkhnd W. Hutchinson (killed in action)
Dkhnd J. Thomas (killed in action)

Chap Rev F. Jackson, RN
Surg S. S. Beare, RN
Surg R. Buddle, MB, RN
Surg B. Collins, RN
Payr H. Woolley, RN
Ord Sea J. Burns, RNVR
Sen Res Att H. Hill
Jun Res Att A. Roscoe
AB A. Wood
Dkhn H. Jarvest, RNR
Ldg Mech W. Grice, RNAS
Ch Motor Mech W. P. Yates, RNVR
Dkhnd M. Vigar, RNR
Dkhnd G. Hancock, RNR
Dckhnd A. Morrison, RNR
Dkhnd P. Humphreys, RNR
Chief Motor Mech H. Underwood, RNVR
Dkhnd R. Gardner, RNR
Air Mech L. Sensicle, RNAS
Ch Motor Mech A. Saunders, DSM, RNVR
Ch Motor Mech E. Windley, DSM, RNVR

CASUALTIES AT ZEEBRUGGE AND OSTEND
23rd APRIL, 1918

OFFICERS
Killed
Capt H. Halahan
Lt-Col F. Brock, RAF
Lt-Com A. Harrison
Lt-Com G. Bradford
Lt-Com D. Young
Lt A. Chamberlain, RN
Lt C. Hawkings
Lt C. Paynter
Lt O. Robinson
Lt-Col B. Elliot
Maj A. Cordner
Maj C. Eagles
Lt C. Rigby
Lt. J. Jackson
Lt W. Sillitoe
Lt S. Inskip
Lt W. Dollery

Died of Wounds
Com V. Gibbs
Lt G. Spencer
Sub-Lt M. Lloyd,
Lt R. Stanton

Missing
Capt J. Palmer
Capt. C. Tuckey

Dangerously Wounded
Capt R. del Strother

Severely Wounded
Lt H. Walker
Lt. J. Keith Wright
Lt E. Hilton Young
Mid E. Bodley
Sgt Maj C. Thatcher

Wounded
Com R. Sneyd
Com P. Edwards
Lt Com F. Bramble
Lt Com R. Rosoman
Lt A. Cory-Wright
Lt R. Sandford
Lt L. J. Lee
Gnr Mr A. Powell
Capt C. Conybeare
Lt T. Cooke
Hon Lt and Qrmr F. Hore
Sec Lt W. Bloxsom
Sec Lt H. Lovatt

Slightly Wounded
Capt A. Carpenter
Com A. Godsal
Lt H. Campbell
Lt J. Annesley
Lt P. Vaux
Lt E. Billyard-Leake
Mid N. Morley
Art Engr P. Brooker
Gnr T. Galletly

MEN
Killed
Ada, A.
Aylott, H.
Barnes, G.
Baxter, J.
Bingley, J.
Bowlt, F.
Bray, H.
Buckley, J.
Caine, J.
Carpenter, R.
Clark, E.

Cochrane, F.
Daniels, J.
Dunmow, F.
Ellams, L.
Everest, R.
Feran, F.
Gilmour, J.
Hallihan, M.
Hannon, J.
Helliar, H.
Hollis, H.
Howes, C.
Lyons, G.
McDougall, S.
McKruly, G.
McNichol, E.
McShane, T.
Martin, E.
Matthews, A.
Miller, H.
Palliser, H.
Pool, F.
Pratt, S.
Rouse, J.
Scott, F.
Smith, W.
Sutherland, W.
Tobra, E.
Trees, B.
Wilkinson, C.
Wood, J.
Woods, G.

Died of Wounds
Beckett, J.
Bowthorpe, D.
Bult, R.
Cleal, J.
Culmer, J.
Dibben, W.
Hick, A.
Jones, H.
Lucas, F.
McIntyre, A.
Nicholls, S.
Smy, N.

Taylor, A.
Willmore, G.

Wounded
Ahern, J.
Antell, G.
Baker, A.
Bassett, J.
Bendall, H.
Berry, F.
Berry, P.
Blades, E.
Bonsor, F.
Briskham, A.
Brooks, A.
Brown, L.
Bryant, T.
Burton, A.
Bush, V.
Callf, A.
Campbell, T.
Carnochan, A.
Casey, D.
Chalkley, F.
Clark, W.
Clinch, H.
Coates, S.
Cochrane, J.
Connolly, J.
Cook, D.
Cowgill, J.
Cox, L.
Critcher, J.
Cross, W.
Cunningham, D.
Davis, A.
Deighton, D.
Edwards, W.
Eldred, G.
Ellis, C.
Evans, A.
Evans, D.
Fairweather, R.
Field, E.
Fields, J.
Frew, R.

Friday, E.
Frost, W.
Gibson, T.
Gilkerson, E.
Goldsworthy, W.
Goodwin, R.
Grey, D. J.
Hall, E.
Hands, J.
Harding, L.
Harner, W.
Harris, T.
Hayman, J.
Hickey, A.
Hide, F.
Higgins, P.
Hilling, A.
Hindle, H.
Horton, W.
Howell, B.
Howett, A.
Hughes, J.
Humphreys, A.
Hutton, J.
Ireland, J.
Jackson, H.
Johnson, A.
Johnson, E.
Joy, W.
Joyce, F.
Kelland, F.
King, L.
Lambkin, A.
Larrett, W.
Lepper, A.
Lewis, T.
Louch, F.
MacAlister, D.
McCorquodale, R.
McKenzie, A.
Mepham, A.
Mereweather, W.
Merritt, A.
Milroy, J.
Nash, H.
Northcott, R.

O'Donnel, J.
Omans, A.
Orman, T.
Oxenbury, S.
Palmer, J.
Pocock, F.
Popple, G.
Price, A.
Radley, E.
Ripley, T.
Roberts, T.
Robinson, A.
Robinson, E.
Rose, J.
Rowlands, R.
Ryan, E.
Salter, F.
Sanderson, G.
Selth, V.
Smith, A.
Smith, J.
Stapleton, A.
Stephenson, G.
Stone, B.
Sullivan, A.
Summerhayes, F.
Taylor, W.
Taylor, W. B.
Tebbutt, W.
Terney, F.
Terry, A.
Terry, T.
Tillett, J.
Trippier, F.
Turk, E.
Turner, C.
Warrington, G.
Watters, D.
Wells, A.
Wells, A. W.
White, E.
White, F.
Wilson, W.
Winfield, C.
Woodroofe, F.
Wood, F.

Worth, G.
Youlton, E.

Missing
Bennewith, H.
Cassell, A.
Cowley, E.
Digby, S.
Drummond, D.
Eves, H.
Guenigault, C.
Harris, A.
Jarrett, C.
McElhatton, J.
Mayers, J.
Mills, G.
Pearson, C.
Richards, F.
Saunders, A.
Smith, A.
Smyth, A.
Stingemore, W.
Stone, T.
Watson, H.
Yeadon, J.

HMS *North Star*
Killed
Ashley, J.
Baty, A.
Best, H.
Calvert, J.
Cox, P.
Hanniker, E.
Harland, W.
Hayward, L.
Hillier, G.
Johnston, F.
Lee, R.
Napper, A.
Neville, K.
North, R.
Payne, R.
Schoolcraft, O.
Smith, L.
Stevenson, A.
Wilson, A.

Died of Wounds
Coxhedge, J.
Fountain, F.

Wounded
Bailey, W.
Byron, G.
Cockburn, R.
Crabb, G.
Cribben, E.
Curtis, F.
Cuthbert, F.
Divers, T.
Dunn, A.
Hobden, G.
Hughes, G.
Mead, H.
Redmond, T.
Whincup, A.

4th ROYAL MARINE
BATTALION
Killed
Adams, R.
Atkinson, A.
Attwood, E.
Bostock, J.
Brewer, G.
Browne, H.
Butler, F.
Butterworth, W.
Clarke, H.
Coombes, E.
Cornforth, W.
Cowley, W.
Croft, T.
Dale, J.
Demary, D.
Drury, L.
Ede, W.
Edney, A.
Eldridge, T.
Freeman, F.
Gatehouse, R.
Goulden, W.
Hand, C.

Harbour, W.
Harper, L.
Hefferman, C.
Henderson, F.
Hudson, W.
Huggins, W.
Hurley, B.
Hurst, G.
Jackson, S.
Jackson, H.
Janes, S.
Jones, G.
Jones, J.
Jones, R.
Latimer, D.
Linkin, P.
Loxley, A.
Mann, W.
Mason, A.
Matthews, A.
May, W.
Mayled, V.
Steer, C.
Mercer, H.
Merritt, F.
Middleton, G.
Misslebrook, A.
More, T.
Neale, R.
O'Neil, H.
Ormerod, V.
O'Sullivan, D.
Packer, W.
Parks, G.
Pease, R.
Prangnell, H.
Reeder, C.
Rolfe, F.
Rumsby, W.
Russell, R.
Scott, W.
Shaw, J.
Sparkes, B.
Spiers, W.
Smith, G.
Smith, S.

Sunshine, F.
Swan, F.
Thomas, H.
Thwaites, A.
Tickner, F.
Tidman, J.
Towers, G.
Vine, S.
West, G.
Weeks, R.
White, J.
Willavise, W.
Witckwar, E.
Wood, G.

Died of Wounds
Barnes, H.
Berry, A.
Burnell, A.
Davies, W.
Giles, S.
Hildred, B.
Lane, G.
Roberts, H.
Simmons, T.
Thatcher, W.
Tysoe, S.
Ware, H.
Wickham, W.

Wounded
Adams, J.
Airey, W.
Allbones, C.
Aldridge, R.
Alexander, P.
Astley, O.
Atkinson, J.
Baines, W.
Baker, D.
Barter, R.
Barry, F.
Baxter, P.
Baum, H.
Beckford, J.
Belleone, A.
Bell, S.

Beresford, C.
Blake, H.
Bold, C.
Booth, R.
Bowie, S.
Branson, J.
Broad, G.
Brooker, G.
Brown, W.
Brown, G.
Bulmer, H.
Bushell, W.
Camfield, H.
Chambers, T.
Charters, E.
Childs, L.
Chittle, A.
Clacey, C.
Clark, A.
Clarke, D.
Clark, J.
Clarke, W.
Clist, J.
Collins, F.
Cope, G.
Coster, G.
Daniel, J.
Daly, B.
Darby, T.
Davies, E.
Deed, J.
Dewhurst, W.
Donnelly, J.
Eden, J.
Edgar, G.
Edge, J.
Erskine, A.
Finch, N.
Fitzpatrick, F.
Finney, J.
Fort, S.
Franks, B.
Frew, W.
Fryer, J.
Gale, C.
Gallon, W.

Gamblin, E.
Gibson, W.
Gilbert, R.
Gillingham, W.
Goddard, W.
Goodchild, F.
Gordon, A.
Graham, G.
Grant, H.
Green, A.
Gunim, A.
Gleed, G.
Hailstone, W.
Hall, G.
Haly, J.
Hardman, J.
Harris, P.
Hart, P.
Hartnell, G.
Harvey, A.
Hedges, R.
Hewitt, G.
Hewlett, G.
Hildred, B.
Hill, E.
Hinchcliffe, J.
Hitchcock, H.
Holder, H.
Holding, L.
Hole, F.
Holmes, M.
Houston, W.
Ireland, S.
Janes, A.
Jeffery, W.
Jones, H.
Johnes, C.
Keaveny, M.
Kelly, F.
Kelso, C.
Kember, J.
Kerr, R.
Knowles, T.
Lawrence, A.
Lee, A.
Letheren, F.

Lewis, R.
Lock, A.
Locker, G.
Lloyd, J.
Lucas, W.
Lynch, C.
Macaskill, H.
Macpherson, A.
Maddocks, L.
Manners, W.
Manning, H.
Marfleet, A.
Marriott, C.
Martyn, C. H.
May, A.
McDonald
McKenzie, R.
Milton, A.
Milton, F.
Moomey, R.
Moran, G.
Mitchinson, G.
Morrow, A.
Morse, J.
Moss, J.
Mundy, F.
Murfin, W.
Narracott, F.
Noyce, L.
Noves, D.
Oakden, A.
Painter, R.
Palmer, J.
Parker, L.
Patston, C.
Pepper, A.
Phillips, A.
Pitcher, W.
Pook, J.
Poole, H.
Potter, J.
Prince, A.
Press, J.
Quarrington, R.
Radford, F.
Rawlinson, W.

Regan, F.
Rhinde, E.
Ritter, R.
Rogers, J.
Rose, B.
Sandy, H.
Scarratt, W.
Scott, T.
Scotton, H.
Seal, N.
Simmons, T.
Skelton, W.
Smith, A.
Smith, R.
Smith, W.
Snelling, A.
Somners, H.
Stanfield, M.
Stewart, A.
Stark, E.
Street, E.
Stewart, A.
Sutton, G.
Taylor, J.
Taylor, A.
Thompson, T.
Thompson, W.
Toache, A.
Turner, J.
Wadd, J.
Wakefield, W.
Walling, A.
Ward, T.
Wolsby, C.
Watkins, B.
Wheatley, C.
Wheeler, C.
White, W.
White, F.
Whitelegge, J.
Whittle, J.
Williams, E.
Williams, A.
Williamson, J.
Whitley, W.
Wiltshire, A.

Wood, W.
Woodhouse, W.
Wright, B.
Wright, T.
Underwood, G.

Missing
Batt, E.
Becquet, A.
Campbell, H.
Colligan, J.
Garland, J.
Hopson, S.
Hurn, H.
Mann, G.
Middleton, T.
Osborne, G.
Sales, H.
Sneyd, T.
Wright, H.

Previously Reported Missing now Reported Prisoners of War
Taylor, W.
Yeoman, A.

CASUALTIES SUSTAINED IN THE RAID ON OSTEND ON 10th MAY, 1918 :

OFFICERS
Killed
Com. A. Godsal
Lt F. Trumble
Lt G. Ross
Act Sub-Lt A. Maclachlan

Wounded
Eng Lt-Com W. Bury
Lt Sir J. Alleyne
Lt R. McBean
Lt. F. Brayfield
Lt G. Drummond

MEN
Killed
Gillett, C.
Hamshaw, J.

Hutchinson, W.
Keel, G.
Morling, W.
Thomas, J.

Missing
Fisher, C.
Garbutt, E.
Kemp, H.
Linegar, G.
McDonald, C.
Martin, H.
Smithers, P.
Thomas, A.
Wilson, F.

Wounded
Bore, F.
Carroll, N.
Carter, W.
Cavanagh, H.
Chambers, J.
Chivers, E.
Coomber, G.
Elliot, G.
Gilroy, F.
Heale, D.
Hill, W.
Humphreys, P.
Jarvest, H.
Joslin, W.
Kerr, G.
Ling, A.
Lowe, B.
O'Reilly, P.
Rees, D.
Robertson, E.
Russell, F.
Saunders, A.
Statton, J.
Sutherland, H.
Taylor, J.
Wilson, H.

Index